BREAKING FROM THE BUD
NEW FORMS OF CONSECRATED LIFE

BREAKING FROM THE BUD

NEW FORMS OF CONSECRATED LIFE

Maria Casey RSJ

Srs of St. Joseph NSW
Sydney 2001

Published in Australia by   Sisters of St. Joseph NSW
                                   Locked Bag 3031
                                   Burwood   NSW 1805

First Published in August 2001

National Library of Australia
Cataloguing-in-publication entry:

    Casey, Maria, 1941-
    Breaking from the Bud: New Forms of Consecrated Life
    Bibliography
    ISBN 0-9579002-1-X
    1. Monasticism and religious life 2. Spiritual life
    3. Christian life I Title

    248.894

Designed and prepared for printing by Sisters of St. Joseph NSW.
Cover photography: David Dare Parker
Cover design: Michael Casey
Printed and bound in Australia by Southwood Press Pty Ltd
                                   Chapel St, Marrickville, NSW

TABLE OF CONTENTS

ACKNOWLEDGEMENTS

I wish to express thanks and appreciation to my Congregation, the Sisters of St. Joseph of the Sacred Heart, Australia, and, in particular, to the sisters in leadership of the NSW Province. I thank them for having made this study possible giving generously not only financially but with friendship and encouragement. I also thank the many sisters from the NSW and Western Australian provinces who have encouraged and supported me constantly by their friendship and prayer in the course of this study. I am especially indebted to my parents who encouraged me to read widely from an early age and to the members of my family who continue to push the frontiers of knowledge by engaging in spirited discussions on many aspects of life.

The staff of Saint Paul University has made the writing of this book not only possible but challenging. I acknowledge the leadership, encouragement and interest of the Reverend Monsignor Roch Pagé, Dean of the Faculty of Canon Law, the guidance in the early stages and sustained interest of Rev. Augustine Mendonça and the availability of the other members of staff as the need arose for advice and assistance on various issues. I especially appreciate the guidance, respectful direction, challenge and friendship of Rev. Francis G. Morrisey, OMI, under whose direction I studied. Mr. Larry Eshelman and the other library staff of the University have made the research enjoyable and rewarding. I particularly acknowledge the assistance of Mr. Daniel Hurtubise in persistently tracing and obtaining books and documents from other facilities.

In addition, I would like to thank Rev. Alexandre Taché, OMI, for his invaluable assistance while I was doing research in Rome, Rev. Jesus Torres, CMF, and Sr. Sharon Holland, IHM, from the Congregation for Institutes of Consecrated Life and Societies of Apostolic Life for the generosity of their time and expertise, Rev. Michael O'Reilly, OMI, and Rev. John McIntyre, SJ, for their support and advice. The leaders of the three institutes that were studied in chapter four were generous in supplying material as well as with time given for interviews. My thanks and good wishes to them for the future. I also acknowledge with gratitude the cheerful assistance of John Doherty, Tristram Kendall, Michael Casey, David Dare Parker and many other friends who enabled this book to be ready for publication.

Finally, I would like to pay tribute to all the men and women who have sought to consecrate their lives to God over the centuries and who have found new ways of expressing that commitment as circumstances demanded. Thanks to them and to all who have walked the path before me and with me.

ABBREVIATIONS

AAS	*Acta Apostolicae Sedis*
AG	*Ad gentes*
Bull. Rom. Taur.	*Bullarum diplomatum et privilegiorum sanctorum Romanorum pontificum, Taurinensis editio (cura Tomassetti), locupletior facta collectione novissima plurium brevium, epistolorum, decretorum actorumque S. Sedis a S. Leone Magno usque ad praesens [i.e. 1740]*
CCCB	Canadian Conference of Catholic Bishops
CD	*Christus Dominus*
CICLSAL	Congregation for Institutes of Consecrated Life and Societies of Apostolic Life
CL	*Christifideles laici*
CLD	*Canon Law Digest*
CLSA	Canon Law Society of America
DIP	*Dizionario degli istituti di perfezione*
EN	*Evangelii nuntiandi*
ET	*Evangelica testificatio*
FLANNERY 1	*Vatican Council II: The Conciliar and Post Conciliar Documents*, vol. 1
FLANNERY 2	*Vatican Council II: More Post Conciliar Documents*
GS	*Gaudium et spes*
IL	*De vita consecrata deque eius munere in Ecclesia et in mundo: Instrumentum laboris*
L	*De vita consecrata deque eius munere in Ecclesia et in mundo: Lineamenta*
LG	*Lumen gentium*
MR	*Mutuae relationes*
PC	*Perfectae caritatis*
RC	*Renovationis causam*
RM	*Redemptoris missio*
VC	*Vita consecrata*

FOREWORD

The future of Consecrated Life and the place of women in the Church are more than ever critical questions for our times.

A major study then, of new forms of Consecrated life will indeed be warmly welcomed not only within religious orders of women and men but within the wider Church and society.

All life is gift and newness of life exhilarates. When we read in the Introduction the beautiful words of Isaiah, we are charged and full of expectation for the opening of new life in our midst. *Look! Here and now I am doing something new; this moment it will break from the bud.*

Sister Maria Casey through her careful doctoral and canonical research, having identified the meaning of consecrated life, has traced its various forms from the earliest times to the present Pope, John Paul II. With sensitivity and clarity Maria has evoked the richness of the many charisms that are gift to Church and community.

Throughout the work there is a subtle but powerful sense of the utter fidelity of God to his people at every phase of history within the social, ecclesial and cultural milieu of the times.

Maria gives appropriate and emphatic recognition to the dramatic impact of Vatican II and the ever reverberating effect of the Council on the Church and societies throughout the world . She recognizes, too, such inspirational documents as: ***Lumen Gentium, Perfectae Caritatis, Ad Gentium, Mutuae Relationes*** and ***Vita consecrata***.

This work brings into focus the emergence of new theologies which have broken open the Word and revealed all of Creation in radiant newness. Studies such as this one put Consecrated life not only into the context of times past but give to it a whole new perspective.

We are proud of this work and grateful to Maria for tracing this way of life through time in a way that gives testimony to the seeming paradox of both its discipline and its freedom.

Giovanni Farquer RSJ
Congregational Leader
July, 2001

INTRODUCTION

In Isaiah 43, 18-19, we read of God consoling Israel, "Cease dwelling on days gone by and brooding over past events! Look! Here and now I am doing something new; at any moment it will break from the bud. Can you not see it?" In *Lumen gentium* the Fathers of the Second Vatican Council state:

> From the God-given seed of the counsels a wonderful and wide-spreading tree has grown up in the field of the Lord, branching out into various forms of religious life lived in solitude or in community. Different religious families have come into existence in which spiritual resources are multiplied for the progress in holiness of their members and the good of the entire Body of Christ.[1]

Pope John Paul II, in his Apostolic Exhortation, *Vita consecrata,* echoes the sentiment that the Spirit is constantly gracing the Church with new gifts.

> The Spirit, who at different times has inspired numerous forms of consecrated life, does not cease to assist the Church...by giving new charisms to men and women of our own day so that they can start institutions responding to the challenges of our times. A sign of this divine intervention is to be found in the so-called new Foundations, which display new characteristics compared to those of traditional Foundations (VC, 62).[2]

In 1998 the Pope, once more, spoke of the new gifts to the Church in his message to the members of the World Congress of Ecclesial Movements and New Communities. He indicated that he had been following their work attentively and that he had been able to point to them as something new that is still waiting to be properly accepted and appreciated. He went on to say that they represent one of the most significant fruits of that Springtime of the Church foretold by the Second Vatican Council[3] and echoed down the ages since the words of Isaiah were spoken.

From the time of Isaiah to that of the present Pope, God has maintained his utter fidelity to his people, giving them what is needed to call them back repeatedly to his teaching, love and care. Through the life of his Son, he gifted the Church to the world and, within it and integral to it, he established consecrated life.[4] As with the Church, consecrated life developed particular characteristics at particular moments of history and within particular social and cultural settings. At the beginning, it was chiefly a lay movement almost independent of Church authorities. However, as circumstances demanded, the Church took responsibility for the life and enacted a number of decrees, the first dating from the Council of Chalcedon in 451.

These decrees of the Council of Chalcedon marked the beginning of the legalisation and institutionalisation of consecrated life. This process has continued to this day and has had the effect of both protecting and pastorally caring for the life and, at times, of nearly stifling its expression. The law always followed the growth emerging in response to particular needs and circumstances. Many enterprising and holy men and women attempted to respond to the inspiration of the Spirit as the needs manifested themselves at different periods of history. Thus, with the passage of time, new forms of consecrated life came into being. From the early hermits developed the monastic style, then the mendicant and apostolic, right down to secular institutes and societies of apostolic life. The content and elements of the life form also developed and changed with the development of theology, spirituality and canon law.

Always central was the concept of commitment to God. The commitment was expressed through the living of the evangelical counsels in a manner consistent with the form of life adhered to. Even though perfect chastity was foundational, the other two counsels, poverty and obedience, were always understood to be part of the commitment. As time passed, the commitment was formalised through the profession of vows, which were later publicly made and accepted in the name of the Church. Many other elements were added down through the centuries, such as a stable form of living in community, prayer styles and obligations arising from the vows, the wearing of a distinctive habit and, for all women religious, the obligation of cloister.

The Church retained the right to have responsibility for religious life, as it was called, to interpret the counsels and legislate for them, to accept and approve new rules. In recent times this fact was recognised in *Lumen gentium* 45, and in subsequent documents during and after the Council. While diocesan bishops could approve new institutes of diocesan right, the Holy See reserved the right to approve those of pontifical right as well as new forms of consecrated life. This right of the Holy See was codified in c. 605 of the 1983 Code of Canon Law.[5]

In this study, we recognise the importance of the historical contribution to consecrated life both in terms of the development of different forms and in the development and application of canon law to the emerging forms. Chapter One examines the evolution of new forms over time, in response to the needs as perceived in the different eras. Such a brief overview does not permit of a detailed analysis of the social, cultural and ecclesiastical exigencies that gave rise to new forms. They are important, however, in the tempering of the gifts granted by the Spirit at a given moment in history. Until the twentieth century the tendency was to uniformity and conformity to ecclesiastical regulations, without much recognition of the originality of the gift to founders/foundresses.

The second chapter examines the newness of the insights into consecrated life received and acknowledged by the Council Fathers and others in documents such as *Lumen gentium, Perfectae caritatis, Ad gentes* and *Mutuae relationes.* The particular gift of the Council to consecrated life included the recognition that it is part of the mystery of the Church, that each institute has a unique gift to offer through the charism given to the founder/s and that all institutes were to renew themselves by returning to the original charism and to the Gospel as the supreme way of life. These insights and a renewed theology of consecrated life were incorporated into the 1983 Code. We examine the law to establish what forms of consecrated life are enshrined there at this time.

In chapter three we endeavour to establish the conditions that led to the formulation of c. 605. We follow its development through the meetings of the code commission for religious life until the promulgation. We then analyse the canon to ascertain the role of the Holy See and diocesan bishops in the approval of new forms. Prior to and during the 1994 Synod of Bishops there was a growing awareness that many new groups were emerging in the Church. Some were in the traditional forms while others did not fit any of the established forms. An analysis of the documents before, during and after the synod gleans an understanding of the thinking and experience of the synod participants concerning new forms. The insights gained are utilised to undertake an examination of the applicability of the canon.

At any period in history a new form did not arise in a vacuum but was closely linked to social, cultural and ecclesial conditions. Consecrated life was affected by its milieu and, in turn, affected it. In chapter four we take a brief *excursus* through the world situation to get a glimpse of some of the ecclesiastical, social, theological and communication factors affecting the emergence and type of new forms. Cognisant of these factors and the understandings reached from the study of the documents in the preceding chapters, we draw up some principles to assist in discerning new forms, look at three new groups and then envisage some possibilities for new forms of consecrated life.

Even though consecrated life is well established in the Eastern Churches, this study is confined to institutes in the Catholic Church under the Latin Code. It is also more concerned with the life as lived in the so-called western world rather than in Asia or Africa.

The study is undertaken from an existentialist approach rather than an essentialist one. It is always mindful that consecrated life is a living, dynamic entity that changes and grows as it evolves and is affected by its ambience. A historical approach is used in the first chapter, while the second and third chapters employ a critical-analytical approach. The fourth chapter includes some analysis of the present world situation. The principles for discernment and their application employ both deductive and interpretive methodologies.

Notes

[1] SECOND VATICAN COUNCIL, Dogmatic Constitution on the Church, *Lumen gentium*, 21 November 1964, in *Acta Apostolicae Sedis*, 57 (1965), pp. 5-75; English translation of this and other conciliar documents in A. FLANNERY (ed.), vol. 1, *Vatican Council II: The Conciliar and Post Conciliar Documents*, new revised edition, Dublin, Dominican Publications, 1992, pp. 350-426. Here at pp. 402-403.

[2] JOHN PAUL II, Post-synodal Apostolic Exhortation *Vita consecrata*, (= *VC*), 25 March 1996, in *AAS*, 88 (1996), pp. 377-486; English translation, *Consecrated Life*, Sherbrooke, QC, Médiaspaul, 1996, 208 p. Here at p. 108.

[3] JOHN PAUL II, "You Express the Church's Fruitful Vitality: Message for the World Congress of Ecclesial Movements and New Communities", in *L'Osservatore romano*, (English edition), 10 June 1998, p. 2.

[4] See *LG*, 44 which confirms that consecrated life, while not entering into the hierarchical structure of the Church, belongs undeniably to its life and holiness.

[5] *Codex iuris canonici auctoritate Ioannis Pauli PP. II promulgatus*, Libreria editrice Vaticana, 1983, xxx, 317 p. British commonwealth version of English-language translation: *The Code of Canon Law in English Translation,* new revised edition prepared by THE CANON LAW SOCIETY OF GREAT BRITAIN AND IRELAND, in association with THE CANON LAW SOCIETY OF AUSTRALIA AND NEW ZEALAND and THE CANADIAN CANON LAW SOCIETY, London, Collins: Ottawa, Canadian Conference of Catholic Bishops, 1997, p. 139.

CHAPTER ONE

THE EVOLUTION OF CONSECRATED LIFE

INTRODUCTION

The Second Vatican Council affirmed that consecrated life, while not belonging to the hierarchy of the Church, "belongs undeniably to her life and holiness."[1] However, the term "consecrated life" as such did not come into usage as a descriptive term until the post-conciliar period. In fact, it was first used in a definitive sense in the 1983 Code of Canon Law when Part III of Book II, *The People of God*, was entitled "Institutes of Consecrated Life and Societies of Apostolic Life.[2] In this context, "consecrated life" embraced Institutes of Religious Life, Secular Institutes, Hermits or Anchorites and the Order of Virgins, but not Societies of Apostolic Life.[3] The 1994 IX Ordinary Synod of Bishops reflected on the subject of "The Consecrated Life and Its Role in the Church and in the World"culminating in the papal exhortation, *Vita consecrata.*[4]

In this chapter we look at some of the terminology used in relation to consecrated life, then examine the evolution of the currently recognised forms of consecrated life from a historico-existential perspective as well as from an ecclesiological one. Having noted the conditions of a period, we examine the forms that emerged in response to its needs and their gradual movement towards acceptance and juridical recognition by the Church. In examining the ecclesiastical legislation, we note its effects on the shaping of such forms and the struggles that often ensued to allow their birthing, their growth to maturity and, even sometimes, to decay and inevitable death. We note the progression from the early forms in the desert to the monastic forms, the mendicants, the apostolic institutes and, finally, the secular institutes, each form with its accompanying legislation. In so far as their members lead consecrated lives, we also examine briefly societies of apostolic life and associations of the faithful with vows.

SOME VOCABULARY

To facilitate later discussion without the ambiguity arising from the use of common terms without a common understanding of them, we will examine the terms "consecration", "charism" and "form" as they are applied to consecrated life.

Consecration

According to J. Arragain, "the term 'consecration' is far from being a perfectly clear notion from the theological and canonical points of view or even from the linguistic point of view."[5] While the word "consecration" was used in the Vatican II Council documents more than forty times, it referred to the baptised, priests, bishops, and religious.[6] In the 1983 Code of Canon Law it has been reserved to refer to institutes whose members are "consecrated" by the practice of the three evangelical counsels.[7] Hence to avoid misunderstanding, the legislator does not use the word "consecration" in Book IV in reference to the sanctifying office of the Church.[8] What then is the understanding of the concept of consecration in the context of "consecrated life"?

Consecration emanates from baptism.

> Christ, the Lord, high priest taken from among men (cf Heb.5: 1-5), made the new people "a kingdom of priests to God, his Father" (Apoc. 1: 6; cf 5: 9-10). The baptised, by regeneration and the anointing of the Holy Spirit, are consecrated to be a spiritual house and a holy priesthood (LG, 10).

B. Secondin believes that religious consecration is "a *radicalisation* of baptismal consecration, destined to draw from it greater fruits of permanent conversion and of significant *sequela.*"[9] L. Boisvert further attests that religious consecration supposes a serious desire to follow Christ according to the teaching of the Gospel. "Incorporated into the people of the Covenant by baptism and totally consecrated to God, he is called to live integrally his baptismal condition, to make his entire existence an offering pleasing to God."[10] To follow Christ seriously he[11] must love God with his whole heart and soul (Luke 10, 27) and love his neighbour as himself. However, this is the call of all Christians. What, then, makes the consecrated person different? Boisvert claims that it is "the desire to centre his life on God and his Reign"[12] and it is this which "theologically specifies religious consecration."[13] Thus "consecrated life" may be seen as a specific way of living out every Christian's call to holiness spelled out in CIC 83 in c. 210 where we find the injunction that "all of Christ's faithful, each according to his or her own condition, must make a whole-hearted effort to lead a holy life." [14]

It is posssible to distinguish between the theological consecration and the juridical or canonical one. The former is the prerogative of every baptised person and of those who wish to make a further personal, private commitment to God even with vows. The latter is that special consecration which began as a personal state but transformed itself into a juridical one recognised by the Church as such. To this are attached special obligations undertaken by the consecrated person with a view to attaining union with God.[15]

Charism

Living a consecrated life is not undertaken on a whim. It involves a call from God and a response from the person called.

> This is the meaning of the call to the consecrated life: it is an initiative coming wholly from the Father (cf Jn 15: 16), who asks those whom he has chosen to respond with complete and exclusive devotion. The experience of this gracious love of God is so deep and so powerful that the person called senses the need to respond unconditionally dedicating his or her life to God, consecrating to him all things present and future, and placing them in his hands.[16]

This response is expressed in a closer following of Christ who is the Way, the Truth and the Life, leading all to the Father under the guidance of the Holy Spirit who "awakens the desire to respond fully; it is he who guides the growth of this desire, helping it to mature into a positive response and sustaining it as it is faithfully translated into action" (*VC,* 19). This is a special gift of the Spirit to the Church, a gift that Paul VI, in *Evangelica testificatio,*[17] was the first to label "charism" specifically in relation to religious institutes.[18] He explains, "the charism of the religious life, far from being an impulse born of flesh and blood or derived from a mentality which conforms itself to the modern world, is the fruit of the Holy Spirit, who is always at work within the Church" (*ET,* 11). The charism is spoken of as a gift to the founder or founders, "their own particular way of understanding and concretising the following of Jesus in the People of God."[19] J. Beyer affirms that a charism is "a particular and specific gift," but that "received from the founder, lived and expressed by him, it is the font of a fidelity which will become tradition and will experience a development of graces and of forces that pertain to the patrimony of every institute, a patrimony which its members receive and must maintain with the power of their divine vocation."[20] He goes on to say that this "charism is collective, even if in the beginning it was personal in the person of the founder. It becomes and remains personal in each of the members of the institute called by the divine gift to participate in the common charism."[21] According to the Second Vatican Council,[22] the charism is a gift that the Lord gave to His Church. "This gift determines the identity of the institute, its nature, its spirit, its finality and its particular character: terms the Code uses to indicate the elements of a charism of consecrated life."[23]

This special gift of the Spirit entrusted to an institute is not solely for the institute but for the good of the Church and the world.[24] As stated in *Lumen gentium,*

> all men are called to belong to the new People of God. This people, therefore, while remaining one and only one, is to be spread throughout the whole world and to all ages in order that the design of God's will may be fulfilled: he made human nature one in the beginning and has decreed that all his children who were scattered should be finally gathered together as one (cf. Jn 11:52) (LG, 13).

This is the purpose of consecrated life, to share in the mission of Jesus which is the realisation of the reign of God focussing on the Church which he gave to the world as sacrament and servant.[25] Since the world is constantly changing, the charism or gift is also being received anew in the circumstances of time and place. Hence it is not a static gift but a "lived and living reality. It is a seed planted in a fertile ground that takes root and grows and multiplies abundantly."[26] "It is unforeseen, like the Spirit who blows where he will; like the Spirit it is unpredictable and creative, and to receive it we always need a new discernment and a new 'conversion'."[27]

Forms of Consecrated Life

The flowering of the gifts of the Spirit has given rise to "new forms" of consecrated life down through the centuries and continues to do so to-day, as individuals are called and respond in appropriate ways to the exigencies of their times. They concretise their response to God and to the promoting of his Kingdom in a form of life which expresses it and favours it.[28] The 1983 Code recognises religious institutes, secular institutes, hermits and consecrated virgins as the "forms" of consecrated life currently approved by the Church authority.[29] Thus, "consecrated life" could be regarded as the *genus* and the others as *species*. However, in the *lineamenta* for the Synod of Bishops: IX Ordinary General Assembly, the concept of "form" includes what we could call *sub-species* of religious institutes. In quoting the decree, *Perfectae caritatis,* the authors of the *lineamenta* refer to "many forms of consecrated life" including "institutes of canonical and monastic life, the mendicant orders, lay institutes and secular institutes" (*PC,* 7-11).[30] They go on to assert that

> religious institutes include a great variety of forms: 1) orders (canons regular, monks, mendicant orders, religious clerics; 2) religious clerical congregations; and 3) religious lay congregations. Among these, it is necessary to mention also religious institutes who through a particular vow are bound either to the contemplative and monastic life or to evangelization and the mission ad gentes.[31]

In the present code, these forms have the requirement that

living be according to the three evangelical counsels, chastity, poverty and obedience and vows taken in public and received in the name of the Church. (c. 573, §2). These and their implications will be examined in depth in a later chapter. The relationships of the members to each other and to the Church, as well as special apostolic endeavours undertaken in the mission of the Kingdom, are spelled out in the proper constitutions of each institute. It is these constitutions that allow for the expression of the unique character of the charism given to the founder/foundress.

Within the institutes, be they religious or secular, the charism is embodied "in an entire way of life, a comprehensive culture, not merely in various norms and particular practices."[32] Any one form, such as "religious institute", is an abstract concept and "does not take into account the particularity of the actual group of people who live the life together in accordance with the special gift of the Spirit."[33] Neither does it reflect the richness of expression of the ways in which institutes participate in the realisation of the Kingdom. This is allowed for in the individual constitutions which were shaped by the ecclesiological, theological, social and canonical elements prevailing at the time of foundation as well as the manner in which they have developed historically.[34] What then, was the evolution of what are now considered to be institutes of consecrated life as delineated in the 1983 Code of Canon Law?

EARLY FORMS OF CONSECRATED LIFE

Even though consecrated life, as we know it, developed in the Church founded by Christ, it had its roots in pre-Christian times. The ideal of celibacy[35] was well respected in Greek and early Roman civilisations, especially in women. "Premarital chastity was such an essential requirement in brides that young women were thrust into marriage just after puberty to eliminate any possibility of a sexual lapse."[36] Goddesses watched over virginity and "stormed and stalked, loved and hated, avenged and persecuted each other and the mortals"[37] exerting, for centuries, a strong influence through mythology. In Rome, the Vestal Virgins had an exalted position not only because of their virginity but because they were the keepers of the "official fire of state". Such was their status that, "alone of Roman women, they enjoyed the same legal rights as men."[38] If they transgressed, however, their fate was death in a sealed tomb with only a little food and water provided. The lover was beaten to death in a public place. Hence, for the Vestal Virgins, virginity was not merely an end in itself but a means to safeguard Rome, a means determined by society.

Several other groups[39] appeared practising both life in common and enforced periods of sexual abstinence,[40] but it was the Essenes who withdrew from society and established male monastic-style communities where strict celibacy was practised. In this period the whole approach to asceticism and celibacy was linked with theories of the body and a lack of understanding of how the body really functioned[41] — an understanding that was to come many centuries later with the development of the sciences of biology, chemistry and, even later, psychology that explored the mind and its relation to the body.

It is not surprising, then, that the Christians of the early Church were people of their day and incorporated into the beginnings of Christianity, and of consecrated life, the social mores, the philosophical thinking, the attitudes to women and the understanding of the body then prevalent. Celibacy was honoured as a form of asceticism that helped control the body under the tutelage of the soul which "had been sent down from heaven for a time to act as an administrator to the murmurous and fertile province of the body."[42] Some of the early Christian women lived as virgins dedicating themselves to God and to works for the Christian community living either at home with their families or in small groups.[43] What their motivations were, is not known, but there is the possibility of a range of motives according to the understandings of the time; the following of Christ according to his Gospel was prominent. The early Christians were endeavouring to live the community life as presented in Acts,[44] that is, they were selling their goods and living in common supporting each other in prayer, life and good works. "It is now recognized that these descriptions witness to the community's ideal rather than to precise historical facts."[45] The virgins and widows, too, "dwelt in the midst of Christian communities during the time of persecutions, where they led lives of edifying holiness dedicated to attaining Christ's conditions of evangelical discipleship"[46] with no laws or rules as yet defined. This form of consecrated life had the rudiments of what later evolved into more precise forms. They pledged themselves to a way of life that was permanent,[47] in relationship with God, according to the teachings of Jesus, but without any specific vow other than the evangelical counsels given for all Christians.

EARLY MONASTIC FORMS
The Desert Fathers and Mothers

The persecutions, which frequently resulted in martyrdom of Jews and Christians, were begun by Nero and followed by those of other emperors, "relieved by intervals when Christians were tolerated, and reached a climax about 250."[48] Christians fled to the desert to escape such persecutions and were joined by others fleeing the cities because of economic burdens.[49] Individual Christians who had been living ascetic lives in the community relished the solitude of the desert, a symbol of the wilderness but also as the place where they confronted the demons which "had retreated after being driven out of the cities by the triumph of the recently established Church."[50] There was also "a rural dimension to the monastic movement from the beginning."[51] T.P. Rausch avows that, as Christianity spread beyond the cities, "it took root in a peasantry who preferred to live as far away as possible from the imperial officials and tax collectors of the cities."[52] Thus the initial growth of monasticism was related to political, social, economic and spiritual influences and pressures.

By the fourth century when peace from persecutions was established, and Constantine had declared Christianity the official state religion, the urgency of the second coming as mentioned by St Paul — "the appointed time has grown very short... the form of this world is passing away," (1Cor. 7: 29-31) — had diminished. This "brought a sense of security and creeping worldliness in its train; and in this situation those who hankered for a more intense religious commitment were increasingly attracted by the idea of total withdrawal from the community."[53] "Paradoxically, the religious peace ... led others to search in solitude, renunciation, penitence, for a kind of replacement martyrdom, martyrdom being the compulsory way to sanctity."[54] Thus life in the desert, for both men and women, was one of renunciation, penance, fasting, prayer and self-immolation in order to become one with God. It was a movement for lay people rather than for clergy or ordained ministers. They left behind family, friends, possessions, choosing to live a simple life of celibacy, eating what food was available or provided, and engaging in manual labour. They based their spiritual lives on prayer forms rather than on the sacraments.

"The monastic movement[55] began in the East, primarily in the desert hinterlands of Egypt, Syria and Palestine. Many of these first monks were hermits."[56] They lived alone, visiting a master ascetic, called *abbas* (from which comes the word abbot), for sharing of wise words and direction. As numbers grew, there were colonies of hermits, *lauras,* often with several thousand hermits "living in caves or huts out of sight, and generally out of earshot, of one another."[57] The life was not structured by a rule. The daily pattern was left to the individual often resulting in the development of excesses in penances, fasting and forms of bodily mortifications[58] fired by the ideas of perfection, body, sex and sexuality popular in that era.

There were not only men living this ascetic life in the deserts. Many women lived solitary lives of prayer and penance often acting as spiritual advisors, despite official censure. Just as the monks' leader was called *abba,* so the female counterpart was referred to as *amma.* Sara and Syncletica are among the few women whose sayings are included in *The Sayings of the Fathers.*[59] While women were numbered among the hermits, life was not always accommodating for them. J. Anson indicates three motifs in their lives: 1) flight from the world, occasioned either by impending marriage or a life of sin; 2) the assumption of male attire and subsequent seclusion and; 3) discovery and recognition, usually after the death of the saint.[60] Much of the history of the early desert mothers is intertwined with the socio-cultural thinking of the day which saw man as the peak of perfection and woman as the lesser of the species and also liable to be the temptress of man. Whatever the motivation for the flight to the desert, many of the women lived exemplary and holy lives along with the thousands of male hermits.

The most famous of these male hermits is Antony. "As his reputation grew, others began to follow his example and to seek out his advice."[61] They lived in huts, under his direction, and were called "monks", from the Greek word, *monos,* meaning alone. His *laura* was reputed to have had several thousand hermits and it was a logical next step that saw them organised into communities.

To Pachomius is attributed the inspiration of organising the large groups of hermits into monasteries with a rule to guide them and a "highly centralized system of government characteristic of a fully organized congregation or order."[62] "His communities were still eremitical from the modern point of view, but they represented a development towards cenobitism, because each group had its own abbot, usually a famous ascetic."[63] As time went on more and more communities began to take on a cenobitic style. If Pachomius gave the first rule to the monasteries in the deserts of Egypt, it was Basil who did likewise in Cappadocia, but moving his monasteries to the cities and introducing the element of ministry. "He made of his monasteries homes of charity, containing orphanages, hospitals, workhouses, farms and hospices."[64] He "helped to integrate what could have easily become a separate movement into the wider community of the Church."[65]

Everywhere throughout the Mediterranean Basin, as the Church was established, monasteries sprang up independently giving a rich diversity of form. However, we can recognise the rudiments of what later came to be called consecrated life. The members accepted to live chastely, dispossessed of goods, obedient to a leader/abbot and with an outward thrust to ministry either in prayer or service to the poor. There were no formal vows yet.[66] Men and women participated in this development of desert life lived for God so that both men's and women's groups often appeared together.

Conciliar Legislation

Until the fifth century there was no ecumenical church legislation governing members of consecrated life, the first official decrees coming from the Council of Chalcedon in 451. As is often the case with legislation, it was introduced to counteract abuse.[67]

The Council decreed, in canon 4, that the monks were subject to the bishop especially with regard to foundations and stability.[68] "...it has been decided that no one is to build or found a monastery or oratory anywhere against the will of the local bishop; and that the monks of each city and region are to be subject to the bishop" (canon 4). While this canon specifically mentions monks it also applied to women in the consecrated life. P.F. Anson claims that this legislation ensured that monasticism became a recognized part of the life of the Church and that the foundation of monasteries was subject to the approval of bishops.[69]

FORMS OF CONSECRATED LIFE IN THE WEST FROM 500 - 1200

During these centuries, consecrated life developed apace. Monastic forms flourished and new forms such as the Hospitallers, the Military Orders and Templars emerged and were all affected by conciliar legislation.

Monastic Forms

While the eremitical way of life was flourishing in the East and evolving into the cenobitic form, asceticism was also practised by both men and women in the West. Monasticism had been introduced but it remained to Benedict of Nursia to provide a rule that became foundational for the West.[70] It is credited with forging a unified whole, a living organism, rather than an aggregation of units, no matter how numerous.[71] The rule can be viewed from two perspectives, namely, as a *spiritual* document meant to inspire, or as a *juridical* code to govern even the minutiae of monastic life.[72] It was the former interpretation that prevailed for Benedict who saw his rule as a changing entity as life unfolded. It was considered a moderate rule more suitable for beginners as Benedict adhered to the notion that monastic life was but a preparation for the eremitical one to which few were called.[73]

The widespread adopting of Benedict's rule was enhanced by its acceptance by Charlemagne, who wished to rule the Church as well as serve it and who imposed it on all the monasteries of his realm.[74] His son, Louis the Pious, was assisted by Benedict of Aniane to enforce this edict but, despite great initial enthusiasm, the project did not last long and reform was needed again. The second factor enabling the spread of Benedict's rule was the support from Pope Gregory the Great (590-604) who was a monk prior to being pope. In 596, "he sent a group of monks to England under St. Augustine."[75] Here they encountered monks from the Celtic monastic tradition in which austerity tended to the extreme and peregrination was an accepted part of life as they went into exile to spread the Gospel and convert the "heathen" in Europe. This "going out" was a new feature of monasticism and contrasted with the stability of Benedict's monks. Gradually, however, the Irish monks came to accept variations of Benedict's rule[76] so that the benedictine form of monasticism became dominant in Europe.

Monasteries developed as separate entities, becoming centres of learning, study, education, hospitality, caring for the ill and the wayfarer. They grew into monolithic systems of enclosed communities including not only the monks but a whole slice of society brought together in a symbiotic relationship involving lands, commerce, succour and lifelong support. In addition, what was essentially a lay movement changed to being predominantly clerical as more and more of the brethren became ordained members. They became enmeshed in the fabric of the feudal society, being both affected and infected by it, accumulated corporate wealth and, inevitably, lost some of their pristine ideals, often becoming decadent, leading to the inauguration of some of the more drastic Church legislation and many attempts at reform.[77]

Monasteries for women had developed along similar lines to those of their male counterparts but they were less numerous and more dependent on the male monasteries because of the need for the sacraments and support in maintenance of lands and buildings. Double monasteries were developed where a monastery for men was erected beside a monastery for women with a joint head.[78] Often the abbess ruled over both and exercised jurisdiction over the appointment of clerics, the establishment and transfer of parishes, the imposing of censures, the admission of persons to the religious life.[79] A certain equality of persons before

God was recognised.

Because of the evolving social situation for women in the middle ages, laws of inheritance, need for dowries, attitude to sex and sexuality, and the perceived higher status of monastic life, many women were placed in monasteries for purely social reasons, or reasons of care, without a true calling.[80] These monasteries, with the complicated system of endowments and inheritance, often grew far from the exalted ideal of following Christ and expended much energy in endeavouring to survive financially especially when dowries and endowments were withdrawn, returned to families or were plundered by greedy lords and, occasionally, greedy bishops.

The Hospitallers, Military Orders and Templars

In the eleventh century, with the onset of the crusades and the reforms of some of the monasteries seeking a more penitential and poor way of life with more emphasis on a pastoral outreach, there emerged the Hospitallers, Military Orders,[81] and the Templars. They "were originally founded for the practice of works of mercy towards pilgrims and the sick. Shortly after adopting a rule requiring the three solemn vows (1118), the Hospitallers assumed a military character and took up arms in defense of the Faith."[82] The Templars adopted a rule requiring the three vows but which divided the members into three classes: knights, serving brothers and chaplains. "The Holy See granted them important privileges of exemption"[83] so that they became a very strong international organisation. They set up a system of finance foreshadowing modern banking, but the excesses which developed from the accrued wealth eventually led to their suppression.

D.A. Walsh points out that

> the establishment of the Military Orders had a twofold significance. In the first place, recognition of this type of life demonstrated the Church's willingness to approve new forms demanded by changing conditions... the Church was not slow to approve unprecedented institutes to cope with

the new problems and dangers of the times. Secondly, a definite milestone in the evolution of the juridic states of perfection was to be noted in the emergence of groups pursuing perfection while engaged in the active life. Hitherto, perfection had implied a life of solitude, prayer, and contemplation.[84]

One group that combined both the hospitaller and military vocation was the Sovereign Military and Hospitaller Order of Saint John of Jerusalem, of Rhodes, and of Malta. This group

arose from a group of hospitallers of the Hospice of Saint John of Jerusalem who had been called upon by circumstances to augment their original charitable enterprise with military service for the defence of pilgrims to the Holy Land and of Christian civilization in the East.[85]

This Order continues to this day and "is a lay religious Order, by tradition military, chivalrous and nobiliary, which in time became sovereign on the islands of Rhodes and later of Malta."[86] It has three classes of members;

Knights of Justice, also called Professed (with the three vows of poverty, chastity and obedience), and Professed Conventual Chaplains who have made religious vows. They are religious for all purposes of canon law but are not obliged to live in community.

Members in Obedience, also in three categories and including men and women in each. These members make the Promise, which obliges them to strive for perfection in conformity with their state, in the spirit of the Order.

Members who do not make religious vows or the promise but who live according to the norms of the Church and are prepared to commit themselves to the Order and the Church. There are six categories. Both Class 2 and 3 include men and women, married and single. Members of this class and class 2 contribute to the finances of the Order as fixed by the General Chapter.[87] The Order was founded in Jerusalem in the eleventh century retaining links that go back to the year 600 to a hospice for Latin pilgrims established by the Abbot Probus. It received its ecclesiastical approval from Pascal II in a Bull, *Pie postulatio voluntatis,* dated 15 February 1113.[88] The Knights of Malta have had a long and somewhat turbulent history and are to be found today in several countries having survived and having found new life after reform in recent years.[89]

These military orders and hospitallers represent a new form that received ecclesiastical approval in response to perceived needs. They are significant for this study in that their members included men and women at different levels of commitment; the members were engaged in an active apostolate while seeking perfection and there was centralised government with many branches.

Conciliar Legislation

The second Council of Nicaea (787 AD) condemned double monasteries and "obliged those already existing to adopt Basil's rule." "We decree that from now on no more double monasteries are to be started... If there are persons who wish to renounce the world and follow the monastic life along with their relatives, the men should go off to a male monastery and their wives enter a female monastery; for God is surely pleased with this" (Canon 20).[90] This was the death knell for double monasteries and, even though they reappeared in the twelfth century in the north and east of Europe, that form is now lost to the Church.[91]

The second Lateran Council in 1139, called by Pope Innocent II, legislated against women living as nuns in the world.

> We decree that the pernicious and detestable custom which has spread among some women who, although they live neither according to the rule of Blessed Benedict, nor Basil nor Augustine, yet wish to be thought of by everyone as nuns, is to be abolished. For when, living according to the rule in monasteries, they ought to be in Church or in the refectory or dormitory in common, they build for themselves their own retreats and private dwelling places where, under the guise of hospitality, indiscriminately and without any

shame they receive guests and secular persons contrary to the sacred canons and good morals.[92]

This legislation also served to enforce the ideal of living life in common sharing all things, including food, and not merely dwelling under the same roof. A further import of this legislation was to circumscribe the evolution of new institutes and new forms.

Even though the Councils just mentioned influenced the development of new forms, it was the Fourth Lateran Council in 1215 that had the most far-reaching influence. There had been a proliferation of new institutes with and without the permission of the ecclesiastical authorities. Canon 13 addressed the problem:

> Lest too great a variety of religious orders lead to grave confusion in God's Church, we strictly forbid anyone henceforth to found a new religious order. Whoever wants to become a religious should enter one of the already approved orders. Likewise, whoever wishes to found a new religious house should take the rule and institutes from already approved religious orders.[93]

Moreover, no one was to found a new institute without the approval of the Roman Pontiff, and anyone who did must adopt one of the four approved rules.[94] This legislation effectively removed the approval of new institutes from the authority of the bishops and placed it right in the hands of the pope, a centralising move. Henceforth, the responsibility for the development of new forms was to be the prerogative of the central authority of the Church.

The need to adopt one of the approved rules had the effect of restricting the expression of new charisms and, conceivably, of aborting the emergence of more new forms. However, the Holy Spirit was not to be stifled and, before long, there appeared more new forms in the Church.

THE MENDICANT ORDERS

Several factors combined to prepare the way for the emergence of a new form in the thirteenth century: the mendicant orders. The first of these factors was that of exemption whereby the control of an institute was removed from the local bishop and placed directly under that of the pontiff.[95] While the bishop could approve the opening of new houses of an institute in his diocese he could not interfere in the governance of the institute nor could he approve its foundation. This, together with other privileges granted by the Holy See, gave some institutes great freedom for movement and, consequently, greater effectiveness in the spreading of the Gospel.

Another factor that favoured the development of the mendicants was the emergence of the orders or congregations that had appeared as a result of the cluniac reforms. One motherhouse could have several other dependent houses following the same rule and under the same abbot.

During the previous centuries, as stated above, the discipline had become lax in many of the monastic settlements. Indeed that is what they had become— large estates with huge tracts of lands, an attendant population dependent on them for economic and spiritual survival, complex relations with both civil and ecclesiastical authorities and a wealth that often belied the initial call of monastic poverty. Moreover, there was a shift from a land-based commerce to a money-based one along with growth in urban centres. The lay people were beginning to be more educated and in need of a spirituality that expressed their way of life; numerous heresies were making their presence felt in Europe and, despite the reforms of Gregory VII (1073-1085), there was a strong anti-clerical feeling.[96]

In this troubled milieu, two men received the inspiration to have a band of men who would be willing to live total poverty, who would not be confined to monastic discipline, and who would preach the Gospel to the people in towns and villages. Dominic, an Augustinian canon, founded an institute that, from the beginning, was clerical, while Francis, a layman, envisioned that laymen could preach the Gospel to their fellow laymen. They depended on alms insisting that both individuals and communities were to reflect evangelical poverty. This, together with the freedom of individuals to move from house to house, as the need arose, ushered in a new form of religious life. "Poverty and preaching were key. Granted this internal identity, the founders related themselves to the universal Church through the pope."[97] This meant that, though the members were often scattered and eventually organised into local structural units, they were one group subject to the one leader, unlike the monastics whose monasteries, on the whole, were autonomous and subject to enclosure. Instead of withdrawing from the world to find their perfection, they withdrew in spirit but brought their sense of Christ's Gospel message to the world preaching to the people, reaching out to them and helping them. It was not a reform but an authentic innovation, the first centralised institutes from birth.[98]

Both Dominicans and Franciscans inspired the foundation of women's institutes but the women did not achieve freedom from the enclosure.[99] On the contrary, they were subjected to it, even though the full papal enclosure was not yet enacted. What became the Second Order of Dominicans was given the enclosure by Dominic. "The bull, *Ne hostis antiquus,* of October 23, 1232,[100] by which Gregory IX confirmed the rule of the Dominican Sisters, gave papal sanction to the perpetual enclosure which St. Dominic had introduced."[101] Similarly, the Second Order of Franciscans were enclosed by Francis and refused permission to live absolute poverty. It was only on her death-bed that Clare received approval for such poverty and then only for her own Convent of San Damiano. In other words, the privileges of the men's institutes were not extended to those of the women for reasons arising from prevailing social and ecclesiastical situations.

In addition to the first and second orders of Friars (as the mens's and women's orders respectively became known), there arose lay groups of single and married people who wished to follow a similar rule to that of Francis and Dominic. Francis drew up a rule that would be compatible with their secular state and married life, if applicable. At first these groups lived at home and took no vows but eventually they began to live in community and "more and more withdrew themselves from the world, so that before very long they added to their rules the obligations of solemn vows and of the observance of the cloister."[102]

Papal Legislation in the Thirteenth Century

In the thirteenth century, one of the most significant pieces of legislation was the bull, *Supra montem,* of Nicholas IV, approving the Franciscan Third Order in 1289.[103] It recognised the possibility of sanctity for lay people living a consecrated life in the world. They could share in the spirituality and devotions of the Friars without the enclosure for women or the obligation to live in community and the commitment to strict poverty that was entailed.

However, a far more significant legal enactment was that of Boniface VIII who issued the constitution, *Periculoso,* in 1298.[104] This constitution declared that "vows taken in a community approved by the Holy See were solemn vows."[105] It imposed the cloister on all women religious without exception. This included both passive and active cloister. At a later period, the penalty of excommunication was imposed for any breach.[106] This constitution was to affect the forms of consecrated life permitted to women for centuries. Henceforth, all women who wished to be religious had to observe cloister, join an already existing order and take solemn vows. They were not to have a share in the apostolate to the poor and needy in the way enjoyed by their male Franciscan and Dominican counterparts, following the tradition of the apostles.

If the thirteenth century ushered in new orders full of fervour and apostolic activity coupled with a commitment to total poverty, the fourteenth century saw the pendulum swing to a laxity that rivalled the initial fervour. The latter half of the century was filled with controversies. The papacy became more centralised causing much resentment. Heresies flourished and were combatted by the Dominicans and Franciscans. At the same time, art and architecture developed to new heights, education was more available to the people, the pope moved to Avignon and the great schism occurred amidst a period of severe turbulence in the Church.[107] Corruption was widespread as the granting of benefices was abused, local clergy were often poorly educated. In the following century the New World was discovered, Luther precipitated the Protestant revolt, and printing was making widespread learning a possibility.[108] The time was ripe for new developments in consecrated life.

APOSTOLIC INSTITUTES (1500-1800)

In this period, many men and women flocked to Apostolic Institutes whose focus was apostolic works rather than the contemplation that was paramount in monastic life.

Apostolic Institutes of Men

In response to the woes of Church and society there arose in the Church groups known as Clerks Regular,[109] among whom were the Jesuits founded by Ignatius of Loyola (1491-1556). They emerged in response to the needs then apparent and "must be seen as fundamentally a continuation of the traditions that began with the mendicants and a powerful expansion of them."[110] They were principally available for the ministry of the word. Ignatius had provided for three types of houses in the *Constitutions* — houses of probation, colleges, professed houses — but in terms of "apostolic mobility" the fourth type was "the world".[111] This approach to "houses" indicates a distinctive break with monastic tradition. It also reflected the connection with the fourth vow taken by the members, namely, that of complete obedience to the pope to be sent wherever he wished. To assist in this mobility "they would not be bound by choir or by a distinctive religious garb, and they would set no limits on the place or circumstances of their ministries, so long as these were ordered to 'the greater glory of God'."[112]

To facilitate optimal availability, Ignatius developed the vow of obedience in ways that had not been expressed previously. He "developed a centralized government that is authoritarian and monarchical,"[113] ruled that the only election would be that of the superior general who would appoint all other superiors and he demanded complete obedience to such superiors. He also forbade his men to accept ecclesiastical preferments so that there would not be a drain on resources. It is asserted that Ignatius

> set aside four ancient and key forms of the monastic structure: lifelong residence in one community; decision-

making on major issues by individual communities in chapter assembled; the choosing of its superior by each individual community; the chanting of the divine office in choir... and elected that detachment, mobility, disposability be the Jesuit marks.[114]

The Jesuits presented themselves to Paul III, who approved their Rule, *Formula Instituti,* in his decree *Regimini militantis Ecclesiae,* 27 September 1540. Pope Julius III confirmed the Society by a decree *Exposcit debitum,* 21 July 1550.[115] They were accepted for the ministry of preaching and soon dispersed throughout the world.

Three papal interventions are important in [their] journey towards approval: the decree of Pius V, *Lubricum vitae genus,* (1568),[116] the bulls of Gregory XIII, *Quanto fructuosius* (1583), and *Ascendente Domino* (1584).[117] The first one reaffirmed past practice especially concerning solemn vows. The latter two are particularly significant in that they set precedents: scholastics and members with simple vows were recognized as religious and a new Rule was accepted.[118]

For the first time since the Fourth Lateran Council in 1215 Rome approved a new Rule and those with simple vows (but with solemn effects) were recognised as religious. A new form of consecrated life had evolved, opening the door to possibilities for other men and women to begin new apostolic orders to meet the needs that were so apparent.

Apostolic Institutes of Women

Many women endeavoured to live consecrated life and meet the needs of the poor at the same time, but they were not recognised as religious. Angela Merici (1474-1540) envisioned a group of women who would vow chastity, live at home and minister to the sick and the elderly, and work for the education of girls. Her group, the Ursulines, received approval from the Vicar General of Brescia in 1536[119] but eventually this group was cloistered and had to take solemn vows, a situation that lasted until the reforms of cloister in the twentieth century. Only a group of secular Ursulines remained as a remnant of Angela's ideal of freedom to minister to the needy.

The vision for a non-cloistered group of women, with simple vows and able to attend to the needs of the poor, was shared by Mary Ward, an English lady (1585-1645). The pursuit of her ideals led her, through many vicissitudes both in France and in England, to decide to adopt the Ignatian *Constitutions* to a feminine mode. This she presented to Paul V in 1615 and, later in 1621, to Gregory XV.

> Such a move was radical on several counts...[it] sought (a) to follow a mixed life of contemplation and apostolic activity 'by means of education of girls or by any other means that are congruous to the times'; (b) to be subject to the pope alone and not to the jurisdiction of any male religious order; (c) to dispense with enclosure in order to pursue the apostolic work of the Institute; (d) to be characterized by no habit but rather to wear the dress of the time, and (e) to be allowed to dismiss persons from the Institute even after profession, for grave reasons.[120]

The world, and indeed the Church, was not ready for such innovations. Despite initial cautious approval by the Congregation of the Council of Trent and the protection of the bishop of Blaes, there was growing antagonism to the "English Ladies" (for that is how they were then known).[121] Amid growing controversy, linked with a detestation of the Jesuits by the English clergy, Mary Ward's institute was suppressed by the bull, *Pastoralis Romani Pontificis*[122] issued by Urban VIII in 1631. Mary was accused of heresy and imprisoned in a Poor Clare convent in Munich where she was deprived of the sacraments for nine weeks. The document had condemned the members' way of life as being a danger to themselves and a scandal to others. (They had refused to undertake enclosure in 1624 and local bishops had tolerated the situation).

> They wander about freely not restricted by the laws of enclosure, under the guise of helping souls and very many other works in no wise suited to the weakness of their sex and powers or to womanly modesty, especially virginal purity — works, which men experienced in the knowledge

of Sacred Scripture and of tested integrity of life in the conduct of such affairs undertake with difficulty and not without grave caution.[123]

The members were released from their vows, forbidden to live in houses of the institute and all offices of governance were declared invalid. This effectively destroyed the institute. However, Mary opened a house in Rome but later returned to England where she and some followers continued to work as before but in secret. Some of her women continued in Germany and some opened houses in Ireland so that, eventually, three branches operated independently. Mary died in 1645 but the institute flourished and, without acknowledging her as foundress, received episcopal approbation in 1680 and some papal recognition through acceptance of the *Rules* by Clement XI in 1703.[124] However, the institute was not recognised until 1749 when Benedict XIV issued the Apostolic Constitution, *Quamvis iusto.*[125] The implications of this document will be discussed in the next section.

Papal and Conciliar Legislation 1500-1800

The edicts of *Periculoso* were reinforced at the twenty-fifth session of the Council of Trent because women, in particular, were ignoring cloistered orders and banding together to live a simple lifestyle so that they could engage in charitable works. Chapter 5 of the Decree on Regulars and Nuns states:

> Renewing the constitution of Boniface VIII which begins Periculoso, the holy council commands all bishops, calling the divine justice to witness and under threat of eternal damnation, to ensure that the enclosure of nuns in all monasteries subject to them by ordinary authority, and in others by the authority of the apostolic see, should be diligently restored where it has been violated, and preserved most carefully where it has remained intact; they should coerce any who are disobedient and refractory by ecclesiastical censures and other penalties, setting aside any form of appeal, and calling in the help of the secular arm if need be. [126]

It went on to declare

> that (1) all women religious were to keep their rules faithfully, observing whatever the rules demanded (for women, this meant strict enclosure); (2) no professed member of a monastery was permitted to work outside the monastery without the permission of the superior (this was addressed to monks); and (3) women religious everywhere were to keep strict enclosure unless they had a lawful reason and the permission of the bishop to depart temporarily. Severe penalties were listed for violation of these regulations.[127]

From this point onwards, religious life for women required complete cloister, solemn vows and approbation from the Apostolic See for a new order. Pius V enacted further legislation in an effort to enforce the application of the rule of cloister. Doubts had arisen whether strict cloister and solemn vows were mandatory. As the awareness of the needs of the poor, sick and uneducated was heightened, many tertiaries and lay groups emerged. Some wore distinctive garb, took simple vows, lived either at home or in common and gave themselves to charitable works with the aim of alleviating the perceived needs. To remove any confusion Pius V issued three statements.

The first was the constitution, *Circa pastoralis,* 27 May 1566,[128] which stated that the regulations of *Periculoso* and the Council of Trent were to be observed; that all women who took solemn vows were to be enclosed and even tertiaries who took simple vows and wore a distinctive garb. As there was still some confusion Pius V followed with another constitution, *Decori,* 1 February 1570.[129] This further reinforced the cloister permitting that only fire, leprosy and an epidemic could warrant leaving the confines of the monastery.[130] These constitutions effectively removed women religious from any active apostolates and decreed that contemplative life was the only option for them as religious. They also implied that any new charisms given to the Church could not be followed within a lawful ecclesiastical situation. Religious life was legally defined for women but the acceptance of both a new rule and of simple vows for the Jesuits offered some glimmer of hope. The Holy Spirit was active and, with the creative co-operation of clerics, bishops and enterprising women and men, the development of new forms continued to bless the Church.

As noted above, one of many women to address the needs of her day was Mary Ward. The journey for her was fraught with difficulty, culminating with the suppression of her institute. However, the tenacity of her followers was rewarded when Benedict XIV issued the Apostolic Constitution, *Quamvis iusto* in 1749 recognising the Institute of the Blessed Virgin Mary as it became officially known after its resurgence.[131] This document, even though addressed to one institute, was a milestone in the development of new forms of consecrated life for women. It stated that, while these women had simple vows distinguishing them from monastic nuns, they were not true religious. It delineated the role of the Superior General giving her jurisdiction over the houses, the right of visitation and, hence, an acknowledgement that the institute enjoyed central government.[132] While strengthening the role of the Superior General, the pope, however, did not give her full jurisdiction but made it subject to that of the bishop to whom she had to report after visitation and consult on many issues of governance. However, the Constitution set the scene for the development of future institutes after having acknowledged the legitimacy of simple vows and the concept of central government for women. According to C.R. Orth,

> though directed to one particular institute this constitution was to be the form for all similar cases of religious congregations in their relations to the local Ordinary. Through this constitution religious congregations may be considered as having been granted legitimate and juridical existence. Thus the foundations were laid for their great future evolution and the first scheme or plan of the constitutions of religious congregations of women was enunciated.[133]

This constitution tacitly approved congregations for women with simple vows but did not approve the institutes themselves or recognise the women as true religious. In the seventeenth century "France... reached the zenith of its cultural leadership in Europe" so that the thrust for ensuring an apostolate for women was centred there.[134] France also contributed the effects of Jansenism as well as the questioning of the Church and its values through the so called Enlightenment. These factors, together with the upheavals in France in the aftermath of the Revolution at the end of the eighteenth century, had profound effects on consecrated life. Many of the monasteries were suppressed, religious disbanded and secularized and, often enough, their properties appropriated.[135]

The beginning of the nineteenth century heralded the proliferation of congregations of men and women with simple vows. They dedicated themselves to the task of educating the masses and of caring for the sick. That they were not recognised as true religious did not hinder their flourishing. Many had the approval of their bishops and some even had their constitutions approved by Rome but not their institutes.[136] There were numerous institutes with members having simple vows involved in the work of the Church both at home in Europe, in the mission fields (as the colonial expansion from Europe was in full swing) both in the United States and Australia. "Finally Leo XIII's Constitution *Conditae a Christo*[137] issued on 8 December 1900 and the *Normae* of the Congregation of Bishops and Regulars on 28 June 1901[138] adapted the law to life by recognizing as religious the congregations of simple vows."[139]

The Constitution *Conditae a Christo* enacted many of the basic principles that the Congregation of Bishops and Regulars had developed during the nineteenth century. It clarified that there were two classes of congregations with simple vows, those with episcopal approval called *diocesan* and those with pontifical approval. It set out the relationship between bishops and superiors especially those of institutes of pontifical right and it acknowledged the reality of central government for such institutes.[140] Most of all "it represented a new era in the pattern of what the Church was requiring in order for a person to be juridically known as a woman religious in the Church."[141] The new form — apostolic religious life with simple vows — had come of age after several centuries of struggling evolution.[142]

The *Normae*, of the Congregation of Bishops and

Regulars issued on 28 June 1901, set out the procedures to follow for institutes with simple vows seeking full papal approbation and, while they were not law, they were often adhered to slavishly giving all institutes a uniform pattern. They had stated that there was no place in constitutions for material that was not juridic. "This had the unfortunate effect of removing from the constitutions the distinctive character and spiritual motivation of the different institutes."[143] The recovery of the distinctive charisms of institutes did not occur until the Second Vatican Council (1962-1965).

Many of the canons on religious in the Code of Canon Law promulgated in 1917, to come into effect in 1918,[144] relied on the Constitution *Conditae a Christo* and the *Normae* for their sources. The Code determined the nature of the state of consecrated life at this time in history. In Book II, Part II, *de Religiosis,* consecrated life was codified and it delineated as religious life those orders with solemn vows and congregations with simple vows. This was not a static situation. There were constant developments and adjustments to respond to questions, problems arising and lived experience until the promulgation of the 1983 Code of Canon Law.

SECULAR INSTITUTES

As with other forms of consecrated life, secular institutes did not arise in a vacuum. They have a history dating from the time of Angela Merici in the early sixteenth century. She and many other founders had no intention of beginning religious institutes but discovered that ecclesiastical law and the popular perception of who and what religious were, forced them to adopt the norms of religious life if they were to survive as an institute in that period.[145] Several attempted to have institutes of consecrated lay members who would live and work from home meeting the needs of the poor. It was not until the aftermath of the French Revolution, when Europe had been shaken to its foundations with upheaval in society and in the Church, and in Church-State relations, that the laity, once again, began to conceive of the possibilities of consecrating themselves to God and meeting the perceived needs. As Walsh states, "the upheaval... made demands and presented opportunities for good that the cloistered nuns, in their obligatory seclusion of life, could not meet."[146] Even though the new apostolic institutes endeavoured to keep pace with the demands for education, care of the sick, the aged and the poor, they were constrained by the slowness of their acceptance both by the Church and society.

> The desperate conditions brought on by the French Revolution necessitated unprecedented modifications in the customary forms of religious life...Towards the end of the eighteenth century and during the nineteenth century, there arose societies which lacked certain elements that had previously characterized religious institutes. Some societies reduced to a minimum or excluded completely the element of the common life, and at the same time discarded all external manifestations (e.g., the religious habit) by which their members would be recognized as religious.[147]

One of the earliest groups, The Daughters of the Heart of Mary, was founded in 1790 by Pierre Joseph Picot de Clorivière (1735-1820) who brought together a group of women who wished "to seek perfection while living in the world and without the obligation of wearing any distinctive dress."[148] Many similar groups appeared in both France and Germany. Because they "resembled religious institutes in their internal administration and bound their members to the practice of evangelical perfection in a fixed and settled way, the absence of the common life and of a distinct religious habit was considered juridically unimportant."[149] They had the same process for approval as those congregations with simple vows, but by 1880 some societies were refused the decree of praise because of the lack of a religious habit and of the fact that the members had vows and were continuing to live in their own homes.

Ecclesiastical Legislation for Secular Institutes

In 1889 the Congregation of Bishops and Regulars issued the Decree, *Ecclesia catholica*[150] to clarify the questions (1) whether the decree of praise could be given to those institutes without life in common and a distinctive garb and (2) whether the decree of praise or approval could be given to such institutes who had no external sign of membership "and who even seek to hide both the Institute itself and its nature."[151] This decree responded that

> 1) the new societies and their members do not possess the juridic character of religious, and, 2) societies which are secret in reference to ecclesiastical authoritity are not to be tolerated in the Church.[152]

The decree was in force for a short period and seems to have been ignored by both *Conditae a Christo* and the *Normae* and was not incorporated in the 1917 Code of Canon Law. Therefore it lost all effectiveness. The societies themselves were not included in the 1917 Code of Canon Law[153] despite the fact that their numbers were increasing and their contribution to the apostolate of the Church was significant and acknowledged by popes who gave approval to several institutes.

The Church studied the characteristics of these institutes both at a regional level and at international conferences. In the meantime, new ones were founded and spread to many countries in Europe. Finally, after several international meetings and examination of the question of their status by a special commission of canonists, Pius XII issued an Apostolic Constitution, *Provida Mater Ecclesia,* which gave definitive recognition to these institutes which came to be called secular institutes.[154] A new form of consecrated life had been formally and juridically recognised. Within a short period, Pius XII followed with a motu proprio, *Primo feliciter,*[155] praising and confirming secular institutes while the Congregation of Religious also issued an Instruction, *Cum Sanctissimus Dominus,*[156] which set out "the supreme norms which may rightly be regarded as fundamental for the solid initial establishment and regulation of secular institutes."[157] They became, in the terminology of the day, "a recognized *state* of perfection,"[158] in other words, a new form of consecrated life.

This legislation gave the parameters for recognising secular institutes. They are defined as "societies, whether clerical or lay, whose members in order to attain Christian perfection and to exercise a full apostolate, profess the evangelical counsels in the world."[159] They are those only which, in their internal constitution, in the hierarchical order of their government, in the full dedication, unlimited by any other ties, which they require of their members strictly so called, in their profession of the evangelical counsels, and finally in their manner of exercising the ministry and apostolate, bear a closer essential resemblance to the canonical states of perfection, and especially to the Societies without public vows, even though they do not practice the religious life in common, but make use of other external forms.[160]

They are not religious; their vows, oaths or promises are not public vows of *religion* in the canonical sense; their consecration is a "consecrated secularity" with an apostolate in the world. Paul VI confirmed and reaffirmed this in his address on the occasion of the 25th anniversary of *Provida Mater*. He stated that

in the soul of every secular institute ...there has been profound concern for a synthesis, the longing for simultaneous affirmation of two characteristics: 1) full consecration of life according to the evangelical counsels, and 2) full responsibility for a transforming presence and action within the world, in order to mould, perfect and sanctify it.[161]

He again urged the members to emphasize their *secular character* in their relationship with the world. It "is not just a sociological condition, an external fact, but an attitude: to be present in the world... and thereby sanctify it from within... to be reflected in all things."[162] John Paul II, commenting on *Provida Mater* on its fiftieth anniversary, held that "the constitution recognized that the perfection of Christian life could and should be lived in every circumstance and existential situation, since it is the call to universal holiness."[163] The Pope went on to explain that he wished

to re-examine several considerations of my venerable predecessor, Paul VI, who had spoken of secular institutes as the answer to a deep concern: that of finding the way of combining the full consecration of life according to the evangelical counsels and the full responsibility for a presence and transforming action within the world, to mold, perfect and sanctify it.[164]

This statement of Paul VI, as quoted, would summarise the essence of secular institutes, namely, the characteristics of full consecration according to the evangelical counsels and an apostolate to and in the world. The 1983 Code of Canon Law in Book II, Title III, gave formal juridical recognition to this new form of consecrated life.

SOCIETIES OF APOSTOLIC LIFE

Societies of Apostolic Life trace their origin to the Beguines and the Beghards,[165] who "belong to the blossoming and multiplicity of the religious life that, with the *vita apostolica* as the premise for reform, accompanied urbanisation and the increasing articulation of laymen in spiritual matters during the High Middle Ages."[166] They were both lauded as religious persons and condemned as heretics. The women were often well-to-do widows and single women who either lived at home or in group housing with walled enclosure, the *beguinage,* helping the poor and the sick. The men's groups often included "fullers, dyers, and weavers in the Flemish cloth industry, reflecting wider recruitment from the lower classes."[167] While they lived in community they promised to live chastity but they kept personal property and were free to leave to marry or embark on other lay pursuits. Through periods of persecution, and especially through the tempestuous times of the French revolution, they endured and some are to be found to this day in Belgium.

The *beguinages* gave rise to a multiplicity of societies "that had the dual aspect of following the religious and that of doing their apostolate without being restricted by the religious vows or the cloister."[168] "They had no vows in the strict sense, but a promise or a contract or some other means of incorporation in the society...they were not religious nor were they juridically organized as the religious."[169]

One such society in the sixteenth century, was founded by Louise de Marillac (1591-1660) who received the inspiration to dedicate herself to the service of the poor as a consecrated person. When her husband died she took a vow of widowhood and discussed her dreams with her spiritual director, Vincent de Paul. Under his direction she established a "type of charitable organization that would support young girls who had come to the city of Paris to serve the poor."[170] Working in partnership with Vincent, Louise, in 1633, structured a format for her company, which included both rural and city women. She did not envisage that this company would become a religious institute as both she and Vincent wanted the members available for the active apostolate, which, because of the policy of cloister, would be impossible if they were religious. They received both episcopal and civil approval in 1645 and 1657 respectively and initial papal approval in 1668. The members lived in community, wore secular dress (rather than a habit), devoted themselves to the sick and the poor in the hospitals and to other charitable works. Final papal approbation, in 1882, recognised that the company was a confraternity, which included women who were consecrated and worked in the active apostolate. They were not subject to the local bishop as their Superior General but to the Superior General of the Congregation of the Missions, whom Louise felt would understand their aims and spirit because of their common founder, Vincent de Paul.

Vincent and Louise had founded what came to be known as "a quasi-religious society" in the 1917 Code of Canon Law and as a Society of Apostolic Life in the 1983 Code. Such societies were regarded as imitating religious life rather than being included in the category. Their members live in common and have a primary apostolic focus. Some of the societies have members who profess some or all of the evangelical counsels either by vow, oath or promise renewed annually, as in the case of the Daughters of Charity. That they did not have public vows received in the name of the Church precluded them from being included in the religious life category or, later, in the consecrated life category.[171]

ASSOCIATIONS OF THE FAITHFUL WITH VOWS

From the very earliest times the Christian faithful have organised themselves into associations for mutual support, for solidarity in an apostolate or for sharing in the spiritual privileges and charisms of various religious institutes.[172] There were two basic types: (1) those established by bishops and given juridical status and which were known as ecclesiastical societies or associations and (2) those which had no official ecclesiastical recognition but were governed and directed by lay people. These were the lay societies.[173] In the eighteenth century some of the new apostolic institutes were approved by the Congregation of Bishops even though they were not regarded as true religious and generally lacked some of the elements seen as necessary for religious life. With the upsurge of new apostolic institutes in the nineteenth century the practice continued. The 1917 Code distinguished between associations and institutes. The 1983 Code of Canon Law recognises that the faithful may associate either as a private group giving rise to a private association of the faithful or with public recognition by the competent ecclesiastical authority to work in the name of the Church. This latter association is recognised as a public association of the faithful. Some associations remain so for their duration and may include persons who profess the evangelical counsels.

However, in order to give some juridic standing to emerging institutes, the practice of recognising them as associations of the faithful as part of their journey to becoming fully fledged institutes remains. Many of these associations have members living the evangelical counsels either through vows, oaths or promises. While they are not juridically recognised as members of the consecrated life, they are considered as theologically consecrated people.

CONCLUSION

The forms of consecrated life that are juridically recognised in the present Code of Canon Law have been evolving almost since the foundation of the Catholic Church. That some of the early Christians lived lives consecrated to God is indisputable. What was private consecration gradually became more public and social, evolving to the *lauras* of the hermits, then to the monastic forms with an emphasis on withdrawal from the world, the practice of chastity, a simple lifestyle and life in common with a fixed rule. The proliferation of such groups together with problems of laxity of discipline and lack of accountability to bishops over a prolonged period invited the concern of the ecclesiastical authorities. Various regional and ecumenical councils enacted legislation that took these institutes from private groups to canonical ones with formal Church recognition, set norms for foundation, approval and mode of living.

As society developed, and with it evolving social, human, philosophical, educational and political interactions, new needs emerged in answer to which new forms of consecrated life came into being at different points of history. The structure of these often mirrored or paralleled the history of the development of the primacy of Rome and the role of the papacy in the Church. From the thirteenth century onwards new institutes were subject to the approval of the Holy See and women's institutes were subject to a strict enclosure thereby depriving the world of the richness of the apostolate that religious women's gifts could offer to the poor and needy. In time (nearly seven centuries later), this anomaly was corrected when Leo XIII's apostolic constitution recognised congregations with simple vows and with very limited cloister as true religious. Less than fifty years later Pius XII, in 1947, recognised secular institutes as institutes of consecrated life — a new form, the latest in the Church.

With the promulgation of the present Code of Canon Law in 1983, there is canonical recognition of two distinct species of consecrated life, namely, religious life properly so called and secular institutes. Religious life has sub-species, contemplative, apostolic and mendicant. In addition there is recognition of hermits and virgins as legitimate forms of consecrated life. What is obvious in this evolution is the overall action of the Spirit calling into life new forms at "the appointed time." The transformation from the private consecration of the individual to the canonically approved consecration in an institute was the result of ecclesiastical intervention. The forms that were recognised manifest fundamental coherence, organic growth and diversity within set parameters. Popes, bishops and councils formulated laws and it is these that protect consecrated life though there were times in history when they almost stifled it. What is critical is that the notion of consecration perdures and the means by which individuals and groups enact that consecration change with time. In this new millennium when there are new needs, as never before, it is not only possible but imperative that more new forms be permitted to emerge, to break from the bud. The Supreme Legislator has made provision for such a possibility in the 1983 Code of Canon Law, more specifically in c. 605.

NOTES

[1] SECOND VATICAN COUNCIL, Dogmatic Constitution on the Church, *Lumen gentium (=LG)*, 21 November 1964, in *Acta Apostolicae Sedis (= AAS),* 57 (1965), pp. 5-75; English translation of this and other conciliar documents in A. FLANNERY (ed.), vol. 1, *Vatican Council II: The Conciliar and Post Conciliar Documents,* (= FLANNERY 1), new revised edition, Dublin, Dominican Publications, 1992, pp. 350-426, here at p. 405.

[2] *Codex iuris canonici auctoritate Ioannis Pauli PP. II promulgatus,* Libreria editrice Vaticana, 1983, xxx, 317 p. British commonwealth version of English-language translation: *The Code of Canon Law in English Translation,* new revised edition prepared by THE CANON LAW SOCIETY OF GREAT BRITAIN AND IRELAND, in association with THE CANON LAW SOCIETY OF AUSTRALIA AND NEW ZEALAND and THE CANADIAN CANON LAW SOCIETY, London, Collins: Ottawa, Canadian Conference of Catholic Bishops, 1997, p. 133.

[3] These Societies do not have public vows canonically recognised by the Church. However their members live in the spirit of the evangelical counsels and have a strong common life and apostolate. Their mode of consecration may well be assessed as being a new form of consecrated life in the future. See J. BEYER, *Religious Life or Secular Institute,* Rome, Gregorian University Press, 1970, p. 111. The author argues that the essential of consecration "is not the form of the commitment but the commitment itself. It is not taking vows that is the most important element, but rather the evangelical counsels themselves, inasmuch as they are means of perfection and signs of a yet deeper consecration."

[4] JOHN PAUL II, Post-synodal Apostolic Exhortation *Vita consecrata,* (= VC), 25 March 1996, in *AAS,* 88 (1996), pp. 377-486; English translation, *Consecrated Life,* Sherbrooke, QC, Médiaspaul, 1996, 208 p.

[5] J. ARRAGAIN, "La Vie consacrée par la profession des conseils évangéliques", in *Claretianum,* 36 (1996), p. 259. "Or, cette 'consécration' est loin d'être une notion parfaitement claire au point de vue théologique et canonique. Et même au point de vue linguistique" (p. 259). See also M. COLRAT, *Vie consacrée,* Strasbourg, Université des sciences humaines, 1984, p. 10, where she writes of the search for a term that applied equally well to members of religious institutes and to

those of secular institutes.

6 COLRAT, *Vie consacrée,* p. 11.

7 M. TRAPET, "Les dangers d'une réduction de la vie consacrée à la vie religieuse", in *L'année canonique,* 30 (1987), p. 87. "L'étude des textes conciliaires laisse, en définitive, apparaître que si le terme de 'consécration' recouvre des réalités très diverses, l'expression de 'vie consacrée' n'a été utilisée — de manière au demeurant insuffisante — que pour qualifier la vie 'des hommes et des femmes qui, par la pratique des conseils évangéliques, suivent plus librement le Christ et l'imitent plus fidèlement' (*PC*)." There is some debate regarding the verb "to consecrate". Who does the consecrating? Is it the person consecrating himself to God or God consecrating the person he has called? See M. CONTI, "La vita consacrata e la sua missione nella Chiesa e nel mondo", in *Antonianum,* 68 (1993), pp. 46-47 and U. BETTI, "Si sono consacrati a te", in *L'Osservatore romano,* 3 July 1996, n. 150, pp. 1, 4. See COUNCIL OF THE GENERAL SECRETARIAT OF THE SYNOD OF BISHOPS, *De vita consecrata deque eius munere in Ecclesia et in mundo: lineamenta* (=*L*), Roma, Libreria editrice Vaticana; English translation, *The Consecrated Life and its Role in the Church and in the World, Lineamenta,* Ottawa, Canadian Conference of Catholic Bishops, 1992, p. 11. See also P. ETZI, "Il concetto di 'consacrazione religiosa' nel supremo magistero dal concilio Vaticano II all'esortazione apostolica post-sinodale 'Vita consecrata'", in *Antonianum,* 72 (1997), p. 571. Here the author claims that John Paul II, in his final revision of the Code, declares that "consecration" is to be understood in the following manner: "It is not God who consecrates the one making profession, but the one making profession who consecrates himself to God through the ministry of the Church." The author analyses the *Magisterium* from Vatican II to *Vita consecrata* concluding that "this is the doctrine that the Roman Pontiffs have constantly put forward in their teaching."

8 TRAPET, "Les dangers d'une réduction de la vie consacrée à la vie religieuse" p. 87.

9 B. SECONDIN, "La théologie de la vie consacrée", in *Vie consacrée,* 66 (1994), p. 240. "Il s'agit d'une *radicalisation* de la consécration baptismale, destinée à en tirer des fruits encore plus grands de conversion permanente et de *sequela* significative", p. 240. Theologians hold differing views on the concept of consecration and this debate will be dealt with more fully in chapter four. See J. AUBRY, "La consacrazione nella vita religiosa", in AA. VV., *La teologia della vita consacrata,* Roma, Centro Studi USMI-Roma, 1990, pp. 99-100. "...con

la consacrazione religiosa quella battesimale viene 'approfondita, radicalizzata, sviluppata, perfezionata, completata, portata a compinento o a pieno attuazione, esplicitata, concretizzata e prolungata in una certa direzione'", pp. 99-100. See also E. GAMBARI, *Religious Life: According to Vatican II and the New Code of Canon Law,* English translation, Daughters of St Paul, Boston, St Paul Editions, 1986, p. 92, where he says that religious consecration "drives its roots into the baptismal consecration and is its most precious fruit in the sense that it is a development or maturation of this consecration to which not all the faithful are called. Religious consecration is the continuation or fuller expression of that of Baptism" (p. 92). Another school of thought believes that the consecration through the vows is a new consecration different from that of baptism. M. PASINI, "Vita consacrata e consigli evangelici (II): La distinzione tra "consacrazione" e "professione", in *Commentarium pro religiosis,* 77 (1996), p. 349, footnote 10, where the author summarises very briefly the opinions of P.R. Régamey, J. Galot. J. Beyer and P. Molinari. "La consacrazione mediante i consigli evangelici deve essere considerata innanzittutto come opera di Dio, costituisce quindi una consacrazione nuova che, pur legandosi al battesimo, deve essere tenuta distinta dalla consacrazione battesimale, con la conseguenza che i consigli evangelici e i correlativi voti religiosi costituiscono le condizioni sostanziali della consacrazione religiosa." See also COUNCIL OF THE GENERAL SECRETARIAT OF THE SYNOD OF BISHOPS, *De vita consecrata deque eius munere in Ecclesia et in mundo: Instrumentum laboris,* Roma, Libreria editrice Vaticana; English translation, The *Consecrated Life and Its Role in the Church and in the World, Instrumentum laboris,* Ottawa, Canadian Conference of Catholic Bishops, 1994, n. 50. Here is summarised and reinforced the Council Fathers' understanding of consecration in consecrated life in relation to baptismal consecration and its demands. See too, *VC* 30, where the Holy Father refers to a "New and Special Consecration" — one that is separate from that of baptism.

[10] L. BOISVERT, "La consécration religieuse", in *La vie des communautés religieuses,* 52 (1994), p. 3. "Incorporé au peuple de l'Alliance par le baptême et totalement consacré à Dieu, il est appelé à vivre intégralement sa condition baptismale, à faire de son existence entière une offrande agréable à Dieu" (p. 3). See J. BEYER, "La vita consacrata: prospettive di avvenire", in *Vita consacrata,* 30 (1994), pp. 698-700.

[11] "He" in this context refers to both male and female and will be used accordingly in this study to avoid the confusion of s/he or he/she.

[12] Boisvert, "La consécration religieuse", p. 5.

[13] Ibid.

[14] See J.M. Arnaiz *et al*, "Comment comprendre et présenter aujourd'hui la vie consacrée dans l'Église et dans le monde", in Union des Supérieurs Généraux, *Charismes dans l'Église pour le monde,* Paris, Médiaspaul, 1994, p. 198. "L'existence de la vie religieuse démontre que ce qu'il y a de plus profond et de plus authentique est commun à tous les hommes et à toutes les femmes; que dans le fond de toute personne humaine de quelque race, culture, religion, peuple ou nation qu'elle soit il y a une tendance irrésistible vers la 'sainteté', vers le 'Mystère', une recherche passionnée de Dieu" (p. 198).

[15] S. Canals Navarrete, *Secular Institutes and the State of Perfection: The Priesthood and the State of Perfection,* Dublin, Scepter, 1959, p. 12ff. The author defines the juridical state as a "personal and stable condition which influences the external and social life of a person and which arises from a permanent cause imposed by law, or at least recognised by it, concerning juridical liberty or the lack of it" (p. 18).

[16] *VC*, 17. See also D.L. Fleming, "Choose Life", in D.L. Fleming and E. McDonough (eds), *The Church and Consecrated Life,* St. Louis, MO, Review for Religious, 1996, p. 6, where he elaborates on consecrated life as "a configuring with Christ... a deepening of this discipleship identity... It is to make real and concrete in one's life a response to Jesus' description of a follower as one who chooses 'to leave everything,' ... for him and for the reign of God" (p.6).

[17] Paul VI, Apostolic Exhortation on the Renewal of Religious Life, *Evangelica testificatio, (= ET),* 29 June 1971, in *AAS,* 63 (1971), pp. 497-526; English translation in Flannery 1, pp. 680-706, here at *ET,* 11, p. 685 where he speaks of the charisms of the founder. The Council Fathers had, in *Lumen gentium,* described 'charism' in the context of the Holy Spirit making holy the People of God. "Allotting his gifts according as he wills, he also distributes special graces among the faithful of every rank. By these gifts he makes them fit and ready to undertake tasks and offices for the renewal and building up of the Church", (*LG,* 12). See P.R. Régamey, "Carismi", (art.) in G. Pelliccia e G. Rocca, *Dizionario degli istituti di perfezione,* Roma, Edizioni Paoline, 1975, vol. 2, pp. 299-315, where he examines the biblical and theological aspects of charisms in relation to religious life.

[18] W. Harrington, "Charism", in J. A., Komonchak, M. Collins

and D. A. LANE (eds), *The New Dictionary of Theology,* Wilmington, DE, Michael Glazier Inc., 1987, p. 180, states that the word "charism" owes its use in religious language to St. Paul. "It is a supernatural gift bestowed by the Holy Spirit for building up the body of Christ. A charism is a gift which has its source in the *charis* — grace or favor — of God and which is destined 'for the common good,' (1 Cor 12: 7)." Paul goes on to describe some of the gifts of the Spirit to the Church. See also B.J. SWEENEY, *The Patrimony of an Institute in the Code of Canon Law: A Study of Canon 578,* Roma, Pontificia studiorum Universitas a S. Thomas Aquinas in Urbe, 1995, pp. 46-51. While the Council did not use "charism", the author says that, in placing consecrated life within the context of life and holiness in the Church, it placed it within the charismatic structure of the Church.

[19] J. ARNAIZ, "Comment comprendre et présenter", p. 221. "Ils ont été rendus capables de comprendre et de concrétiser la marche à la suite de Jésus dans le peuple de Dieu d'une manière particulière." This echoes the statement in "The Consecrated Life and its Role in the Church and in the World: *Lineamenta",* where the Synod Secretariat quotes Paul VI from *ET.* The *"charisms of Founders and Foundresses* are revealed as an *experience of the Spirit,* transmitted to their disciples to be lived, safeguarded, deepened and constantly developed by them, in harmony with the Body of Christ continually in the process of growth" (*ET,* 16).

[20] J. BEYER, "Charisms, Religious Institutes and Particular Churches", in *Consecrated Life,* 15 (1990), p. 316.

[21] Ibid. See P. NEUNER, "Charisme/Ministère", in B. LAURET (ed.), *Nouveau dictionnaire de théologie,* Paris, Les Éditions du Cerf, 1996, where he uses M. Weber's definition: "Le charisme est la qualité exceptionnelle d'une personne à qui l'on attribue des aptitudes et forces surnaturelles, surhumaines ou au moins hors du commun, ou bien que l'on considère comme envoyée de Dieu ou encore comme exemple et guide" (p. 119). See JOHN PAUL II, "Religious Live Baptismal Vows Intensely", in *L'Osservatore romano* (English edition), 5 October 1994, p. 11. The Holy Father says that "collective charisms are generally bestowed on men and women who are destined to establish ecclesial works, especially religious institutes, which receive their distinctive mark from their founders' charisms, live and work under their influence and receive new gifts and charisms for each individual member and for the community as a whole."

[22] SECOND VATICAN COUNCIL, "Decree on the Up-to-date Renewal

of Religious Life", *Perfectae caritatis,* (= *PC*), 28 October 1965, in *AAS,* 58 (1996), pp. 702-712; English translation in FLANNERY 1, 1(b), p. 611.

23 J. BEYER, "Charisms, Religious Institutes and Particular Churches", p. 317. The Code, itself, does not use the term, "charism", there being too great difficulty in defining its nature. In the 1982*Schema,* the term was used eight times, four in reference to religious institutes and four to secular institutes. For a fuller discussion see B.J. SWEENEY, *The Patrimony of an Institute in the Code of Canon Law: A Study of Canon 578,* pp. 53-60.

24 G. GHIRLANDA, "Carisma di un istituto e sua tutela", in *Vita consacrata,* 28 (1992), p. 470, summarises his understanding of charism: "Un carisma è un dono esteriore di grazia fatto da Cristo a una persona, per mezzo dello Spirito Santo. Esso puó essere:

— per l'utilità spirituale di chi lo riceve o per l'utilità comune della Chiesa, cioè per un qualche servizio o ministero da esercitare in essa;

— temporaneo o permanente, individuale o collettivo; se è permanente e collettivo dà origine a un ministero stabile o istituito, come il ministero gerarchico, o a un'altra forma stabile di vita, come la vita consacrata.

ordinario o straordinario: il secondo è una momentanea e individuale manifestazione prodigiosa dello Spirito, e non dà luogo a un ministero istituito né a un'altra forma stabile di vita."

25 JOHN PAUL II, Encyclical letter, *Redemptoris missio,*(= *RM*), 7 December 1990, in *AAS,* 83 (1991), pp. 249-340; English translation in *Origins,* 20 (1990-1991), p. 545. See BOISVERT, "La consécration religieuse", p. 6, where he states that the consecrated person cannot focus on giving his/her life to God without being equally concerned for the coming of the Kingdom. "Ces deux aspects (contemplatif et apostolique) sont d'ailleurs si intimement liés que, se vouer à Dieu, c'est inséparablement se vouer à l'instauration du Règne."

26 E. MCDONOUGH, "Charisms and Religious Life", in *The Church and Consecrated Life,* p. 133.

27 F. CIARDI, "Theology of the Charism of Institutes", in UNION OF SUPERIORS GENERAL, *Religious Life 20 Years after Vatican II: Evaluation and Prospective,* Roma, Unione superiori generali, 1986, p. 17.

[28] BOISVERT, "La consécration religieuse", p. 8. "Le propos de centrer son existence sur Dieu et le Règne se concrétise habituellement, quoique non nécessairement, dans une forme de vie qui l'exprime et tend à le favoriser."

[29] L. BOISVERT, *La consécration religieuse: consécration baptismale et formes de vie consacrée,* Paris, Éditions du Cerf, 1988, p. 45. "Les formes de vie consacrée sont des façons particulières de vivre chrétiennement, reconnues par l'autorité de l'Église."

[30] *L,* 18.

[31] *L,* 18 a.

[32] McDONOUGH, "Charisms and Religious Life", p. 133.

[33] W.F. HOGAN, "Canonical Room for Charisms", in *The Church and Consecrated Life,* p. 145.

[34] See B. SECONDIN, "La théologie de la vie consacrée", p. 228, where he distinguishes between an "essentialist" vision and a "historical-existential" vision in relation to charism. The former concentrates on essential elements, while the latter focuses on the charismatic identity of the founder and the ecclesial mission of the initiator and of his disciples. The former risks being an abstract deduction beginning from "above" while the second considers the fruit of discernment applied to the historical developments from "below" and allows more for the creativity and varieties of consecrated life.

[35] Celibacy is the state of being unmarried, a condition freely chosen, but not necessarily implying lack of sexual activity. Consecrated celibacy involves abstention from sexual activity as its form of chastity to which all are called in whatever state. For a full discussion see S. SCHNEIDERS, *New Wineskins,* Mahwah, NJ, Paulist Press, 1986, pp. 207-213. See E. ABBOTT, *A History of Celibacy,* Toronto, Harper Collins, 1999, p. 3, where, from a secular point of view, she utilises the Webster dictionary definitions. See also E. GAMBARI, *Religious Life: According to Vatican II and the New Code of Canon Law,* p. 266, where he is careful to point out that chastity (as he refers to consecrated celibacy) "deeply involves the whole personality." He goes on to say that it is not merely a renunciation of sexual activity and pleasure but "the choice of a closer and more complete relationship with the mystery of Christ and the Church for the good of all mankind" (p. 267). Virginity is described as the

state where there has been no sexual activity. Its spiritual elements will be discussed later.

36 ABBOTT, p. 10.

37 Ibid.

38 Ibid., p. 29.

39 A. VEILLEUX, "The Evolution of the Religious Life in its Historical and Spiritual Context", in *Cistercian Studies,* 6 (1971), p. 9 explains that "Pythagoras of Samos established at Croton a group of disciples dedicated to seeking God and to the contemplation of his mysteries. This was a fraternal life of asceticism and contemplation which already foreshadowed that of the Christian ascetics." V. CODINA and N. ZEVALLOS, *La vie religieuse: Histoire et théologie,* traduit de l'espagnol par E. URIBE-CARRENO, Paris, Les Éditions du Cerf, 1992, p. 22, speak of stoics interpreting the Pythagorean ideal so that "one kept above all a sense of community life, an asceticism centred on the renouncing of goods and sexual relations, towards the goal of attaining impassibility which permits one to arrive at the contemplation of God and higher things." See also ABBOTT, pp. 34-35, where she discusses the influence of Pythagoras and Plato on the emerging Christian community.

40 ABBOTT, p. 34.

41 P.R. BROWN, *The Body and Society: Men, Women and Sexual Renunciation in Early Christianity,* New York, Columbia University Press, 1988, p. 26. Sexual activity for men was regarded as everything from a duty "to bequeath a copy of himself to posterity" (p. 7), to a need to preserve his physical strength by not losing "a decisive surplus of heat and fervent vital spirit" amassed in the womb (p. 10). "Biologically, the doctors said, males were those fetuses who had realized their full potential...Women, by contrast, were failed males" (pp. 9-10), and had no status other than that accorded by marriage.

42 Ibid., p. 26.

43 *Acts* 21: 8-9 tells of "the four daughters of Philip the evangelist, virgins with the gift of prophecy who lived in their father's house", VEILLEUX, "The Evolution of the Religious Life", p.10. He says that in "the numerous writings of the second and third century ... it becomes clear that these 'virgins' come from every social class and

occupation."

44 *Acts,* 4: 32.

45 VEILLEUX, "The Evolution of the Religious Life", p. 10.

46 L. CADA, et al., *Shaping the Coming Age of Religious Life,* New York, Seabury Press, 1979, p. 14.

47 See BROWN, *The Body and Society,* p. 6. "Citizens of the Roman Empire at its height...were born into the world with an average life expectancy of less than twenty-five years." It is reasonable to assume that conditions were similar for the emerging Christian communities so that life-long commitment was limited by comparison with to-day. However, Justin, Martyr, in his *Apology I,* is quoted as saying that "many men and women, disciples of Christ since their childhood, have remained virgins to the age of sixty or seventy" (JUSTIN, *Pro Christianis,* in S. SCHNEIDERS, "Non-Marriage for the Sake of the Kingdom," in *Widening the Dialogue: Reflection on 'Evangelica testificatio',* Ottawa, Canadian Religious Conference, 1974, p. 153).

48 P.F. ANSON, *The Call of the Desert: The Solitary Life in the Early Christian Church,* S.P.C.K., London, 1964, p. 9. In all "there were roughly ten persecutions between AD 64, when Nero treated Christians in Rome as criminals, until Constantine and Licinius proclaimed complete religious liberty throughout the empire with the so-called Edict of Milan in 313."

49 ANSON, *The Call of the Desert,* p. 9. They likewise had the example of the Essenes and of John the Baptist as well as the precept to be perfect, "Go sell what you have and give to the poor and come follow me" (Matt. 19:21).

50 CADA, *Shaping the Coming Age,* p. 15. See ANSON p. 9 where he says that the urge to flee was strengthened by the belief in the immanence of the parousia.

51 T.P. RAUSCH, *Radical Christian Communities,* Collegeville, MN, Liturgical Press, 1990, pp. 38-39.

52 Ibid., p. 39.

53 C.H. LAWRENCE, *Medieval Monasticism: Forms of Religious*

Life in Western Europe in the Middle Ages, London, Longman, 1984, p. 3. See RAUSCH, *Radical Christian Communities,* p. 39, where he points out that "with the passing of the age of martyrs Christianity became not only acceptable but respectable as well" and baptism was often sought as a means of social advancement.

54 M. DRIOT, *Les Pères du désert: vie et spiritualité,* Paris, Médiaspaul, 1991, p. 13. "Mais, paradoxalement, la paix religieuse qui a suivi en a amené d'autres à rechercher dans la solitude, le renoncement, la pénitence, une sorte de martyre de remplacement, le martyre étant alors le passage obligé vers la sainteté." See RAUSCH, *Radical Christian Communities,* p. 40, where he suggests that this new "white" martyrdom replaced death that was the lot of many Christians, and especially virgins, during the persecutions.

55 SCHNEIDERS, *New Wineskins,* describes a movement as having two characteristics. "First, a movement engages a *group of people who are animated by a common concern..* It may engage many aspects of its members' thought and life or only one; it may be highly centralized and tightly organized or it may be very decentralized and amorphous... The second characteristic of a movement is that it admits of *degrees of participation* (p. 29). She goes on to assert that the degrees of participation in a movement are not usually formalized and that the time of belonging could be fluid. See S. FAGAN, "The Identity of Religious", in A. FLANNERY, (ed.) *Towards the 1994 Synod of Bishops,* Dublin, Dominican Publications, 1993, pp. 18-19, for a further elucidation on movement versus institution.

56 RAUSCH, *Radical Christian Communities,* p. 41.

57 LAWRENCE, *Medieval Monasticism,* p. 5. *Laura* comes from the Greek word meaning footpath which connected the caves to one another. The settlement had a common set of buildings with bakeries and a church where they gathered for Mass and prayer in common.

58 Ibid., p. 6. See D. CHITTY, *The Desert a City: An Introduction to the Study of Egyptian and Palestinian Monasticism under the Christian Empire,* Oxford, Basil Blackwell, 1966, gives a detailed description of monastic life in a *laura.* See also ANSON, pp. 17-38, for descriptions of eremitical settlements in Egypt, Syria and Palestine.

59 See M.H. KING, "The Desert Mothers: A Survey of the Feminine Anchoretic Tradition in Western Europe", <http://www.peregrina.com/matrologia/desertmothers. html> (5 June 2000), p. 2.

[60] Ibid., p. 3. See J. ANSON, "The Female Transvestite in Early Monasticism: The Origin and Development of a Motif", in *Viator,* 5 (1974), pp. 1-32. See also ASPEGREN, K., *The Male Woman: A Feminine Ideal in the Early Church,* Stockholm, Almqvist & Wiksell International, 1990, pp. 115-143, where the author explores the approach to chastity in the first two centuries of the Church. This is part of a study of the role and duties of women in both non-Christian and Christian environments ranging from 400 B.C. to 300 A.D.

[61] RAUSCH, *Radical Christian Communities,* p. 37.

[62] J. RYAN, *Irish Monasticism: Origins and Early Development,* Dublin, Four Courts Press, Reprinted 1992, p. 38.

[63] ANSON, *The Call of the Desert,* p. 28. See D. KNOWLES, *From Pachomius to Ignatius: A Study in the Constitutional History of the Religious Orders,* Oxford, Clarendon Press, 1966, p. 4, where he outlines Pachomius' strategies for organisation of the many houses that comprised the monastery.

[64] KNOWLES, *From Pachomius to Ignatius,* pp. 4-5. See VEILLEUX, "The Evolution of the Religious Life", p. 12. See also RAUSCH, *Radical Christian Communities,* p. 17, where he speaks of the danger of spiritualizing and privatizing the Gospel, "ignoring the hard sayings about our responsibility to others." Jesus' message was principally to bring good news to the poor.

[65] RAUSCH, *Radical Christian Communities,* p. 43.

[66] The taking of vows and their relation to religious profession will be dealt with later.

[67] L. JARRELL, *The Development of Legal Structures for Women Religious Between 1500 and 1900: A Study of Selected Institutes of Religious Life for Women,* Washington, DC, Catholic University of America, 1984, p. 7. Monks were leaving their monasteries and travelling about extensively without the necessary authorization and frequently acting independently of the bishop in erecting a monastery in a diocese. There were several pieces of legislation in the course of the centuries regulating consecrated life but only those pertaining to the evolution of new forms will be addressed in this study.

[68] J.D. MANSI (ed.), *Sacrorum conciliorum nova et amplissima*

collectio, (=MANSI), Parisiis, H.Welter, 1901-1927, vol. 6, col. 1226: "...placuit neminem ullo modo aedificare, nec instituere monasterium... aedem sine voluntate civitatis Episcopi. Monachos vel, qui sunt per singulas civitates & provincias, subjectos esse Episcopo, & quietem deligere, & operam dare jejunio & orationi, in quibus locis abnunciaverunt observantes; ... nec communionem habere relinquentes sua monasteria, nisi forte praeceptum eis fuerit propter necessariam utilitatem ab Episcopo civitatis." Canon 4 of the Council of Chalcedon, from the translation in N.P. TANNER (ed.), *Decrees of Ecumenical Councils,* original text established by G. Alberigo et al. in consultation with H. Jedin, London, Sheed and Ward; Washington, Georgetown University Press, 1990, p. 89. Bishops now had the sole right to permit the founding of monasteries, that is, new religious communities, since each was autonomous. It was only later that papal approval for new institutes became necessary.

[69] See M. GALLAGHER, *The Common Life: An Element of Apostolic Institutes of Women,* Doctoral dissertation, Ottawa, Faculty of Canon Law, Saint Paul University, 1995, p. 8-9, where she summarises the effects of the legislation of the Council of Chalcedon. See also C.R. ORTH, *The Approbation of Religious Institutes,* Washington, DC, Catholic University of America, 1931, pp. 15-19, where he elucidates the effects of the Council on monasteries of the day and on religious life for the future. At this period, since Christianity was the state religion, the laws had both civil and ecclesiastical effects, having been incorporated into Justinian's law, so that monasteries having permission for erection were also graced with juridic recognition which was so important for endowments, wills and civil business.

[70] I.G. SMITH, *Christian Monasticism: From the Fourth to the Ninth Centuries of the Christian Era,* London, A.D. Innes, 1892, p. 62. Until this period "there were as many rules as there were monasteries" and "a great diversity of practice, even amongst those professing to follow the same Rule" (p. 63). See A. VEILLEUX, "The Interpretation of a Monastic Rule", (art.), in M.B. PENNINGTON (ed.), *The Cistercian Spirit: A Symposium in Memory of Thomas Merton,* Spencer, MA, Cistercian Publications, 1970, p. 52, where he points out that Benedict's rule "is the objectification of a transcendant and permanent reality (the evangelical doctrine on the perfect Christian life) in contingent and changing historical forms." It is situated in a particular moment of history and expresses a spiritual attitude that cannot exist in the abstract. The ancient rules were spiritual documents, the expression of values and norms. See also J. LECLERQ, "A Sociological Approach to the History of a Religious Order" (art.), in M.B. PENNINGTON (ed.), *The Cistercian Spirit:*

A Symposium in Memory of Thomas Merton, Spencer, MA, Cistercian Publications, 1970, p. 140. "The rule is the mediator in the dilemma which might arise from the confrontation of personal experience and common institution, for it makes an attempt at respecting each member's personal religious experience which can never be sacrificed to the institution nor absorbed by it." He goes on to say that the rule is what provides for life in common, giving a sense of collectivity and community but is often sacrificed by institutionalization and the making of constitutions which can stifle the spirit leading to "observance", conformity, ritualism and rigidity. Examples abound in later church legislation.

71 SMITH, *Christian Monasticism,* p. 63.

72 VEILLEUX, "The Interpretation of a Monastic Rule", p. 55. The author would suggest that the rule was not juridical but spiritual and had not yet attained a legalism that came later. He also contends that, "in any given monastery, the monks might have been using several rules simultaneously for their spiritual orientation" (p. 57).

73 H. LEYSER, *Hermits and the New Monasticism: A Study of Religious Communities in Western Europe, 1000-1150,* London, Macmillan Press, 1984, p. 12. Clearly hermits seek the "perfection of the monastic life" and are described as "those who not in the first fervour of their conversion but after long probation in a monastery... go out well armed... to the solitary combat of the desert." Quoted from J. McCANN, *The Rule of St Benedict,* London, Burns Oates, 1952, p. 14. This was a reversal of the previous experience of the hermit becoming a monk.

74 See VEILLEUX, "The Interpretation of a Monastic Rule", p. 57 and VEILLEUX, "The Evolution of the Religious Life", p. 17. The Carolingian reform succeeded in the widespread adaptation of Benedict's rule but it had the concomitant effect of turning it from a spiritual document to a legal, juridical one. "With this development, the Western religious tradition was tainted by a legalism that it has never succeeded in ridding itself of completely."

75 RAUSCH, *Radical Christian Communities,* p. 50.

76 B. MURRAY, *Les ordres monastiques et religieux,* Paris, MA Editions, 1986, p. 27. "La règle colombanienne elle aussi, même en Irlande où elle correspondait mieux à l'austérité du pays, fut progressivement adoucie et absorbée dans le courant bénédictin."

[77] The most famous of these was the Cluniac reform. It began with the founding of a monastery in southern Burgundy which enjoyed such success because it obtained the first exemption both from civil and episcopal rulers and was answerable only to the pope. It created a system of dependencies foreshadowing the later orders where groups of houses would follow the same rule and be dependent on one motherhouse. See D. KNOWLES, and D. OBOLENSKY, *The Christian Centuries: A New History of the Catholic Church,* London, Darton, Longman and Todd, 1969, vol. 2, pp. 117-128, for a study of the impact of monasticism as it developed.

[78] S. SHAHAR, *The Fourth Estate: A History of Women in the Middle Ages,* translated by C. GALAI, London, Methuen, 1983, p. 31. Such monasteries existed throughout western Europe but with considerable resistance from the beginning because of the supposed "danger of moral laxity and the dishonouring of monasticism." Some double monasteries were St. Brigid's of Kildare, Whitby Abbey in England and Fontevrault in France. The demise of the double monastery came at a time when the cult of Mary was coming into prominence as the antithesis of Eve who was the temptress, the seducer of men and the cause of Adam's sin, p. 33.

[79] E. CONNOR, "The Royal Abbey of Las Huelgas and the Jurisdiction of its Abbesses", in *Cistercian Studies,* 23 (1988), p. 146. Connor gives a detailed description of the jurisdiction, both civil and ecclesiastical, enjoyed by the abbess of this monastery until its loss in 1873 as a result of the bull, *Quae diversa,* issued by Pius IX placing all religious institutes under the jurisdiction of the diocesan bishop. The question of jurisdiction for laity was and remains a controversial one.

[80] SHAHAR, *The Fourth Estate,* p. 38. See J.A. MCNAMARA, *Sisters in Arms: Catholic Nuns through Two Millennia,* Cambridge, MA, Harvard University Press, 1996, pp. 176-201, where there is a detailed exposition of social and ecclesiastical conditions of the day. See also MURRAY, *Les ordres monastiques et religieux,* p. 29.

[81] See D.A. WALSH, *The New Law on Secular Institutes: A Historical Synopsis and a Commentary,* Washington, DC, Catholic University of America, 1953, p. 17, where the author indicates "a surprising innovation", namely the relaxation of the vow of chastity, which allowed some members to marry. The Order of Calatrava and the Order of St. James "required the vow of conjugal chastity together with the usual vows of poverty and obedience." Both received approval from Pope Alexander III, the former by *Petentibus Garcia,* 25 September

1164, in J. MIGNE (ed.), *Patrologiae cursus completus,* Series latina, Parisiis, Montrouge, 1844-[1960], vol. 200, pp. 310-312: and the latter by papal Bull, *Benedictus Deus,* 5 July 1175, in *Bullarum diplomatum et privilegiorum sanctorum Romanorum pontificum, Taurinensis editio (cura Tomassetti), locupletior facta collectione novissima plurium brevium, epistolorum, decretorum actorumque S. Sedis a S. Leone Magno usque ad praesens [i.e. 1740],* (= *Bull. Rom. Taur.*), A. Taurinorum, S. Franco et H. Dalmazzo editoribus, 1857-1872, vol. II, pp. 781-785.

[82] WALSH, *The New Law on Secular Institutes,* p. 16. See H. JEDIN, and J. DOLAN, (eds), *History of the Church,* (translation of *Handbuch der Kirchengeschichte,* 1962-1979), London, Burns & Oates, 1981, vol. 3, p. 464, where he describes the origin of the Templars.

[83] JEDIN, and DOLAN, (eds), *History of the Church,* p. 464.

[84] WALSH, *The New Law on Secular Institutes,* p. 18.

[85] *Constitutional Charter and Code of the Sovereign Military Hospitaller Order of St. John of Jerusalem, of Rhodes and of Malta,* promulgated 27 June 1961, revised by the Extraordinary Chapter General, 28-30 April 1997, Roma, Tipografia Arte della Stampa, 1998, p. 9.

[86] Ibid.

[87] Ibid., pp. 17-19.

[88] See Bull, *Pie postulatio voluntatis,* 15 February 1113: original in the Palace of the Grand master in Valletta; English translation in KNIGHTS OF MALTA, *The Rule, Statutes and Customs of the Hospitallers, 1099-1310,* with Introductory Chapters and Notes by E.J. KING, London, Methuen & Co. Ltd., 1981, pp. 16-19.

[89] See H.J.A. SIRE, *The Knights of Malta,* New Haven, Yale University Press, 1994, pp. 258-279 for some recent historical developments. SIRE states that there are presently more than 10 000 knights continuing the apostolate begun almost nine hundred years ago.

[90] J.D. MANSI (ed.), *Sacrorum conciliorum nova et amplissima collectio,* vol. 13, col. 755: "A praesenti statuimus non fieri duplex monasterium, quoniam hoc sit multis scandalum & offensio. Si qui autem

volunt cum cognatis mundo renunciare, & vitam sequi monasticam, viros quidem oportet in virorum monasteria discedere; faeminas autem ingredi in mulierum monasteria: hoc enim est Deo acceptum. Quae autem huc usque duplicia fuerunt, serventur secundum canonem sancti patris nostri Basilii, & secundum ejus constitutionem ita regantur", Canon 20. English translation in TANNER, pp. 153-154. See GALLAGHER, *The Common Life,* p. 12. See also SMITH, *Christian Monasticism,* p. 230, where he claims that the edict even included, in cases of consanguinity, the forbidding of a nun to see a monk except in the presence of the abbess.

[91] See H. LECLERCQ, "The Second Council of Nicaea", <http://www.newadvent.org/cathen/11045a.htm> (15 March 2000). Canon 20 of the 22 canons on discipline forbade double monasteries. However, several began in Europe after this period, one of the most famous being at Fontevrault, where the men followed the rule of Augustine and the women that of Benedict. The women's section was finally suppressed in 1790.

[92] MANSI, vol. 21, cols 532-533; "Ad haec perniciosam & detestabilem consuetudinem quarumdam mulierum, quae licet neque secundum regulam B. Benedicti, neque Basilii, aut Augustini vivant, sanctimoniales tamen vulgo censeri desiderant, aboleri decernimus. Cum enim juxta regulam degentes in cenobiis, tam in ecclesia quam in refectorio atque dormitorio communiter esse debeant: propria sibi aedificant receptacula, & privata domicilia, in quibus sub hospitalitatis velamine passim hospites & minos religiosos, contra sacros canones & bonos mores suscipere nullatenus erubescunt"; English translation in TANNER, p. 203. See GALLAGHER, *The Common Life,* p. 12.

[93] MANSI, vol. 22, col. 1002: "Ne nimia religionum diversitatis gravem in ecclesia Dei confusionem inducat, firmiter prohibemus, ne quis de cetero novam religionem inveniat, sed quicumque voluerit ad religionem converti, unam de approbatis assumat. Similiter qui voluerit religiosam domum fundare de novo, regulam & institutionem accipiat de religionibus approbatis." English translation in TANNER, p. 242.

[94] The four approved rules were those of Benedict, Augustine, Basil and Francis. See ORTH, *The Approbation of Religious Institutes,* for a fuller rationalisation of the need and desire for such legislation, pp. 27-35.

[95] M.A. DONOVAN, *Sisterhood as Power: The Past and Passion of Ecclesial Women,* New York, Crossroad, 1989, p. 11. See R.W. CROOKER in W.J. MCDONALD, (ed. in chief), *New Catholic Encyclopedia,* New York,

Mc Graw Hill, 1967-, vol. 5 for a treatment of exemption in the Church. "The first known instance of episcopal exemption... is the one granted by Pope Honorius I to the monastery of Bobbio in 628" (p. 717). This is contradicted by M.C. McCarthy, *The Rule for Nuns of St. Caesarius of Arles: A Translation with a Critical Introduction,* Washington, DC, The Catholic University of America Press, 1960 (p. 66), where she claims that Caesarius of Arles (470-542) "believed that it was necessary to exempt his community of nuns even from the authority of bishops lest they change the ideal of life he had set up; therefore, he secured the extraordinary papal privilege for his nuns of exemption from episcopal authority" (p. 66). Later, exemption was granted to the *Humiliati* because the Pope was thought to believe that he, through them, could best refute the heresies of Lombardy at the time. Full exemptions were given to religious when congregations formed that spread over many dioceses and this became the norm for religious in the late medieval period. The balance was restored by later legislation.

96 Lawrence, *Medieval Monasticism,* pp.193-196. He points to the lack of any serious education on the part of the clergy in rural areas where most were from among the peasants. See Donovan, *Sisterhood as Power,* pp. 11-12, where she confirms that the schools were largely attached to monasteries. See also Murray, *Les ordres monastiques et religieux,* p. 41, where he attests to the burgeoning of the arts and the construction of the great cathedrals flowing from the enthusiasm of the laity after the crusades.

97 Donovan, *Sisterhood as Power,* p. 13.

98 Codina, and Zevallos, *La vie religieuse: Histoire et théologie,* p. 52. They contend that, despite the insecurity of the poverty, these new mendicants drew more young people than the security of the monasteries. They were integrated into the "new civilisation, and in a true paradox of the incarnation, their radicalisation of the Gospel awoke the fervour of the masses", p. 55. The Dominicans received papal approval from Honorius III on 22 December 1216 with the papal Bull, *Religiosam vitam,* in *Bull. Rom. Taur.,* vol. 3, pp. 309-311. Francis received verbal approval from Innocent III in 1209 and approval for his rule at the IV Lateran Council, (it was recognised as one of the four approved rules for the future), he did not receive written papal approval until 29 November 1223 with the issue of the papal Bull, *Solet annuere,* by Honorius III (found in *Bull. Rom. Taur.,* vol. 3, pp. 394-397). While the mendicants were to combine the active apostolate with the contemplative in daily life, the eremitical was not absent from the foundation. Indeed, Francis withdrew to the Carceri on Mount Subasio

for times of prayer and fasting. Others of his friars also withdrew to the Carceri and other hermitages. Three other foundations of mendicants at this period are significant as both came from an eremitical heritage. These were the Carmelites, the Servites and the Augustinian friars. See KNOWLES, *From Pachomius to Ignatius,* pp. 55-57 and KNOWLES and OBOLENSKY, *The Christian Centuries,* p. 263. See also W. HINNEBUSCH, "Origins and Development of Religious Orders", in *Review for Religious,* 29 (1970), p. 67.

99 What began as a practical means of providing security within monasteries from marauding hordes became in the course of time a characteristic of monastic life and an essential of female religious life. The first forms of enclosure or cloister were walls built around monasteries for protection from external forces — wild animals, thieves or invaders. As the attitude to women changed and a spirituality demanding a cut-off from the world developed, the cloister took on another significance. See M. DORTEL-CLAUDOT, "La clôture des moniales des origines au code de droit canonique", in C. FRIEDLANDER (ed.), *La clôture des moniales: Trente ans d'expectative,* Namur, Vie consacrée, 1997, pp. 67-73, where he outlines the development of the cloister from the fourth to the thirteenth century. From being a "common sense" requirement of Pachomius and Basil for the sensible interaction of male and female monastics it became an essential, by the thirteenth century, for women wishing to live religious life. In the course of time it was legislated for both by civil and Church authorities for spiritual as well as economic and moral reasons but it was not until the thirteenth century that full papal enclosure was enforced. See also J. PROU, *La clôture des moniales,* Paris, Les éditions du Cerf, 1996, pp. 39-89, where the author explains that the cloister is both an interior attitude as well as an external expression in law. It was both for a spiritual good as well as a deterrent, especially in the middle ages, for those who would sometimes violate their vow of chastity either because of weakness or of being forced to be in a monastery against their will for economic or family reasons. Cf. McNAMARA, *Sisters in Arms,* pp. 373-376.

100 *Bullarium Ordinis Fratrum Praedicatorum,* T. RIPOLL (ed), Romae, 1739, vol. 7, pp. 410-413.

101 V.T. SCHAAF, *The Cloister,* Cincinnati, OH, St Anthony Messenger Press, 1921, p. 27.

102 WALSH, *The New Law on Secular Institutes,* p. 23. Eventually there were Third Order Regulars and Third Order Seculars.

103 *Bull. Rom. Taur.*, vol. 4, pp. 90-99.

104 FRIEDBERG, A., *Corpus iuris canonici,* Lipsiae, ex Officina B. Tauchnitz, 1879-1881, vol. 2, cols. 1053-1054.

105 See WALSH, The New Law on Secular Institutes, p. 19.

106 J.T. SCHULENBURG, "Strict Active Enclosure and Its Effects on the Female Monastic Experience (ca. 500-1000)", (art.) in J. A. NICHOLLS and L. T. SHANK (eds), *Medieval Religious Women I: Distant Echoes,* Kalamazoo, MI., Cistercian Publications Inc., 1984, pp. 68-70. This author reviews the legislation on enclosure from Carolingian times indicating the progression to this point and the unequal requirements for men and women. See J.R. CAIN, *The Influences of the Cloister on the Apostolate of Congregations of Religious Women,* Rome, Pontificia Universitas Lateranensis, 1965, for a review of the effects of the imposition of cloister on women religious until recent times. See also E. MAKOWSKI, *Canon Law and Cloistered Women: Periculoso and Its Commentators 1298-1545,* Washington, DC, The Catholic University of America Press, 1997, for a detailed analysis of the reasons for the decretal of Boniface VIII and its impact on monasteries and women religious. Both authors outline the effects of the decretal on the spirituality of the women as well as its effects on the economy.

107 See KNOWLES and OBOLENSKY, *The Christian Centuries,* pp. 385-425. They examine the social, historical and cultural influences on the Church in this period. See also DONOVAN, *Sisterhood as Power,* p. 15. She discusses the influence of the 100 Years War and the Black Plague on the Church. See also A. RAVIER, *Ignatius of Loyola and the Founding of the Society of Jesus,* translated by M. DALY et al., San Francisco, Ignatius Press, 1987, pp. 36-54 for further discussion on aspects of Christianity in this period.

108 CADA, *Shaping the Coming Age,* p. 34. See CAIN, *The Influences of the Cloister,* p. 1, where he elaborates on the state of society where, among other problems, "religious were now faced with a populace that bore little respect for them or their form of life."

109 J.W. O'MALLEY, "Priesthood, Ministry, and Religious Life: Some Historical and Historiographical Considerations", in *Theological Studies,* 49 (1988), p. 223. The author defines these as "priests living in a religious order or congregation under a rule." He goes on to examine the relationship between priesthood and ministry especially as exemplified by the Jesuits.

[110] Ibid., p. 238.

[111] J.W. O'MALLEY, "To Travel to any Part of the World: Jeronimo Nadal and the Jesuit Vocation", in *Studies in the Spirituality of the Jesuits,* 16/2(1984), pp. 5-6.

[112] Ibid., p. 1.

[113] HINNEBUSCH, "Origins and Development of Religious Orders", p. 69.

[114] DONOVAN, *Sisterhood as Power,* p. 16 quoting W.V. BANGERT, *A History of the Society of Jesus,* St. Louis, The Institute of Jesuit Sources, 1972, p. 44. BANGERT goes on to say that Ignatius had recovered one of the key concepts of consecrated life in the early Church, namely, that the role of the superior was to be in every way that of a spiritual father to the individual subject. This offset the practice of *commendam* whereby, in medieval times, the office of abbot was "commended" to one who was not necessarily a member of the order or even a catholic. The restoration of the role of spiritual guide and mentor ensured the vitality of the life.

[115] *Bull. Rom. Taur.,* vol. 6, pp. 303-306 and pp. 422-427 respectively.

[116] *Bull. Rom. Taur.,* vol. 7, pp. 725-726.

[117] *Bull. Rom. Taur.,* vol. 8, pp. 406-409; 457-465.

[118] GALLAGHER, *The Common Life,* p. 31.

[119] Ibid., p. 28. See F.J. PARENTY, *Life of St Angela Merici of Brescia: Foundress of the Order of St. Ursula,* New York, P.J. Kenedy, 1857, pp. 67-105, for a fuller description of the evolution of the order. Angela's significance to this study is in the fact that she had the foresight to establish a group without cloister, devoted to the poor and to the education of girls. That her effort did not succeed as planned points to the strength of the perceptions of religious of the time and to the strength of Church legislation.

[120] D. ROFE, "Journey into Freedom", in *The Way Supplement,* 53 (1985), p. 9.

121 See M. WRIGHT, *Mary Ward's Institute: The Struggle for Identity,* Sydney, Crossing Press, 1997, xvi, 248 p., for a fuller account of the founding of Mary Ward's Institute, later known as the Sisters of Loreto.

122 See URBAN VIII, Bull, *Pastoralis Romani Pontificis,* 13 January 1631, in L. CHERUBINI (ed.), *Magnum bullarium Romanum a beato Leone magno usque ad S.D.N. Benedict XIV,* editio novissima, Luxemburgi, Gosse, 1742, vol. 4, pp. 180-182; English translation in Archives of the Institute of the Blessed Virgin Mary, Toronto.

123 URBAN VIII, Bull, *Pastoralis Romani Pontificis,* §2.

124 WRIGHT, *Mary Ward's Institute: The Struggle for Identity,* pp. 53-57.

125 See BENEDICT XIV, Apostolic Constitution, *Quamvis iusto,* 30 April 1749, in *Magnum bullarium Romanum: bullarum, privilegiorum ac diplomatum Romanorum Pontificum amplissima collectio continuatio,* Graz, Akademische, Druck-u, Verlagsanstalt, 1963-1964, vol. 3, pp. 54-68; English translation from the Archives of the Institute of the Blessed Virgin Mary, York in WRIGHT, *Mary Ward's Institute: The Struggle for Identity,* pp.196-213.

126 MANSI, vol. 33, cols. 174-173. "Bonifacii VIII constitutionem, quae incipit *Periculoso,* renovans sancta synodus, universis episcopis, sub obtestatione divini iudicii, & interminatione maledictionis aeternae, praecipit, ut in omnibus monasteriis sibi subjectis ordinaria, in aliis vero sedis apostolicae auctoritate, clausuram sanctimonialium, ubi violata fuerit, diligenter restitui, & ubi inviolata est conservari maxime procurent; inobedientes atque contradictores per censuras ecclesiasticas, aliasque poenas, quacumque appellatione postposita, compescentes, invocato etiam ad hoc, si opus fuerit, auxilio brachii saecularis." English translation in Tanner, pp. 777-778.

127 JARRELL, *The Development of Legal Structures,* p. 16.

128 *Bull. Rom. Taur.,* vol. 7, pp. 447-448.

129 *Bull. Rom. Taur.,* vol. 7, pp. 808-810.

130 JARRELL, *The Development of Legal Structures,* p. 22.

131 See WRIGHT, *Mary Ward's Institute: The Struggle for Identity,*
pp. 43-77. Here the author details the history of the foundation of the
institute and the vicissitudes endured in attempting to form an institute
that did not conform to the ecclesiastical laws then in force. She outlines
the move towards central government for the institute, the development
of the relationship with the local bishops and the relationship between
the bishop and the Superior General.

131 See WRIGHT, *Mary Ward's Institute: The Struggle for Identity,* p. 75.

132 WRIGHT, *Mary Ward's Institute: The Struggle for Identity,* p. 75.

133 ORTH, *The Approbation of Religious Institutes,* pp. 54-55. See
B.F. FARRELL, *The Rights and Duties of the Local Ordinary Regarding
Congregations of Women Religious of Pontifical Approval,* Washington,
DC, Catholic University of America Press, 1941, p. 26. This author
reiterates that "this constitution served as a basis for all subsequent
juridical decisions for similar institutes during the next century and a half,
and can be considered as the first juridical outline of a constitution for
congregations of women of simple vows."

134 CADA, *Shaping the Coming Age,* p. 37.

135 See CADA, *Shaping the Coming Age,* pp. 37-38. See also
HOSTIE, *Vie et mort des ordres religieux,* pp. 216-221; VEILLEUX, "The
Evolution of the Religious Life", pp. 28-29; FARRELL, *The Rights and
Duties of the Local Ordinary,* pp. 30-31 and also JEDIN, and DOLAN, (eds),
History of the Church, vol. 7, pp. 3-50. These authors outline the
exigencies of this period leading to the decline of religious orders, the
need for religious that were not cloistered but who were free to live and
work with the people. See also DONOVAN, *Sisterhood as Power,* pp. 17-
20 for a synopsis of the results of the Enlightenment on religious.

136 VEILLEUX, "The Evolution of the Religious Life", p. 29. There
was no new development in terms of there being a new form but this
period saw the journey towards recognition and acceptance of the form
that had developed after Ignatius and Mary Ward.

137 LEO XIII, Apostolic Constitution *Conditae a Christo,* in *Acta
Leonis XIII Pontificis Maximi,* Romae, ex Typographica Vaticana, 1881-
1905, vol. 20, pp. 317-327; English translation in D.I. LANSLOTS,
*Handbook of Canon Law for Congregations of Women Under Simple
Vows,* 9th edition revised and enlarged to conform with the new Code of
Canon Law, New York, F. Pustet Co., Inc., 1920, pp. 246-258.

138 The full title is *Normae secundum quas S. Congregatio Episcoporum et Regularium procedere solet in approbandis novis institutis votorum simplicium.* This pamphlet was edited and printed separately by Typis S. Congregationis de Propaganda Fide, 28 June 1901. The Sacred Congregation forbade the printing of other editions. These *Normae* followed the *Methodus quae a Sacra Congregatione Episcoporum et Regularium servatur in approbandis novis Institutis votorum simplicium* which had been issued on 22 September 1854. *Methodus* is found in SACRA CONGREGATIO EPISCOPORUM ET REGULARIUM, *Collectanea in usum Secretariae Sacrae Congregationis Episcoporum et Regularium,* A. BIZZARRI (ed.), Romae, Ex typographia polyglotta, S.C. Propaganda fide, 1885, pp. 772-773. This document outlined a process for institutes to follow as they sought papal approbation. Both documents are an indication of the measure of regard that the Holy See had for the correct approbation of and care for new institutes.

139 VEILLEUX, "The Evolution of the Religious Life", p. 29.

140 F.J. CALLAHAN, *The Centralisation of Government in Pontifical Institutes of Women with Simple Vows,* Rome, Gregorian University, 1948, p. 69.

141 JARRELL, *The Development of Legal Structures,* pp. 280-281. See WALSH, *The New Law on Secular Institutes,* p. 36, where he contends that the Constitution *Conditae a Christo* "gave to institutes whose members were professed with simple vows a permanent and specific standing in the common law of the Church, but did not explicitly make them an integral part of the religious state." This admission to the religious state occurred with the publication of the Code of Canon Law in 1917.

142 Complete enclosure was not enforced but the rudiments of cloister had to be observed in each house. Cloister remained in place for some congregations founded in the eighteenth century. Either the students had to come to a specified part of the house or the sisters could go to an attached school. However, some creative bishops defined the cloister for their diocesan religious as they considered appropriate. One archbishop in the west of Ireland decreed that the cloister for two communities of Presentation Sisters' (founded in 1906 and 1909 respectively), was the limits of the surrounding garden. For a foundation on Achill Island in 1919, it was to be the whole island, whereas a fourth community founded in 1935 enjoyed the freedom of two islands. He even provided a horse with cart and driver to enable them to travel within their cloister. This situation continued until the change in Constitutions in

the 1970s after the Second Vatican Council. (*Annals of "Iona" Presentation Sisters Convent, Achill, 1919* and personal communication).

[143] WRIGHT, *Mary Ward's Institute: The Struggle for Identity,* p. 149. See also VEILLEUX, "The Evolution of the Religious Life", p. 29, for further comment on this consequence of the use of the *Normae.*

[144] See *Codex iuris canonici, Pii X Pontificis Maximi iussu digestus, Benedicti Papae XV auctoritate promulgatus,* Romae, Typis Polyglottis Vaticanis, 1917, pp. 96-136.

[145] Cf Angela Merici, Mary Ward (1585-1645), Catherine McAuley (1781-1841) whose foundations all became recognised as congregations of religious with simple vows. Louise de Marillac (1591-1660), with the assistance of the foresight and creativity of Vincent de Paul, managed to have her members remain with simple vows, taken privately and were therefore not true religious and not subjected to the cloister. They lived in common, were free to serve the poor in a consecrated lifestyle and are now known as a Society of Apostolic Life.

[146] FARRELL, *The Rights and Duties of the Local Ordinary,* p. 32.

[147] WALSH, *The New Law on Secular Institutes,* pp. 44-45. See also VEILLEUX, "The Evolution of the Religious Life", p. 29.

[148] See WALSH, *The New Law on Secular Institutes,* p. 45, footnote 4. This society eventually received papal approval in 1918 with privileges absolving its constitutions from complete conformity to the new Code of Canon Law. It maintains these privileges to this day and was not affected by the later Constitution, *Provida Mater,* of Pius XII in 1947.

[149] Ibid., p. 47.

[150] SACRED CONGREGATION OF BISHOPS AND REGULARS, Decree *Ecclesia catholica,* in *Acta Sanctae Sedis,* Romae, Typis polyglottis Vaticanis, vol. 23, pp. 634-636.

[151] WALSH, *The New Law on Secular Institutes,* p. 48.

[152] Ibid., p. 49.

153 CANALS NAVARRETE, *Secular Institutes and the State of Perfection,* p. 52. There was a state of flux in the new institutes and CANALS proposes that the Code Commission was not ready to include them as the juridical position "was not, as yet, clear and definite", p. 54.

154 PIUS XII, Apostolic Constitution *Provida Mater Ecclesia,* 2 February 1947, in *AAS,* 39 (1947), pp. 114-124; English translation in *Canon Law Digest* (=*CLD*), Milwaukee, Bruce Publishing Co., vol. 3, pp. 135-146.

155 PIUS XII, Motu proprio *Primo feliciter,* 12 March 1948, in *AAS,* 40 (1948), pp. 283-286; English translation in *CLD,* vol. 3, pp. 147-151.

156 SACRED CONGREGATION OF RELIGIOUS, Instruction *Cum Sanctissimus Dominus,* 19 March 1948, in *AAS,* 40 (1948), pp. 293-297; English translation in *CLD,* vol. 3, pp. 151-157.

157 *CLD,* vol. 3, p. 152.

158 P.M.J. CLANCY, "The Nature of Secular Institutes in the Light of Papal Documents", in J.E. HALEY (ed.), *Dedicated Life in the World: Secular Institutes,* St. Meinrad, Indiana, Grail Publications, 1955, p. 17. For discussion and definition of "state of perfection" see CANALS NAVARRETE, *Secular Institutes and the State of Perfection,* pp. 12-23.

159 *Provida Mater,* § 1 of the "The Law Governing Secular Institutes" in *CLD,* vol. 3, p. 142.

160 *Provida Mater,* in *CLD,* vol. 3, p. 139.

161 PAUL VI, "The Unique Witness of Secular Institutes", 2 February 1972, in *L'Osservatore romano,* 3 February 1972; English translation in *The Pope Speaks,* 17 (1972), pp. 27-28.

162 Ibid., in *The Pope Speaks,* p. 30.

163 JOHN PAUL II, Address in Italian to members of Secular Institutes marking the fiftieth anniversary of *Provida Mater,* "Witnessing Christ in Secular Life", 1 February 1997; English translation in *The Pope Speaks,* 42 (1997), pp. 230-233.

164 Ibid., p. 231.

165 E.W. McDONNELL, "Beguines and Beghards", in W.J. McDONALD, (chief ed.), *New Catholic Encyclopedia,* New York, Mc Graw Hill, 1967-, vol. 1, pp. 224-226. See G. DUCHET-SUCHAUX et M. DUCHET-SUCHAUX, *Les ordres religieux: Guide historique,* Paris, Flammarion, 1993, pp. 37-39. See also P. PÉANO, "Beghine", in G. PELLICIA, and G. ROCCA, (eds), *Dizionario degli instituti di perfezione,* Romae, Edizione Paoline, (G. PELLICIA 1962-1968 and G. ROCCA 1969-), vol. 1.

166 McDONNELL, "Beguines and Beghards", pp. 224-225. These groups have links with the recluses, with the mendicants and also with heretical groups.

167 Ibid., p. 225.

168 F. MASCARENHAS, *The Identities of Societies of Apostolic Life: An Analysis of c.731,* Rome, Pontificia Universitas Urbaniana, 1990, p. 6.

169 Ibid., p. 7. See A. MACHA, *The Juridical Identity of the Societies of Apostolic Life Compared to Institutes of Consecrated Life in the Light of the Present Code of Canon Law, Canon 731: A Comparative Study,* Rome, Pontificia Universitas Urbaniana, 1994, pp.20-24 and also C.J. DUSTER, *The Canonical Status of Members of Missionary Societies of Apostolic Life of Pontifical Right,* Rome, Pontificia studiorum Universitas a S. Thomas Aquinas in Urbe, 1994, xii, 280 pp. 7-94 for the background to the development of clerical Societies of Apostolic Life.

170 JARRELL, *The Development of Legal Structures,* p. 149.

171 See B.J. RISTUCCIA, *Quasi-Religious Societies: A Historical Synopsis and a Commentary,* Washington, DC, The Catholic University of America Press, 1949, pp. xv-xvi and J. BONFILS, *Les sociétés de la vie apostolique: identité et législation,* Paris, Les Éditions du Cerf, 1990, pp. 17-19 for a fuller discussion of these societies and pp. 139-144 for listings of such societies both of pontifical and diocesan right.

172 See J.R. AMOS, *Associations of the Christian Faithful in the 1983 Code of Canon Law: A Canonical Analysis and Evaluation,* Ann Arbor, MI, University Microfilms International, 1988, pp. 6-21 where the author outlines the historical development of associations of the faithful.

173 See T.J. CLARKE, *Parish Societies,* Washington, DC, The Catholic University of America Press, 1943, pp. 3-7.

CHAPTER TWO

VATICAN II AND POST-CONCILIAR TEACHINGS ON VARIOUS FORMS OF CONSECRATED LIFE AND RELATED FORMS

INTRODUCTION

Consecrated life was a feature of Christian life from the early days of Christianity. It was undertaken in imitation of Christ, poor, chaste and obedient, sent by the Father to be one like us, so that he could redeem humanity. Jesus took human nature on himself so that "he could be poured out" for us ultimately through his death on the Cross — a death which is the very foundation of the Church and Christianity.[1]

Jesus, the Word of the Father, was spoken in the world, so that the Trinity could be manifested to the world in an ineffable expression of love, that is, the all-embracing God was particularised in one human being — the generic became the particular. Jesus wanted his life to be remembered, wanted to continue to be a living presence to his Apostles and disciples but mere words would not ensure this remembrance. "And he knew, that to achieve this, he would have to breathe out his Spirit in dying, so that from beyond death he might breathe it intimately into them."[2] This Spirit was not just to be a lively remembrance of him who once was, but also to allow him to remain present in person.[3] Thus it was that Christ left his Church to the world as the living embodiment of his presence and active love in the world — "something humanly tangible that would guarantee the immediacy of his presence."[4]

Just as the Church incarnates or particularises the presence of Christ in the world, so too consecrated life incarnates, in a very specific way, the presence of the poor, chaste and obedient Christ in the Church.[5] He, who was one with the Father, could truly say to his Apostles, "All authority in heaven and on earth has been given to me. Go, therefore, make disciples of all nations; baptise them in the name of the Father and of the Son and of the Holy Spirit" (Matt. 28; 18-19). Thus, from the outset, the Church did not exist for itself but for the mission of Christ. Because of this, consecrated life finds its meaning in the context of Church and shares in its mission. It is caught up in the mystery that is Church. It has Trinitarian, Christological and missionary dimensions. Likewise, it has love both as its source and as its end for that was and is the greatest commandment, "Love one another as I have loved you" (John 15:12), that is, even unto death.

From the beginning, the evangelical counsels of chastity, poverty and obedience were accepted as constitutive of the state of life being aspired to.[6] They were embraced without being defined and were lived in the seclusion of the desert; later, they found their expression in monasteries and religious houses as institutes formed and spread around the world. In the course of centuries the commitment to the invitation of Jesus to accept the gift of the counsels[7] was concretised in the three vows of chastity, poverty and obedience[8] which came to be normative for living the religious life. As seen in Chapter One, consecrated life was originally a lay movement and not regulated by early Church authorities until the proliferation of wandering monks became a problem in some towns and cities. The Church then took responsibility for it, for the manner of its living and for the many forms that evolved over the centuries.[9]

So stringent was the control that even in the twentieth century institutes had to satisfy a pre-determined formula[10] so that there was little scope for a genuine expression of a founder's charism. This situation was rectified during the Second Vatican Council which took a serious look at consecrated life and its place in the Church and the world.

In this chapter, we examine the treatment of consecrated life as found in the conciliar documents *Lumen gentium, Perfectae caritatis,* and *Ad gentes,* as well as in the significant post-conciliar document, *Mutuae relationes.* We analyse the documents under five themes:

Relationship of consecrated life to the Church;

Basis of consecrated life;

Purpose of consecrated life;

Relationship of consecrated life to the world; and,

Plurality of forms of consecrated life.

We then examine the forms of consecrated life that are canonically recognised in the 1983 Code of Canon Law, and look at other possible forms, including societies of apostolic life and those associations of the faithful that include persons who profess the evangelical counsels.

THE CONCILIAR AND POST-CONCILAR DOCUMENTS

Much has been written about the fact that the Council Fathers took a great deal of time and discussion to arrive at the decision to treat consecrated life in a separate chapter in the Dogmatic Constitution of the Church, *Lumen gentium*.[11] There were those Fathers who, during the second session of the Council, felt that religious were adequately included in the chapters, "The People of God and the laity", and "The vocation of all to holiness; religious", which highlighted the universal call to holiness as a response to baptism.[12] Others felt that religious should not be considered only "from the viewpoint of their vocation to sanctity, but also from the viewpoint of their educational, charitable, social, pastoral, and especially missionary work, which is of the greatest importance for the life of the whole Church."[13] Strong representation was made to the Theological Commission, before the third session of the Council, for the inclusion of a special chapter on Religious. As a result, chapter 6, "On Religious" was added to the revised schema of the Constitution on the Church.

Some of the reluctance on the part of a number of the Council Fathers to treat religious separately was due to a lack of understanding of what the religious life was about and of its role in the structure of the Church. There were those who saw it mainly as a workforce, those who considered it in terms of living the evangelical counsels, and those who had an appreciation of the fact that both elements needed to be combined.[14] Moreover, there was a problem of clarity of terminology. The term "religious" was taken to include all who were leading a consecrated life with a commitment to the evangelical counsels either through vows, promises or other bonds, that is, members of religious institutes, secular institutes and also societies of apostolic life.[15] However, despite the lack of clarity in terminology, *Lumen gentium* was a watershed document as far as consecrated life is concerned. For the first time in history, consecrated life was treated as an integral element in the Church and has enjoyed this position as a birthright in documents that followed.

Relationship of Consecrated Life to the Church

In the documents, *Lumen gentium, Perfectae caritatis, Ad gentes* and *Mutuae relationes* consecrated life will be seen as integral to the Church, how the Church took responsibility for the life, how it relates to the hierarchy and its place in the mission of the Church.

Consecrated Life Integral to the Church

Despite the initial problems, the inclusion of Chapter 6, "Religious", in the Dogmatic Constitution on the Church, *Lumen gentium,* definitively sets consecrated life[16] in the context of the Church and, consequently, in a relationship to the world. Neither exists in a vacuum but in a socio-cultural setting with all its relationships, privileges, problems, questions and challenges. *Lumen gentium* 43 situates consecrated life precisely as a structure **in** the Church with its "own place in relation to the divine and hierarchical structure of the Church."[17] However, *LG* 44 stresses that, while consecrated life does not enter into the hierarchical structure **of** the Church, it belongs undeniably to its life and holiness.[18] It is an intimate part of the mystery of the Church (*PC*, 1), and has been part of it since the beginning, following the example of Christ. While the different forms of consecrated life have their origins in history, consecrated life as such had its origins with the Lord.[19] This tracing of the origins to the Lord is reiterated in *Perfectae caritatis*, 1.[20] Thus consecrated life, which the Church, by virtue of its authority, gladly accepted and approved (*PC*, 1), will always be present in the Church even if different institutes, or even different forms, come and go.

Church Accepts Responsibility for Consecrated Life

Lumen gentium, 43 as well as *PC,* 1 attest to the historical role of the Church in a right interpretation of the counsels, in regulating their practice and setting up stable forms of living embodying them. The Church assumes a canonical role as well as a pastoral one in giving institutes a juridical status.[21] Eventually, this responsibility of the Church was translated into new canonical language in the 1983 Code of Canon Law. Canon 573 defines consecrated life theologically and canonically and c. 576 assigns responsibility to the competent authority to interpret the counsels, direct their living and take care that they grow and flourish according to the mind of the founders.[22] During the Council, the Church, through the Fathers, continued to exert its responsibility by issuing the decree for the up-to-date renewal of religious life, *Perfectae caritatis.* The Fathers recognised the need for updating and renewal if consecrated life were to flourish and participate meaningfully in the mission of the Church in modern times.

This decree, however, was more than a directive to update. *Lumen gentium* had referred to a "state" of life (*LG,* 44) but *Perfectae caritatis* referred to "the up-to-date renewal of the religious life" (*PC,* 1). This change from the static, neutral and lifeless term "state" to the dynamic term "life" constitutes a significant move in the thinking regarding consecrated life. It signals a view of consecrated life that is alive, growing, changing and subject to change.[23] The change in terminology, as well as the development in theology, function as a detonator, releasing a potent energy long repressed.[24] The released energy burst forth in an unprecedented process of renewal and updating of institutes of consecrated life, thereby establishing new relationships within the Church and with the Church.

The Council Fathers realised that much in the living of consecrated life had become outmoded and unsuited for many aspects of the modern world. They wanted the gift that consecrated life was to the Church to be burnished anew and restored as it was originally intended. They wanted the accretions of centuries of customs that had become meaningless, the legalisation and legalism that often replaced spontaneity and dedication, the ritualisation of life in modes that were not conducive to growth in holiness or to availability for mission, to give way to a genuine renewal of mind and heart.[25] This renewal called for conversion, for a constant return to the sources of scripture and tradition, to the spirit and aims of each founder and to the institute's sound traditions (*PC*, 2 b).[26] So important were these elements that they were later incorporated into c. 578 that spells out the patrimony of an institute. For the first time, the Church authorities recognised the role of the founder/s and the inspiration that was received from the Spirit at the outset. This richness of the initial gift of the Spirit was eventually crystallised into the word "charism" in an allocution by Pope Paul VI when he addressed members of general chapters in Rome in 1964[27] and used decisively in *Evangelica testificatio* 11.[28] The return to the Gospel and to the understanding of the original charism were seen as foundational to renewal.

Molinari sees the charismatic element as being of the highest importance. The grace given to the founders is a rich treasure and religious must therefore understand that it is in a certain sense continually projected in themselves.[29] However, because it is a living inheritance, religious must seek to enhance it by a continual reflection so that it does not suffer distortion but be vital and available to true adaptation to the contemporary scene. This, as pointed out in *PC*, 4, is the responsibility of all members of consecrated life, not just those in authority. Thus the Council Fathers recognise the principles of subsidiarity and responsibility inherent in community life.[30] They realise that renewal involves not only the institute as a whole but each member in the depth of his being having a wealth of gifts and experience to contribute. They see a living, evolving organism that must take cognisance of its base on the Gospel and on its founding spirit which must be developed and used for the mission of the Church but always guided by its competent authorities.

Relationship of Consecrated Life to the Hierarchy of the Church

Lumen gentium presents the Church as mystery, sacrament, *communio*, Body of Christ and People of God, which includes bishops, clergy, lay persons and members of institutes of consecrated life. It is the way to holiness mediated by its leaders, especially the Pope and Bishops in ecclesial communion. The Council declares "that Jesus Christ, the eternal pastor, set up the holy Church by entrusting the apostles with their mission as he himself had been sent by the Father. He willed that their successors, the bishops namely, should be the shepherds in his Church until the end of the world" (*LG,* 18). This shepherding responsibility should not imply division but rather a deeper awareness of the call to unity since *Mutuae relationes*[31] decrees that "it is necessary to acknowledge, as a basis, the universal call to union with God for the salvation of the world" (*MR,* 4). The dialogue includes the whole Church because "everyone, as a sign of his ecclesial communion, must recognise *life in the Spirit...* From this common baptismal vocation to *life in the Spirit* there come to light clearer demands and effective means in what concerns relations between Bishops and Religious" (*MR,* 4).[32] Since consecrated life, though belonging to the universal Church, is lived in a particular Church, the relationship with the diocesan bishop is paramount.

LG, 45 strongly reminds members of consecrated life that they must show respect and obedience towards bishops in accord with Canon Law, both for harmonious relations in apostolic work and to acknowledge their pastoral authority in individual churches. The Constitution also asserts that the hierarchy has the task of making wise laws for the regulation of the practice of the counsels (*LG,* 45). They should do so in docile response to the promptings of the Holy Spirit, for building up the body of Christ and in order to allow the religious institutes to flourish in accordance with the spirit of their founders (*LG,* 45), that is, charism.

That there is interdependence between Bishops and Religious is without question. *Christus Dominus* exhorts religious "at all times (to) treat the bishops, as the successors of the apostles, with loyal respect and reverence" (*CD,* 35, 1º) (cc. 273, 678 §1). The bishops are thus given "the power to teach all peoples, to sanctify men in truth and to give them spiritual nourishment" (*CD,* 2). Therefore bishops, in this role of *perfectores,* "must promote the sanctity also of religious" (*CD,* 15; *MR,* 7; 9 c).

> To fulfil such duty, bishops along with their clergy should be convinced advocates of the consecrated life, defenders of religious communities, custodians of fidelity to the religious vocation in the spirit of each institute, but also be "firm guardians of the specific character of each religious family both in the spiritual and the apostolic field (MR, 28).[83]

In order to be guardians of the specific character of each religious family it devolves on the bishop to know this character for each institute in his diocese as far as is humanly possible. Such knowledge is particularly demanded when it is a question of approving new institutes. The call of a founder is not a personal gift "in favor of an individual or a group of persons; it implies necessarily a mission in the Church and for the Church."[34] It is a gift of the Spirit founded on love and activated by love in an ecclesial setting. "Thus the founder and the institute he established enter into relation with the hierarchy, the pastors who are called to direct and co-ordinate the entire salvific mission of the Church."[35] In collaboration with the Holy See, the bishop discerns the charism and missionary endeavour of the new institute and may give it his approval as a local institute until such time as it is sufficiently viable, or until it wishes to become pontifical.[36] This process demands "a scrupulous respect for the character proper to each institute of consecrated life".[37] In return, it also demands a reciprocal respect on the part of the institute for the role of the bishop as leader of the particular church. It leads to "an intrinsic collaboration, because of the charismatic reality that consecrated persons incarnate."[38]

Within the context of this mutual collaboration, the bishop cares for and protects the integrity of the institute (*MR*, 11) and, concomitantly, receives from the institute the "visible testimony of total consecration to God" (*MR,* 14 a) as well as its commitment to the mission of the Church.

The Second Vatican Council expressly declared, "All religious, whether exempt or non-exempt, are subject to the authority of the local Ordinary in the following matters: public worship, the care of souls, preaching to the people, religious and moral education, catechetical instruction and liturgical formation of the faithful, especially of children" (*CD,* 35). *Mutuae relationes* unequivocally endows the Bishops with both pastoral and juridical roles in their relations with religious. It endeavours to endow religious with the necessary pastoral assurance as well as the security of an approved juridic framework. It asserts that "there is, then, *an internal organisation* in religious Institutes which has its proper field of competency and a measure of real *autonomy*, even though in the Church this autonomy can never become *independence* (*MR* 13).[39] Rightful autonomy is recognised in c. 586. Religious Institutes need to be inserted into the local Church but also serve the whole Church.[40]

LG, 45 treats of the often delicate relationships between the hierarchy and institutes of consecrated life. The Pope, as primate over the entire Church, can exercise the privilege of exempting institutes from the control of local ordinaries and subject them to himself alone or he can entrust them to the care of the appropriate patriarchal authorities (*LG*, 45). Exemption refers principally to the internal governance of an institute and is granted so that these institutes may more fully express their identity and devote themselves to the common good with greater generosity and on a wider scale (*MR,* 22). Even though some institutes may be exempt from direct control of local ordinaries, they are strongly reminded that the members must show respect and obedience towards bishops in accordance with canon law (*LG,* 45) both for harmonious relations in apostolic work and to acknowledge their pastoral authority in individual churches. At the same time, the bishops are reminded to acknowledge and appreciate the contribution of institutes of consecrated life to the ministry of the dioceses.

Finally, the Church, through its hierarchy, sets forth liturgically the religious form of life as a state of consecration to God, receiving the vows of those who profess them and bestowing on them a spiritual blessing, associating their self offering with the sacrifice of the Eucharist (*LG,* 45). As P. Molinari points out, the Church not only gives canonical status to consecrated life but through her liturgical action she presents it as a state of consecration to God.[41] In this state of consecration the person is more closely united with Christ for the perfection of charity. This union is expressed through relations with the hierarchy, which must be founded on love.

> This action and reaction in the living relationship and mutual love between Christ and his Church, in all its many aspects, explains to us the basic root of religious life... from first to last the accent is on this love, which, in union with Christ's own, comprehends the whole of his mystical body and is there enriched with the wealth of his saving redemption.[42]

Mutuae relationes presents the relationship as *communio,* through which the hierarchy mediates the call to holiness in a spirit of unity and mutual collaboration. In the particular Church the relationship is more specifically with the bishop who is charged with the task of endeavouring to understand the charisms of institutes in his diocese and of protecting them in a pastoral and juridical manner. *Mutuae relationes* emphasises the mutuality of the relationship and particularises it, whereas *Lumen gentium* spoke of the relationship more in abstract terms with "Church".

Consecrated Life and Mission in the Church

Consecrated life is intimately related to the mystical body of Christ, participates in a special way in redemption and is both mystically and juridically related to the Church on earth. In recalling the wonderful variety of religious communities that came into existence, *Perfectae caritatis* points out that this variety enabled the Church "not merely to be equipped for every good work of the ministry" but also "to appear adorned with the manifold gifts of her children ...and to manifest in herself the manifold wisdom of God" (*PC*, 1). This echoes the sentiment expressed in *Lumen gentium,* 46, that "religious see well to it that the Church truly show forth Christ through them with ever increasing clarity to believers and unbelievers alike." It goes on to confirm that the Council gave its support to the generous service of the most varied kinds from religious institutes to all manner of people.

The theme of service in mission is taken up in *Ad gentes*[43] which expounds profoundly and insistently the Church's pastoral work of salvation and its worldwide missionary function.[44] As T. Corboy writes, "The mission of the Church is derived from the doctrine of the Trinity itself and is further developed from the mission of the incarnate Son of God and his sending of the Holy Spirit."[45] Because of its intimate relationship with the Church, consecrated life shares in this missionary function, a function that "by proclaiming his Gospel to every creature (cf. Mk. 16:15), it may bring to all people that light of Christ which shines out visibly from the Church" (*LG*, 1).

All baptised members of the Church are called to missionary endeavours (*LG*, 13).[46] Not only is this assertion made in the Constitution of the Church but it also states that all are called to belong to the new People of God (*LG*, 13). This imparts a universal character to the mission of evangelisation and aims to heed Christ's prayer to his Father, "That they all may be one like us" (Jn 17: 11).

While every member of Christ's faithful has both the right and the obligation to be missionary, the Decree on the Church's Missionary Activity gives to consecrated life a universal dimension in terms of obligation to bring the Good News to all people. *Ad gentes,* 40 specifies the obligation for institutes of consecrated life. It acknowledges that "religious institutes of the contemplative and active life have up to this time played, and still play, the greatest part in the evangelisation of the world" (*AG*, 40). It exhorts them, because of their commitment to the perfection of charity, to continue untiringly in the work they have begun. In fact, it claims that this vocation "impels and obliges them to a spirit and a work that is truly Catholic." Such an ecclesiology of mission invites all institutes of consecrated life into a Trinitarian relationship in a very profound manner. There are no longer missions, but The Mission of the Church.[47]

Basis of Consecrated Life

Lumen gentium 43 gives the basis for consecrated life, namely the evangelical counsels which have their foundation in "the teaching and example of Christ", chaste, poor and obedient. It claims that these counsels are recommended by the Apostles and Fathers of the Church and also by its doctors and pastors. Even though all Christians are called to holiness[48] (c. 210) and to living the evangelical counsels according to their state, there are some specially called by God to undertake a public, life-time commitment to them[49] (c. 574 §2). The living of the counsels by these members, either through vows or other sacred bonds is not so much from the personal viewpoint as from that of the strict ecclesial significance of this particular form of living.[50] *LG,* 44 makes it clear that the purpose is twofold: to set the person free from hindrances "that could hold him back from fervent charity and perfect worship of God, and, secondly, in order to consecrate himself in a more thoroughgoing way to the service of God." While the paragraph reinforces the call to a life of holiness given to all the People of God, it stresses the invitation to members of consecrated life to derive still more abundant fruit from the grace of baptism.[51] The life is not graced by a new sacrament, nor is it a kind of middle way between the clerical and lay conditions of life. Rather the counsels may be lived by both clerical and lay people "so that they may enjoy a special gift of grace in the life of the Church."[52]

Perfectae caritatis reaffirms the evangelical counsels as the basis for consecrated life and, unequivocally, links their practice to the mission of the Church (*PC,* 1). However, the decree shows a progression in theological thinking in that it moves "away from the overemphasis on vows (regarded strictly juridically) and even from the evangelical counsels (understood chiefly in the ascetical sense) as the essence of the religious life."[53] The evangelical counsels are presented as the means by which the pursuit of perfect charity can trace its origins to the teaching and example of the Divine Master (*PC*, 1). Therefore the role of scripture and tradition is paramount in the understanding and living of consecrated life.[54]

Ad gentes emphasises both the dynamic nature of the Church and hence the dynamic nature of consecrated life. Never again can consecrated life be regarded as a static entity in the Church, either in terms of theology or in relation to its self-perception. It is part of the evolving, living Church emanating from the Trinity and in relationship with all people.

Mutuae relationes reiterates the fundamental nature of the evangelical counsels as the basis for consecrated life (*MR*, 10). It places the life firmly within the ecclesial setting with both charismatic and concrete dimensions. It affirms the necessity for an organic *communio* which is the work and fruit of the Holy Spirit.[55] It stresses the primacy of *life in the Spirit* (*MR*, 9) but acknowledges the expression of that life in a socio-cultural, geographical context within a particular church. It gives serious expression to the primacy of charism in an institute (*MR*, 11) and the mutual respect that bishops and religious must have for that charism. Finally, it gives members of consecrated life the assurance that mission is integral to their life but not independent of the bishop's role.

Purpose of Consecrated Life

LG, 43, in speaking of the many religious families that have come into existence, states that, in the many, there is a multiplication of spiritual resources "for the progress in holiness of their members[56] and for the good of the entire Body of Christ." This purpose of consecrated life as the pursuit of holiness both concurs and contrasts with that emphasised in *Perfectae caritatis*. *LG*, 43 emphasises the helps given to members through belonging to institutes — having a stable and more solidly based way of Christian life, receiving well proven teaching on seeking after perfection and being bound together in the army of Christ. In *Perfectae caritatis* the primary purpose is presented as the pursuit of holiness through the perfection of charity (*PC*, 1). The practice of the evangelical counsels is a means to this end so that the vows, community living and other legal or canonical structures are no more than a framework for the response to the special call to holiness given to members of institutes of consecrated life. This call is more fully realised in the deepening of the consecration which occurs in baptism by means of a life consecrated wholly to God through the evangelical counsels (*PC*, 5).

The words, "For the good of the entire Body of Christ" (*LG*, 43), place the purpose of consecrated life in its ecclesial setting. Consecrated life is not for itself alone or for the individual members or even for the good of the various institutes, but for the Church, to whose saving mission it must contribute. According to the type of institute and its capacities, members "have the duty of working for the implanting and strengthening of the kingdom of Christ in souls and for spreading it to the four corners of the earth." *Perfectae caritatis* stresses that the more members join themselves to Christ by this gift of their whole life, the fuller does the Church's life become and the more vigorous and fruitful its apostolate. They, the religious, should be aware that they are dedicated to its service (*PC*, 5). This reinforces the teaching in *LG*, 43, that they must work to perpetuate the work of Christ and make it effective throughout time.[57] Thus each institute must have a missionary goal with a world-view, working within the Church and in collaboration with it, echoing the Lord's words to the Apostles after the resurrection, "Go, therefore, make disciples of all nations" (Matt. 28: 19).

This same purpose is echoed in *Ad gentes*. This document, in stressing the missionary responsibility of all Christians, includes also members of consecrated life. It is not sufficient that, once the Church is established in a nation, that Christians should merely exercise the apostolate of good example. They should by word and deed proclaim Christ to non-Christians (*AG*, 15). Members of consecrated life play an indispensable role in planting and strengthening the kingdom of Christ. Some institutes are called to a direct and active involvement in this mission. Others are called to support by prayer, sacrifice and encouragement in whatever way is possible and practical (*AG*, 40). Members of consecrated life are encouraged to invite new churches to form indigenous institutes with training and formation compatible with their task in the Church and with their culture. They then have the task of leading each new church to be missionary in turn, that is, by "ceasing to be purely local and becoming *Catholic*, actively relating itself to the total mission of the Church, which according to God's plan is directed to all mankind."[58]

Mutuae relationes contains a similar message — "in the Church there is diversity of ministry but unity of mission",[59] the mission of Christ continued in the world. As with all the faithful, this mission incorporates the call to holiness of each member of an institute of consecrated life. This is seen as a fundamental ministry of sanctification. "Superiors have a special competency, as well as the responsibility, of *'perfecting'*, in various ways, the life of charity, within the rule of the institute" (*MR,* 13 b). Moreover, Superiors must "take care of the special mission of the Institute, develop it and work at its effective insertion into the ecclesial activity, under the direction of the bishop" (*MR,* 13 c). This document makes clear that the purpose of an institute is not for itself but for mission achieved in ecclesial unity[60] with the co-operation of both bishops and religious for the good of the People of God.

Another significant purpose of consecrated life presented in *Lumen gentium* is that of being both sign and symbol. "It is a visible sign of the Church's nature — both of her bridal union with Christ and of her 'other-worldliness'" (c. 607 §1).[61] *LG,* 44 exhorts all members to "fulfill unflaggingly the duties of their Christian calling. The profession of the evangelical counsels shines before them as a sign which can and should effectively inspire them to do so."[62] As well as being a source of inspiration, consecrated life also points to a heavenly reality witnessing to the new and eternal life which we have acquired through the redemptive work of Christ and preluding our future resurrection and the glory of the heavenly kingdom. This eschatological dimension complements the ecclesial one. Consecrated life is a reality within the Church, holding the temporality of this life while it points to the eternal future (c. 599).[63]

The purpose of consecrated life as presented in the

documents just studied is to assist members in their call to holiness, not for the sake of the institutes but for the furthering of the Reign of God. Consecrated life is for mission, but also exists as a sign of the world to come, to point to a reality that is not temporal and call all to an appreciation of the spiritual.

Relationship of Consecrated Life to the World

The eschatological perspective is not to blind members of consecrated life to present realities. *LG,* 46 stresses that renunciation of goods, which undoubtedly deserve to be highly valued, is not "to constitute an obstacle to the true development of the human person".[64] On the contrary, such renunciation is to contribute to that development. According to G. Lesage, *Lumen gentium* places the value of the individual above that of the institute and heralds a new era of appreciation of the person within the institute rather than focusing primarily on the supremacy of the institute. Embracing the evangelical counsels, in accordance with each one's personal vocation, leads to spiritual freedom and, hence, to love so that the person may conform more and more to Christ in love.

Those persons who have renounced the "goods" of the world are not thereby useless for human society (*LG,* 46). They are still in relationship with the world and, as in the case of apostolic members of consecrated life, work in the world while still being separated from it. They have their fellow men present with them in the heart of Christ so that they may work towards building up human society with Christ as the foundation (*LG* 46) (c. 577).[65] This clarification of the relationship of consecrated life with the world had significant repercussions in the later process of renewal and in the developing theology of consecrated life.

Perfectae caritatis does not say anything directly about the relationship of consecrated life to the world even while maintaining that members are there for service to the Church and should endeavour to be associated with the work of redemption and to spread the kingdom of God (*PC,* 5). However, this same paragraph presents a conundrum. It says that members of consecrated life, having accepted a divine call and consecrated themselves to God, should be dead to sin and also renounce the world so that they may live for God alone. It would seem that religious commitment is incompatible with a real relationship to the world despite what the other Council documents have expressed.[66] It would also seem that "living for God alone" presupposes a rejection of the world he created.[67] This supposition places in question the value of the commitment of members of secular institutes. Even though the Council Fathers exhort members of secular institutes to "preserve their own special character — their secular character" (*PC*, 11), they seem to forget that this means they live and work in the world and from the world.[68] This seeming contradiction is overlooked in the document. It could be argued that the dilemma is resolved in the later exhortation that institutes should faithfully maintain and accomplish the tasks that are theirs (*PC*, 20).

Ad gentes established that

> the agents of missionary activity are the "heralds of the gospel sent out by the Church". Their field of activity is in principle the whole world, but in actual fact in their special sphere as missionaries they have to preach the gospel and plant the Church only among those "peoples or groups who do not yet believe in Christ."[69]

That this document sees the mission of the Church as being to the whole world augments the view in *Lumen gentium* that the Church is no longer in isolation but in a relationship to the world, even where Christ is not yet known. In turn, this consolidates the stance that consecrated life is also in relationship to the world for the establishment of the reign of God. For religious this implies a delicate balance between withdrawal from the world and being in it — a fundamental concept of consecrated life (c. 607 §3). It is no longer those referred to as "missionaries" that have such a responsibility. The document makes it clear that even contemplative institutes must include mission fields in their prayer and contemplation and, where possible, establish houses in missionary territories (*AG*, 40). In line with the Church and the thinking of the Council Fathers a new openness is required of all members of institutes of consecrated life.[70]

The document also underlines another shift in the Church's relationship to the world. It "deliberately moves the centre of gravity of the prevailing concept of missions from the geographical and territorial sphere to an almost exclusively human and sociological conception in harmony with the Council's ecclesiology."[71] It does not perceive missionary activity in a vacuum but in the context of historical, social and cultural realities. Christian charity is extended to all without distinction of race, social condition or religion; for this reason Christians ought to interest themselves, and collaborate with others, in the right ordering of social and economic affairs (*AG,* 12). Moreover, there must be a genuine seeking "of ways and means for attaining and organising fraternal cooperation and harmonious relations with the missionary undertakings of other Christian communities, so that as far as possible the scandal of division might be removed" (*AG,* 29). The implications for the way that institutes and members of consecrated life relate to missionary territories are significant. They must understand the whole spectrum of life in such places and transform it with the message of Jesus in a fully integrated manner. This includes all that is understood in the terms "inculturation" and "integration" as applied to evangelisation (c. 787 §1). As the Decree states, "Whoever is to go among another people must hold their inheritance, language and way of life in great esteem" (*AG,* 26). The challenge, then, of *Ad gentes* to the Church and to consecrated life is "how it can show that love of God and love of neighbour always form in a new and epochal way an absolute unity."[72]

In asserting and confirming the missionary aspect of consecrated life, *Mutuae relationes* thereby confirms the relationship of consecrated life to the world, established in previous documents. This is spelled out more definitively in *MR,* 15. "All, pastors, laymen and religious, each one according to his specific vocation, are called to an apostolic engagement." This engagement originates with the Father, is nourished by the Spirit. Thus it is impelled by the same Spirit that impelled Christ, himself. "Therefore the mission of the People of God can never exist solely in the activities of the exterior life ... since every pastoral and missionary initiative is rooted in participation in the mystery of the Church." The document acknowledges that all circumstances of mission are not the same or equal. It supports the fact that "there will be differences which do not flow from the inner nature of the mission itself, but from the circumstances in which it is exercised" (*MR,* 17). Again, the document, recognising the profound changes occurring in the world in terms of values, means of communication and contemporary needs, requires a "search for new methods of apostolic presence" (*MR,* 19). This implies that institutes of consecrated life and their members must have a dual relationship with the world, namely, a spiritual one but also one based on a realistic understanding of all the exigencies of time, place and culture.

Plurality of Forms of Consecrated Life

LG, 43 also introduces another significant dimension of consecrated life. In the second paragraph it mentions "various forms of religious life lived in solitude or in community" that have grown from the God-given seed of the counsels. Having acknowledged the plurality of forms, it does not elaborate at this stage on the concept of form other than that found within what is strictly religious life. Reference is made to religious life lived in solitude or in community but there is no reference to other forms of consecrated living. The hierarchy has the responsibility to authorise officially the rules for religious so that "institutes established all over the world for building up the Body of Christ may develop and flourish in accordance with the spirit of their founders" (*LG,* 45).

Perfectae caritatis recognises a plurality of forms in paragraphs 7-11, speaking mainly of forms of religious life, namely, contemplative, apostolic, monastic and lay religious life. There is a special paragraph, 11, relating to secular institutes but no mention is made, during this description, of societies of apostolic life or other forms of consecrated life. It could be said that they are included throughout because of the general statement in paragraph 1. This states that the general principles given for renewal pertain to the life and discipline of religious orders and, while leaving their special character intact, of societies of common life without vows, and of secular institutes. Almost twenty years after the approval of secular institutes, the

Council Fathers still think basically of consecrated life in terms of religious life and the theology associated with it.[73]

While *Ad gentes* does not deal specifically with the forms of consecrated life, it does make reference to them in treating of the ways that institutes and members can participate in missionary activity. It stipulates that all forms have a responsibility to contribute to the missionary endeavour of the Church (*AG*, 40). However, it simply refers to contemplative and active forms of religious life and details the ways in which they contribute. It would seem that secular institutes are tentatively included but have no other role than "as an example of total dedication to the evangelisation of the world" (*AG*, 40). It is evident that the Council Fathers lack a clear understanding of the new form so clearly approved by *Provida mater* in 1947 and are slow to give it full credence in the scheme of ecclesiastical life.

However, the Fathers encourage the promotion of "different forms of religious life" in the new churches so that they might manifest different aspects of Christ's mission and the life of the Church (*AG*, 18). Whether the Fathers have in mind totally new forms or the adaptation of forms already in existence is not clear. What is abundantly clear is that institutes of consecrated life must abandon forms of life and exercises of piety conditioned by their age or social milieu.[74] The emphasis is not to be on outward forms but on a mentality attuned to listening and striving to hand on the "mystical graces" of the Church in a manner in keeping with the character and outlook of each nation (*AG*, 18). This incarnational approach provides a challenge to existing institutes of consecrated life and sets parameters for impending new forms.

There is no direct reference to forms of consecrated life in *Mutuae relationes* other than the acknowledgement that the document treated religious institutes and societies of common life. Secular institutes are included in what concerns the general principles of consecrated life and the insertion of these institutes into the particular churches (*MR*, Introduction III). However, there is an implicit reference to the need for new forms in the discussion on local and cultural adaptations (*MR*, 17). Women religious are exhorted to put "to good use the inborn qualities of their womanhood, and respond to the concrete needs of the Church and the world by seeking out and contributing new forms of apostolic service" (*MR,* 49). Such a response could simply demand new forms of apostolate or, even more radically, new forms of consecrated life.

The inclusion of consecrated life in *Lumen gentium* established this form of living in its rightful place within the Church but its treatment as a separate chapter highlighted its significance in the context of the Church. The document re-iterated the classical foundation for consecrated life, namely, the practice of the evangelical counsels, without giving due consideration to the forms of consecrated life other than that designated as "religious life". The lack of clear distinction meant that the document seemed to overlook these other forms so that what they could expect from it would have been disappointing. It did establish, however, that consecrated life was a sign to the world both of the holiness of the Church here on earth and a promise of a kingdom not of this world. It showed that consecrated life had a real relationship to the world even though many of its members had withdrawn from the world. While no one document can treat of everything, it is evident that the chapter on religious failed to come to terms with the theologies of the form of living. It alluded to several of these, but lacked a clear statement on any. It touched on the spousal relationship of the religious to Christ and of the Church to Christ, the martyrdom of virginity and the concept of consecration, but did not elaborate on any of them. Neither did it explicitate a scriptural basis for the life. Nevertheless, it affirmed consecrated life in a new and unique position within the Church for the first time in history.

SUMMARY OF ANALYSIS OF DOCUMENTS

The main points determined in the analysis of the documents are summarised under their respective headings.

Relationship of Consecrated Life to the Church

Lumen gentium determined that while consecrated life was a structure in the Church it was not a structure of the Church.

It, nevertheless, belongs to the life and holiness of the Church, which has a right to interpret the counsels, regulate their practice and determine stable forms of living them. *Perfectae caritatis* develops the relationship saying that consecrated life shares in the mystery of the Church, presented as the mystical body, wherein the ultimate aim was the perfection of charity. *Ad gentes* underscores the fact that, in belonging to the Church and sharing in its mystery and general call to holiness, consecrated life is also called to share in the mission of the Church towards all people thus giving a universal dimension to every institute of consecrated life. *Mutuae relationes* stresses the unity of the People of God through the ecclesiology of *communio.* It recognises the role of the Petrine office but, more especially, that of the diocesan bishop in the particular Church. In setting principles for the activity of institutes within dioceses, it underscores the necessity for holiness, the call to perfect charity and, thence, to participation in Mission.

Basis of Consecrated Life

Lumen gentium establishes that consecrated life is not merely an entity midway between the clerical and lay states but is an authentic form in its own right, firmly based on a public, life-time commitment to the evangelical counsels either through vows, or other sacred bonds. While all are called to holiness, this consecrated commitment is a further enhancement of that made in baptism. *Perfectae caritatis* describes the overall goal as the pursuit of the perfection of charity emphasising the paramount importance of the scriptural and traditional bases. *Ad gentes* presents consecrated life as an evolving, dynamic entity with a special relationship to people based on the model of the Trinity, while *Mutuae relationes* stresses the concrete and charismatic dimensions of consecrated life, unified in the Spirit. Through the four documents there is a progression in development and thinking. The basis of consecrated life remains the practice of the evangelical counsels. However, from being of prime importance in themselves, in *Lumen gentium,* they become the means to attaining perfect love in *Perfectae caritatis,* guided towards the spreading of the Kingdom through sharing in a missionary endeavour, in *Ad gentes*. All of this activity is mediated through the gift of the charism to each institute which works in harmony with the diocesan bishop in full *communio* with the Church and the People of God.

Purpose of Consecrated Life

Lumen gentium firmly places consecrated life in an ecclesial setting with its main purpose being the progress in holiness of its members deepening their baptismal call through commitment to the evangelical counsels. It is also presented as both a sign and symbol of bridal union with Christ and of eschatalogical longing. *Perfectae caritatis* reiterates the call for members to realise more fully their baptismal consecration but to do so through the pursuit of perfect charity. Both *Ad gentes* and *Mutuae relationes* acknowledge that the primary purpose of consecrated life is to pursue the call to holiness but these documents together with *Lumen gentium* and *Perfectae caritatis* all see service of the People of God as of the essence of consecrated life. That service has both local and universal dimensions unified in the Spirit through the leadership of the bishops.

Relationship of Consecrated Life to the World

Lumen gentium establishes that the Church is no longer perceived as separate from the world but embedded in it and in relationship with it. Because members of institutes of consecrated life are in relationship with Christ they are, thereby, in relationship with all people. The requirement of withdrawal from the world is seen as somewhat of a contradiction in *Perfectae caritatis* which overlooks the existence of secular institutes whose very mission is in the world. *Ad gentes* presents ministry as occurring with people who do not yet know Christ. It is no longer a geographical factor but includes social, historical and cultural dimensions. *Mutuae relationes* emphasises that mission is not exercised only in exterior circumstances but must be attentive also to the interior and spiritual ones, while, at the same time, taking cognisance of the society with its cultural and media possibilities. That is to say, mission exists in a world that is fully recognised in all its aspects.

Plurality of Forms of Consecrated Life

The Council Fathers and their successors, in all four documents, seem to labour under the prevailing view that consecrated life equals religious life, despite the approval of secular institutes as a new form in 1947. *Lumen gentium* refers only to forms, or sub-species, of religious life and this is consistent in all four documents with the exception of *Perfectae caritatis,* which does treat of secular institutes and societies of common life without vows. Both *Ad gentes* and *Mutuae relationes* call for the development of new forms but do not indicate clearly whether they intend wholly new forms of consecrated life or new forms of religious life.

The documents show some progression in the thinking of the Council Fathers in their theological view of consecrated life in relation to the Church and the world, and in their understanding of its basis and purpose. These documents provide the foundation for the understanding of new forms of consecrated life.

RECOGNISED FORMS IN THE 1983 LEGISLATION

The theological and pastoral foundations of consecrated life presented in the documents from the Second Vatican Council were transformed into juridic norms in the 1983 Code of Canon Law. This new code, replacing the first codification of ecclesiastical law in 1917, takes on the spirit of the Second Vatican Council. As noted above, consecrated life is based on the perfection of charity, on the life of the spirit in communion with the Church and its mission. Therefore, the canons emphasise commitment arising from an interior spirit of freedom in love rather than from an external obligation.[75] The law of Christ is alive and active, and while it must adjust to the vicissitudes of the times it is also open to misuse. The new code proposes a theological framework for consecrated life (cc. 573-575) and then sets forth clear principles from which external actions emanate. These external actions indicate the harmony that exists between the inner and external life and situates both in relationship to the

Church and to the world in mission. Thus there is a mixture of theological, pastoral and juridical norms for consecrated life.

The code recognises consecrated life in a canonical and technical sense. Only those forms officially approved by the Church are considered consecrated life (cc. 573-606).[76]

Religious Institutes

Religious institutes are one of the two canonically recognised forms of consecrated life lived in community.[77] "The new Code specifically states that the following of Christ is the supreme norm of life for religious" (c. 662).[78] However, this norm is elaborated in order to give more theological, pastoral and juridical directions to those embracing the life.

Religious life itself is governed by the general norms for consecrated life.[79] It is a stable form of life embodying the profession of the evangelical counsels under the action of the Holy Spirit, in total dedication to God in whose service the members help to build up his body, the Church, for the salvation of the world. They strive for the perfection of charity and are "a splendid sign in the Church" (c. 573 §1). The institutes to which they belong are to be approved by the appropriate ecclesiastical authority — either the local bishop in the case of diocesan institutes or the Holy See in the case of pontifical institutes (cc. 593-595). This ensures that there is a discernment of charisms as well as the protection of having the rule and constitutions in harmony with Church teaching in both theological and juridical aspects. It also makes adequate provision for the recognition of the authority of the Church to interpret the evangelical counsels and to make wise laws for their practice (*LG,* 45).

The general norms also make provision for fraternal life (c. 602) as well as for the formation of members, the governance of institutes with a rightful internal autonomy and the preservation of the patrimony[80] of each (cc. 576-602). In some instances, "by virtue of his primacy in the universal Church, and with a view to the common good", the Supreme Pontiff may "withdraw institutes of consecrated life from the governance of local ordinaries, and subject them to himself alone, or to some other ecclesiastical authority" (c. 591).

For members of religious institutes the profession of the vows must be public[81] (c. 607 §2); there must be an element of separation from the world (c. 607 §3), and a fraternal life lived in common (c. 607 §2) in accord with the proper law of the institute.[82] The incorporation into the institute brings with it both rights and duties (cc. 662-672) and there are norms for separation from the institute (cc. 684-704). There are also norms for the regulation of the apostolate of institutes so that their ecclesial relationship and the union with the mission of Jesus through the leadership of the bishop are established and recognised for the unity of the Church (cc. 673-683).[83]

The Code makes few provisions for the differentiation of forms of religious life. While it mentions monasteries of nuns (c. 614) and associated institutes of men, autonomous houses "of canons regular or of monks under the governance and care of their own Moderator" (c. 613 §1), it does not distinguish forms as such. The distinguishing of forms pertains now to the proper law of institutes where the charism or special character is brought to life in the constitutions and books of the institute.[84] Thus there is no distinction in the Code between religious of solemn and simple vows as was found in the previous code. The apostolic religious are treated rather by implication than by direct legislation. In other words, the **form** is given life through the proper law of the institute and the manner of living the counsels under the inspiration and guidance of the Holy Spirit. That some institutes have a similar way of enlivening the counsels and participating in the mission of the Church means that similar structures arose historically and were, in time, recognised by the Church. There are, for example, the mendicants, the apostolic religious and those who became contemplatives. As was indicated in Chapter One these varying forms could be said to be *sub-species* of the *species* 'religious life', of the *genus* 'consecrated life'.

Secular Institutes

Secular Institutes belong to the second species of

canonically recognised forms of consecrated life. As such they are seen as equal in dignity to religious institutes.[85] Their members live a consecrated life in the world "without abandoning secular affairs. Rather, they seek the sanctification of earthly realities operating from within as leaven."[86] They are subject to the general canonical norms (cc. 573-602) set out for all institutes of consecrated life. They profess to follow the evangelical counsels by sacred bonds, the nature of which is established by the constitutions of the institute (c. 712). In contrast to members of a religious institute, those of a secular institute do not change status in the Church by reason of their consecration (c. 711).[87]

This consecration entailed through the sacred bonds "is full and complete; there is no question of being 'almost as good as'."[88] Canon 712 emphasises that it is the constitutions that are to determine the sacred bonds by which the evangelical counsels are undertaken in the institute, thus safeguarding the charism of each institute. In addition, canon 712 safeguards "the secular character proper to the institute"[89] while acknowledging "a certain pluralism, at least concerning the meaning of secularity."[90] In addressing the heads of secular institutes, Paul VI gave a definition of secularity telling those assembled that "secularity means that your place is in the world...as your very own field of Christian responsibility."[91]

Consecrated secularity is closely associated with and linked to the concept of mission and apostolate in secular institutes. These "are so inseparably bound one can hardly speak of one without the other. The perspective of each becomes more a nuance than a differentiation. They merge in a vital unity, in the combination of man's endeavour and the action of God operating in him."[92] The secular institute is

> a community which, by remaining in the ordinary conditions of existence, with each person in his own environment, seeks the reordering of temporal values according to Christ and the integral development of the cosmos, of humanity, and of man, using the means suited to the nature of all these.[93]

Paul VI reminded members that "they must listen to the

appeal of Evangelii nuntiandi,[94] as being addressed particularly to them. 'The specific field of their evangelising activity is the vast and complicated world of politics, social matters, economy, but also culture, sciences and arts, international life and the mass media'.'[95] John Paul II re-echoed these sentiments in his address, "To Change the World from the Inside," when he reminded his listeners that "Secular Institutes will become the Church's experimental laboratory for its acid test of its adaptations in dealing with the world."[96] John Paul II continued by saying that he asked the members

to consider three conditions of fundamental importance for effective mission: (a) You must be above all disciples of Christ... You do this in a way that does not change your condition — you are and you remain lay people, and this is very important — but actually confirms and strengthens it. Your secular condition is now consecrated...

(b) The second condition refers to the practical wisdom gained by experience, and the know-how, your competence in this your own field of work...

(c) The third condition which I ask you to think over is the resolve in your hearts, hallmark of your condition as Secular Institute members, to change the world from the inside...You must consider yourselves part of the world, committed to the sanctification of the world, with full acceptance of its rights, its claims upon you, claims inseparable from the autonomy of the world, of its values, of its laws.[97]

This blueprint for members of secular institutes is juridicised in c. 713 §2. Members "participate in the evangelising mission of the Church in the world and from within the world...They also offer their cooperation to serve the ecclesial community in accordance with the secular manner of life proper to them." Their mission "is not to establish and develop the ecclesial community" (*EN*, 70). Neither is their mission one of the institute but a personal one carried out in accord with the spirit of their charism and under the directives of their constitutions. Their duties are those of any of the lay members of Christ's faithful lived in an intensive commitment. Similarly, for clerical members their role is that of clergy through their sacred ministry.[98] Their relationship to the official Church, especially the bishop, is that of the lay person or of the priest who is incardinated in a diocese. What applies to each of these applies to members of the secular institutes. As institutes, the work, is "to form their members' consciousness to maturity and openness"[99] for their consecrated secularity. However, special tasks, such as catechetics, may be assigned to them.

Unlike the situation in religious institutes, members of secular institutes are not bound to live a fraternal life in common. They live their lives in the ordinary conditions of the world, either alone, in their families or in fraternal groups, in accordance with their constitutions (c. 714). However, there may be houses in common for their leaders, for formation or for the sick and elderly or even for specific works.

The flexibility of the secular institutes is indicated in the canons that give the members the right to share in the governance of the institute as well as determine the type of governance, policies for admission and dismissal, administration of goods and the daily organising of life (cc. 716-730).

That secular institutes are a "new form" of consecrated life is beyond doubt. Paul VI declared this as fact in his short address on the occasion of the 30th anniversary of *Provida Mater* — "thirty years ago, on 2 February 1947, the Church recognized a new form of consecrated life."[100]

Societies of Apostolic Life

Although societies of apostolic life are treated in the 1983 Code in the same Part, namely Book II, Part III, as are institutes of consecrated life they are not canonically recognised as forms of consecrated life but are a separate entity under their own title.[101] Canon 731 §1 states that they "approximate to institutes of consecrated life. Their members, without taking religious vows, pursue the apostolic purpose proper to each society. Living a fraternal life in common in their own special manner, they strive for the perfection of charity through the observance of the constitutions." The second paragraph of the canon speaks of some societies "in which the members, through a bond defined in the constitutions, undertake to live the evangelical counsels" (c. 731 §2).

The document, *Perfectae caritatis,* as its title suggests, envisaged consecrated life as the seeking of the perfection of charity, but mediated through the profession of the evangelical counsels (*PC* 1). If the perfection of charity is of the essence of consecrated life, it follows that the means are secondary. Therefore, if the perfection of charity is pursued through a total commitment to God for the sake of the mission of Jesus and the coming of the Reign of God, then such commitment, in a stable form of living and lived in a fraternal life in common, is a form of consecrated life. That so many members of societies of apostolic life also profess the evangelical counsels either by private vows renewed annually, or by oaths or other sacred bonds, strengthens the proposition.[102] What is lacking for such institutes is the public profession of the counsels, although the concept of their extending and deepening the consecration of baptism is evidenced nonetheless. It can be said that, theologically, societies of apostolic life are attuned to consecrated life, but they are not so consonant either juridically or canonically.[103]

The anomaly of a separate category for these societies and their non-inclusion in institutes of consecrated life could be attended to by the canonical re-definition in line with the lived experience. The definitive interpretation of their living of the counsels could be contained in their constitutions so that the practice of poverty, for example, with the missions in mind, could be accommodated. That there are many similarities between institutes of consecrated life and societies of apostolic life is without question. The societies of apostolic life have as their primary focus the mission or apostolate[104] "without taking religious vows" (c. 731 §1). Since vows are not essential for consecrated life and since all members of institutes of consecrated life are urged to be missionary in mind and heart (*Ad gentes*), the canonical differences would appear to be surmountable.[105] For those who undertake living according to the evangelical counsels, the issue of what "public" embraces could be negotiated. One solution would be to recognise the consecration of the members of societies of apostolic life, permit them to develop their special identity but place them as a new form under the genus of consecrated life defined with different modalities. L.A. Luna Barrera suggests that the group without vows could belong to associations of the faithful while the other groups could be assumed into the institutes of consecrated life. "This would require the acceptance and approval of the competent ecclesiastical authority and of the members who would make up the new membership. This they must make known by a vote with a qualified majority."[106]

Societies of apostolic life are subject to cc. 578-597 in common with all institutes of consecrated life but "with due regard, however, for the nature of each society" (c. 732). For societies of clerics, incardination may be in the society or in a diocese, to be determined according to the constitutions (c. 736 §1). The relationship with the bishop, with respect to the apostolate, depends on the place of incardination or on the constitutions. In other words, the provisions are similar to those for institutes of consecrated life.

Hermits

Hermits were the foundational members of consecrated life in the early history of the Church (see Chapter 1). In seeking to dedicate themselves totally to God, they withdrew from the world and lived solitary lives in the desert in prayer, solitude, self-denial and other forms of asceticism.[107] This individual form of consecrated life is recognised in the 1983 Code of Canon Law. "For the first time in the modern era, the Latin Church opens to hermits independent of any institute the possibility of juridic status within the context of consecrated life."[108]

Canon 603 §1 states that "besides institutes of consecrated life, the Church recognises the life of hermits or anchorites." This individual life-choice contrasts with that lived in institutes and acknowledges the right of individual members of the Church to be recognised "by law as dedicated to God in consecrated life if, in the hands of the diocesan Bishop, they publicly profess, by a vow or some other sacred bond, the three evangelical counsels" (c. 603 §2). They can then live a particular form of life under the guidance of the diocesan Bishop. This form of life is in contradistinction to eremitical life lived attached to an institute where the constitutions of the institute provide the norms for life. The essence of this form of consecrated life lies in the profession of the evangelical counsels and the withdrawal further from the world, living life in silence, prayer and penance. The withdrawal does not necessarily mean to isolated places without human contact. It represents a personal withdrawal to a place, even in cities, where the individual can be alone to follow the chosen way of life.[109] This style of life does not preclude mixing with people as hospitality and necessity require.[110]

It is for the individual and the bishop to determine the charter or rule of life tailored to the person. It becomes "a personal document, adapted to each vocation, taking into account, in order to express better the mode of a true eremitical life, the personality of the interested person (life prior to this, needs and possibilities on the physical, intellectual and spiritual levels, etc.)"[111] Conditions for embracing this life are not spelled out in the code. It is presumed that the norms for consecrated life would be followed, that is, that the subject be catholic, be in communion with the Church, be of legal age and of sufficient maturity and stability, both psychologically and physically, to embrace such a life.

That eremitical life is recognised in the Code of Canon Law indicates an acceptance of a previously respected and admired form of consecrated life. It is not new but is re-introduced with the blessing of the Church as a means to respond to the call to holiness by those who are so inspired by the Spirit.

Consecrated Virgins

Consecrated virgins were a feature of the early life of the Church, living either at home with their families or together in groups.[112] After the eighth century the rite of consecration of virgins had practically disappeared, except for use in some rare monastic families which preserved the tradition more as a "crowning" of monastic profession.[113] Despite requests from bishops in the early part of the 20th century,[114] it was not until. the introduction of c. 604 in the 1983 Code of Canon Law that the reality of permitting consecrated virgins in the world was acknowledged anew in canon law. The revised rite for the consecration of virgins had already been approved in 1970. The canon, as well as re-establishing the order of consecrated virgins, also confirmed that it is possible to live a consecrated life in the world without being attached to an institute.[115] It is the bishop of the diocese who "consecrates them according to the approved liturgical rite" (c. 604 §1).[116] The rite does not "necessarily require any form of vow or other sacred bond and does not juridically encompass the evangelical counsels of poverty and obedience."[117] However, the *propositum* of the canon with respect to virginity would meet that exigency since it was undertaken in a solemn and public ceremony.[118] Therefore it is not necessarily a form of consecrated life in canonical terms but "approximates to these forms of consecrated life" (c. 604 §1) and has juridic status.[119] Moreover, the consecrated virgin is not consecrated for herself *per se* but, having been "mystically espoused to Christ, she is dedicated to the service of the Church" (c. 604 §1). She is a public sign of the espousal of Christ to his Church and this takes precedence over any ministry.[120]

The decision to consecrate rests with the bishop and it is for him to decide and then approve the nature of service to the Church to be undertaken by the consecrated virgin. The state of consecrated virginity is thus recognised as integral to the Church and is made so by an official bond through the consecration. However, the canon does not define the relationship with the bishop nor place him under any obligation to determine a way of life for the guidance of the consecrated virgin. It acknowledges the complete autonomy of the person to live a consecrated life. This contrasts with the expectation for the hermit who takes vows.

Associations of the Faithful with Vows

All the faithful, that is, those who have been baptised and who are in full communion with the Church (cf. c. 205), are called to holiness (*LG* 39). They have the right to participate in the apostolic action of the Church (c. 216) and to form associations "which serve charitable or pious purposes or which foster the Christian vocation in the world" (c. 215). From among those faithful, whether cleric or lay, some may choose to consecrate themselves to God by profession of the evangelical counsels (c. 207 §2).

To be recognised canonically as consecrated life, the vows or other sacred bonds must be recognised and approved by the Church (c. 207 §2) in an institute of consecrated life. For those wishing to establish new institutes, the practice has been to begin as associations of the faithful.[121] Associations of the faithful, as distinct from institutes of consecrated life, "strive with a common effort to foster a more perfect life, or to promote public worship or Christian teaching" (c. 298 §1). They are to have their own statutes approved by the competent ecclesiastical authority and may be either private or public associations.

Some associations remain such for the term of their existence but some are transitional, that is, remain so until recognised as institutes of consecrated life or societies of apostolic life. These transitional associations "conduct themselves as though they had the juridical nature of an institute of consecrated life even though, as a matter of fact, they do not yet have that status."[122] On the other hand, there are associations of the faithful where some members are consecrated by the profession of the evangelical counsels either by vow or other sacred bond, and which retain their status as associations by choice.

These associations may include clerics, married couples, lay people and those consecrated by profession of the evangelical counsels. They wish to remain as such for the richness of the witness of a microcosm of the Church. If they become a public association they can take on an apostolate, in the name of the Church and with the blessing of the Church, while the Bishop continues to discern the Spirit and the genuineness of the charism in accord with *Perfectae caritatis,* 19 and *Mutuae relationes,* 51 as well as taking cognisance of the canons on general norms for consecrated life and associations of the faithful.

"The contents of c. 207 §2 represent something new in the Code of 1983, a newness already contained in the apostolic constitution *Provida Mater,* sanctioned by Vatican II and followed as such in the Code."[123] E. Gambari claims that vows pronounced by members of associations according to statutes approved by a Bishop cannot be considered purely private. He wonders if "the recognised and approved by the Church" does not, *in effect*, confer upon such vows a status equivalent to public vows (c. 1192). They are not, he says, equivalent to the vows of religious but could be analogous to those of secular institutes or those of societies of apostolic life. What is certain is that such associations have consecrated persons and could be considered for recognition as a new form of consecrated life if that is the wish of the founder/s.

CONCLUSION

The four documents, chosen from many issued on the subject of consecrated life during the Second Vatican Council and after it, are fundamental for an understanding of consecrated life at this point in history.

Lumen gentium definitively places consecrated life in the context of the Church and acknowledges it as an integral structure in the Church but not of the Church. It recapitulates the theological basis for consecrated life as understood at this moment. It examines the purpose of consecrated life both for the individuals who embrace it, for the Church, and for the world. It takes a fresh look at the relationship with the world acknowledging the goodness of all creation and giving fresh perspectives to the ideal of "flight from the world". Finally, it admits of the reality that there are many forms related to the ever-abundant gifts of the Spirit, the needs of the times and the charisms of founders. However, the concept of consecrated life in this crucial expression of the Church's understanding of itself, is limited largely to the one form — religious life, even though both Secular Institutes and Societies of Apostolic Life had been approved for some time.

Perfectae caritatis reinforces the relationship of consecrated life to the Church and its importance to the mission of the Church. It simultaneously recognises the need for a genuine renewal and adaptation to modern life if it is to be the means of holiness for its members and perceived as more than an anachronism in daily living. It acknowledges the plurality of forms within religious life (strictly so called), encourages this diversity and really calls for a flowering of the fruits of their charisms. While there is still much ambiguity in the treatment of secular institutes and other forms of consecrated life, the document exudes new life. It invites institutes, in the spirit of openness, trust and inclusiveness engendered at the Council, to be revitalised in a manner never before experienced in the Church.

Ad gentes re-echoes the mission of Jesus to the whole world widening the horizons of members of consecrated life to embrace all peoples. It underscores the missionary nature of the Church, the need for renewal as well as a fresh look at the theological underpinnings of institutes. *Mutuae relationes,* 8 concretises the relationship between institutes and the Church in the person of the diocesan bishop who heads the local Church, is responsible for its mission and the mission to the world. Such a relationship is the linchpin to the Church universal.

The teachings of these documents (and others) found their juridical expression in the 1983 Code of Canon Law. There, the Church expresses its care for the protection of the gifts given to it (c. 575), exercises its right to interpret the living of the evangelical counsels, sets parameters for new institutes, seeks to give wise guidelines for the members living in institutes, both protecting their rights and those of the institutes as well as outlining their mutual duties. The most significant and liberating feature of the legislation is the freedom and flexibility accorded to institutes to incorporate the spirit of their charism into their constitutions and statutes. However, the need to categorise institutes within the canonically recognised boundaries of consecrated life does not permit a full recognition of the variety of forms that exist in reality in the Church as a result of the response to the needs of society and the ever-present action of the Spirit. Canon 605 and the reflection engaged in before, during and after the 1994 Synod of Bishops on consecrated life offer a window of hope on the possibilities of new forms and is the subject of exploration in the next chapter.

NOTES

¹ See H. URS VON BALTHASAR, *Church and World,* translated by A.V. LITTLEDALE and A. DRU, Montreal, Palm Publishers, 1967, p. 29.

² H. URS VON BALTHASAR, *New Elucidations,* translated by M.T. SKERRY, San Francisco, Ignatius Press, 1986, p. 88.

³ See ibid., p. 89.

⁴ Ibid.

⁵ F. WULF, "The Call of the Whole Church to Holiness", in H. VORGRIMLER, *Commentary on the Documents of Vatican II,* Freiburg, Herder and Herder, 1967-1969, vol. 1, p. 274. The author says, "because that (religious) state is intelligible only in terms of the mystery of the redemption, it refers men to the inmost mystery of the Church — to the crucified and risen Christ who cloaks himself in and works through her visibility, to the salvation present in him — as no other ecclesiastical state is able to do."

⁶ See H. URS VON BALTHASAR, *Love Alone,* translated by A. DRU, New York, Herder and Herder, 1969, p. 110. Here the author asserts: "There are not really three counsels but one — to *one* form of life: nor are there really three vows, but only one — to vow oneself to the crucified form of love, as to the one and only form of life."

⁷ See P. MOLINARI and P. GUMPEL, *Il capitolo VI "De religiosis" della costituzione dogmatica sulla Chiesa,* Milan, Editrice Àncora, 1985, p. 138. The author distinguishes between "precept" and "counsel" as used in *Lumen gentium.* "I precetti riguardano ciò che si è obbligati a fare, mentre il consiglio va al di là di ciò che è dovuto. Si specifica inoltre che la mancata osservanza di un precetto costituisce un peccato, mentre chi non segue un consiglio otterrà un bene minore, ma non fa nulla di male."

⁸ J. DANIÉLOU, "La place des religieux dans la structure de l'Église", in G. BARAÚNA (ed.), *L'Église de Vatican II: Études autour de la Constitution conciliaire sur l'Église,* Paris, Éditions du Cerf, 1966, vol. 3, pp. 1174-1175. The author points out that "poverty and obedience, in so far as they are expressions of a particular state of life, are only suggested in the New Testament. It is quite different in the case of virginity consecrated to God." He quotes the disciples asking Jesus if it

were better not to marry and the reply, "It is not everyone who can accept what I have said, but only those to whom it is granted" (Matt. 19:10-11). St Paul, in 1 Cor. 7:25, refers to his own "counsel" concerning virgins so that it is clear, concludes the author, that consecrated virginity is not a precept for all but a call of the Lord addressed to a few.

9 E. MCDONOUGH, *Religious in the 1983 Code: New Approaches to the New Law,* Chicago, Franciscan Herald Press, 1985, p. 16. The author explains that legislation is often a response to crisis. "Ecclesiastical law is often a dialectical response to particular, historically situated circumstances. Likewise, church law evolves only in the context of the real world in which this Body of Christ that we call the Church exists."

10 G. BATTELLI, *Religious Life in the Light of the New Canon Law,* Nairobi, Kenya, St Paul Publications – Africa, 1990, p. 55. The pre-determined formula was set out in the *Normae secundum quas S. Cong. Episcoporum et regularium procedere solet in approbandis novis institutis votorum simplicium,* Romae, Typis S. C. Propagande Fide, 1901. The *normae* were revised after the 1917 code and published as *Normae secundum quas S. Congregatio de Religiosis in novis religiosis congregationibus approbandis procedere solet,* Romae, Typis polyglottis Vaticanis, 1922, 16 p.

11 SECOND VATICAN COUNCIL, "Dogmatic Constitution on the Church", *Lumen gentium* (= *LG*), 21 November 1964, in *Acta Apostolicae Sedis* (= *AAS*), 57 (1965), pp. 5-75; English translation of this and other conciliar documents in A. FLANNERY (ed.), vol. 1, *Vatican Council II: The Conciliar and Post Conciliar Documents,* (= FLANNERY 1), new revised edition, Dublin, Dominican Publications, 1992, p. 403. All quotations from Council documents will be from FLANNERY unless otherwise indicated.

12 See A. HASTINGS, *A Concise Guide to the Documents of the Second Vatican Council,* London, Darton, Longman & Todd, 1968, Vol. 1, p. 32 and pp. 52-54. During the Second Vatican Council there was an acceptance of a significant shift in ecclesiology. The Church was no longer seen primarily as "a perfect society" with a "monarchical" structure concerned mainly with the visible and governmental side. The Council placed more emphasis on the Mystical Body, the theology of the People of God, the mystery of the Church, the role of the Church in the world and in relation to it. Consequently, the place of religious had a different starting point from that perceived after the 1917 Code of Canon Law. See ibid., pp. 30-31.

13 R.M. WILTGEN, *The Rhine Flows into the Tiber: A History of Vatican II,* Devon, Augustine Publishing Co., 1979, p. 105.

14 Ibid., pp. 104-105

15 See E. McDONOUGH, *"Lumen gentium's* Chapter 6: Religious", in D.L. FLEMING, and E. McDONOUGH (eds), *The Church and Consecrated Life,* St. Louis, MO, Review for Religious, 1996, p. 24. See alsoMOLINARI and GUMPEL, *Il capitolo VI "De religiosis",* p. 99. See also M.J. SCHOENMAECKERS, *Genèse du chapître VI 'De religiosis' de la constitution dogmatique sur l'Église 'Lumen gentium',* Rome, Gregorian University Press, 1983, p. 98.

16 "Consecrated life" will be used in this dissertation to include all those forms mentioned in relation to "religious" in *Lumen gentium.*

17 F. WULF, "Decree on the Appropriate Renewal of the Religious Life", in H. VORGRIMLER, *Commentary on the Documents of Vatican II,* vol. 2, p. 329. "The religious state is a state within the Church, not just in the sense that it operates within the Church, receives grace from the Church and is legally sanctioned by the Church, but in the sense that it shares in a special way in the mystery of the Church, is one of her organs, through which the Church perfects her own life."

18 See G. GHIRLANDA, "The Consecrated Life in the Church", in *Consecrated Life,* 20-21 (1999), (combined edition), p. 87. The author quotes John Paul II at the Wednesday General Audience on 28 September 1994, just prior to the opening of the Synod on Consecrated Life. "The authoritative interpretation which the Pope gives of this text is important: 'This adverb — "undeniably" — means that all of the jolts that might agitate the life of the Church will never be able to eliminate the consecrated life, characterized by the profession of the evangelical counsels. This state of life will always remain an essential element of the holiness of the Church. According to the Council, this is an "undeniable" truth'." (Quoted in *L'Osservatore romano,* (English edition), 5 October, 1994, p. 11.) The adverb *inconcusse* is translated as "undeniably" or "unshakably". There is a correlative canon to this, c. 207 §2.

19 See E. MARTINEZ SOMALO, "Presentation of the Apostolic Exhortation, *Vita consecrata*", in *Consecrated Life,* 22 (1999), p. 6.

20 SECOND VATICAN COUNCIL, "Decree on the Up-to-date Renewal of Religious Life", *Perfectae caritatis* (= *PC*), 28 October 1965, in *AAS,*

58 (1966), pp. 702-712; English translation in FLANNERY 1, pp. 611-623. Here at p. 611.

²¹ F. WULF, "Chapter VI: Religious", in H. VORGRIMLER, *Commentary on the Documents of Vatican II,* vol. 1, p. 274.

²² *Codex iuris canonici auctoritate Ioannis Pauli PP. II promulgatus,* Roma, Libreria editrice Vaticana, 1983, xxx, 317 p. British commonwealth version of English-language translation: *The Code of Canon Law in English Translation,* new revised edition prepared by THE CANON LAW SOCIETY OF GREAT BRITAIN AND IRELAND, in association with THE CANON LAW SOCIETY OF AUSTRALIA AND NEW ZEALAND and THE CANADIAN CANON LAW SOCIETY, London, Collins: Ottawa, Canadian Conference of Catholic Bishops, 1997, xvi, 509 p. Canon references will be to this edition unless otherwise stated. The numbers of the canons that arose from the documents under analysis will be given in parenthesis.

²³ See C. VENDRAME, *Essere religiosi oggi: Riflessioni di un superiore generale,* Roma, Edizioni Dehoniane, 1989, p. 15. "È significativo anche il cambio del nome: dalla denominazione di "stato" religioso si è passati a quella di "vita" religiosa, con tutto quello che essa significa di dinamismo, crescita, souplesse, ricambio, adattamento, frutti e gioia."

²⁴ Ibid.

²⁵ See P. HINNEBUSCH, "Is an Outmoded Rule a Holy Rule?", in *Sisters Today,* 37 (1966), pp. 299-301. The author sees the Gospel as the form that is to be built into the material of life situations. Since these change with time, constitutions for institutes of consecrated life need to be updated to accommodate such change in order to be congruent with the Gospel. See also B. MEYERS, "Fire, Flood, Earthquake – *Sursum Corda,* Sisters", in *Sisters Today,* 10 (1967), pp. 334-339. This author discusses formalism which gave blindly-accepted customs the undeserved dignity of authentic tradition. She also claims that "trivia, unless repeatedly examined and re-examined, can blow up to an importance that makes for distortion."

²⁶ See K. RAHNER, *The Dynamic Element in the Church,* translated by W. J. O'HARA, Montreal, Palm Publishers, 1964, p. 9, where the author describes charism as "the absolutely unique gift of God to the Church and to the individual in the Church, the outcome of a particular divine prescription." See MOLINARI and GUMPEL, *Il capitolo VI "De*

religiosis", p. 184, where the authors state that "there is no such thing as a divine vocation to live religious life *in genere* but that it is always a question of a call to a specifically determined Institute of consecrated life." Each institute has its own charism. See also WULF, "Decree on the Appropriate Renewal of the Religious Life", p. 336. The Council stresses not only the "charismatic character of the origin of the communities following the counsels, but also the charismatic character of their appropriate renewal." However, it is the Church which will judge the charisms and discern the spirits.

27 PAUL VI, Allocutio *Magno gaudio,* May 23, 1964 in *AAS,* 56 (1964), pp. 565-569.

28 PAUL VI, Apostolic Exhortation on the Renewal of Religious Life, *Evangelica testificatio,*(= *ET*), 29 June 1971, in *AAS,* 63 (1971), pp. 497-526; English translation in FLANNERY 1, pp. 680-706.

29 See MOLINARI, *"Perfectae caritatis* – Introduction and Commentary", p. 17.

30 J.F. KOBLER, "Toward a History of Vatican II", in *Chicago Studies,* 38 (1999), p. 179. The provision of principles rather than directives is in keeping with John XXIII's directives that the Council be pastoral so there would be a "new Pentecost" experienced in a climate of freedom under the inspiration of the Holy Spirit. This same author goes on to indicate the enormity of the shift from an essentialist approach to an existentialist one where the daily problems of the world were assessed in the light of Christianity where justice and love have to be in counterbalance. He also points out that the personal encounter with God is necessary in the life of faith (pp. 180-181).

31 SACRED CONGREGATION FOR BISHOPS and SACRED CONGREGATION FOR RELIGIOUS AND SECULAR INSTITUTES, Directives for Mutual Relations Between Bishops and Religious in the Church,*Mutuae relationes,* (= *MR*), 14 May 1978, in *AAS,* 70 (1978), pp. 473-506; English translation in A. FLANNERY, (ed.), *Vatican Council II: More Post Conciliar Documents,* (=FLANNERY 2), Northport, NY, Costello Publishing Co., pp. 209-243. This document was prepared as a result of joint meetings of the Congregations for Bishops and for Religious and Secular Institutes, following wide consultation with their membership. It was aimed at exploring the mutual expectations between bishops and religious (understood as all forms of consecrated life) and at suggesting practical means for an orderly and fruitful collaboration at all levels.

32 See E. RINERE, "Dialogue Between Bishops and Religious", in *Review for Religious,* 45 (1986), p. 369. The author also points to the fact that "the circle of dialogue...is wider than the two groups which come together... The reality of the Church must be incorporated into any dialogue between those claiming Church involvement."

33 V. DAMMERTZ, "What Do Religious Expect of Bishops?", in *Consecrated Life,* 14 (1989), p. 13.

34 DAMMERTZ, "What Do Religious Expect of Bishops?", p. 12. See G. GHIRLANDA, "Relations Between Religious Institutes and Diocesan Bishops", in *Consecrated Life,* 14 (1989), p. 38. See also E. GAMBARI, "La Costituzione *'Lumen gentium'* e la vita religiosa", in *Vita religiosa,* 2 (1966), p. 38.

35 DAMMERTZ, "What Do Religious Expect of Bishops?", p. 12.

36 See *MR,* 8. "The Bishops, as members of the Episcopal College and in agreement with the will of the Supreme Pontiff", have the tasks of regulating the practice of the evangelical counsels; approving Rules thus recognising and conferring on the Institutes their specific mission at the same time; assigning tasks and duties; protecting the spirit of the Founders and defining exemptions. See also GHIRLANDA, "Relations Between Religious Institutes and Diocesan Bishops", p. 45, where the author points out that an institute "is born in a particular church, but for the universal Church inasmuch as the universal Church exists in and from the universal churches. The diocesan bishop must respect this universal character of institutes; he cannot prevent them from expanding into other dioceses or from asking for pontifical approval."

37 DAMMERTZ, "What Do Religious Expect of Bishops?", p. 13.

38 H. BÖHLER, "Vita consacrata e Chiesa particolare", in *Quaderni di diritto ecclesiale,* 10 (1997), p. 360.

39 See B. MALVAUX, *Les relations entre évêques diocésains et instituts religieux cléricaux de droit pontifical du Concile Vatican II à l'Exhortation apostolique post-synodale Vita consecrata,* Doctoral dissertation, Ottawa, Université Saint-Paul, 1996, p. 43, for discussion on the significance of the public acceptance of the autonomy of religious institutes even though limited to their internal ordering.

⁴⁰ See J. BEYER, "Religious in the New Code and Their Place in the Local Church", in *Studia canonica,* 17 (1983), p. 177, where the author quotes John Paul II addressing Superiors General in 1978. "Your vocation for the universal Church must be carried out then within the structures of the local church...Unity with the universal Church through the local Church is therefore your way" (*Allocutio,* 24 November 1978).

⁴¹ See P. MOLINARI, *"Perfectae caritatis* – Introduction and Commentary", in *Supplement to the Way,* 2 (1966), p. 12.

⁴² Ibid., p. 13. See F. WULF, "Decree on the Appropriate Renewal of the Religious Life", in H. VORGRIMLER, *Commentary on the Documents of Vatican II,* vol. 2, pp. 312 and 329 where the author discusses love as the basis of the counsels and, later, points out that renewal, as proposed in the document, leads back to the gospel sources helping "to supersede a style of thinking that was a blend of legalism and asceticism." See also R. VÖLKL, "Excursus on the 'Church of Love': *Ecclesia caritatis",* in VORGRIMLER, vol. 5, pp. 384-389.

⁴³ SECOND VATICAN COUNCIL, "Decree on the Church's Missionary Activity", *Ad gentes,* (= *AG*), 7 December 1965, in *AAS,* 58 (1966), pp. 947-990; English translation in FLANNERY 1, pp. 813-856.

⁴⁴ S. BRECHTER, "Decree on the Church's Missionary Activity", in H. VORGRIMLER, *Commentary on the Documents of Vatican II,* vol. 4, p. 87.

⁴⁵ T. CORBOY, "A Commentary on the Mission Decree", in A. FLANNERY (ed.), *Missions and Religions: A Commentary on the Second Vatican Council's Decree on the Church's Missionary Activity and Declaration on the Relation of the Church to Non-Christian Religions,* Dublin, Scepter Books, 1968, p.10.

⁴⁶ CORBOY, "A Commentary on the Mission Decree", p. 11. In the decree, "since the notion of 'mission', is derived from the Trinity and the missions of the Son and Holy Spirit, every apostolic activity in the Church must be called missionary." However, the other sense of the word is that used in reference to evangelising those who have never known Christ. See C. ALEXANDER, *The Missionary Dimension: Vatican II and the World Apostolate,* Milwaukee, The Bruce Publishing Co., 1967, pp. 3-4. See also L. RUGAMBWA, "The Church's Mission in the World Belongs to the Church's Essence", in M. Von GALLI, (ed.), *The Council and the Future,* New York, McGraw Hill Book Company, 1966, pp. 236-237.

47 See Y. CONGAR, *Report from Rome,* London, Geoffrey Chapman, 1963, pp. 74-75.

48 Ibid., p. 263. The author points to a new understanding in the Constitution, namely, "Christian holiness is not primarily — much less exclusively — moral perfection, heroic human virtue, but primarily and in the deepest sense the glory and the love of God given to the redeemed without any merit on their part." He goes on to explain that holiness is not received "in a purely private encounter between two persons, but in the Church, (the community of the People of God) and by her intermediary", pp. 263-264.

49 P. GUMPEL, "Capitolo VI: I religiosi", in G. BRESSAN et al., *Lumen gentium: guida alla lettura della costituzione* Roma, Salles, 1996, p. 173.

50 See HASTINGS, *A Concise Guide to the Documents,* p. 55. See also SCHOENMAECKERS, *Genèse du chapître VI 'De religiosis',* p. 255 where the author claims that secular institutes are excluded from such a sign value because of the phrasing used, namely, "the profession of the evangelical counsels". This is only one way to practise the counsels.

51 Ibid., p. 56. The author states that this consecration is "an explicitation and affirmation, by a most deliberate human action, of the baptismal consecration of this Christian and of every Christian."

52 See B. BUTLER, *The Theology of Vatican II,* London, Darton, Longman & Todd, 1981, pp. 71-73. The author claims that the Second Vatican Council did not adequately address the theology of religious life. This, he sees, as a task for theologians in the future.

53 WULF, "Decree on the Appropriate Renewal of the Religious Life", p. 329.

54 See *ET,* 12, "The supreme rule of the religious life and its ultimate norm is that of following Christ according to the teaching of the Gospel."

55 A. DELANEY, "Bishops and Religious — the Document *Mutuae relationes*", in *The Furrow,* 34 (1983), p. 234.

56 See S.M. GONZALEZ SILVA, "In the Church and for the Church", in *Consecrated Life,* 22 (1999), p. 50, where the author states that the

"specific" contribution which consecrated life gives to the Church is not primarily that of helping to spread the Gospel but that of helping others to grow in holiness. Consecrated life is a source of holiness for the entire Church.

57 Ibid. See *LG* 43. See also HASTINGS, *A Concise Guide to the Documents of the Second Vatican Council,* vol. 2, pp. 190-191.

58 ALEXANDER, p. 19. See also A.C. RENARD, *Le concile et les religieuses,* Mulhouse, Salvator, 1966, p. 62.

59 Ibid.

60 See GHIRLANDA, "Relations Between Religious Institutes and Diocesan Bishops", pp. 37-39. The author presents the Church as a communion, both organic and hierarchic. He sees juridic charity as the fundamental principle governing the relations between bishops and religious.

61 HASTINGS, *A Concise Guide to the Documents,* p. 55. See MOLINARI and GUMPEL, *Il capitolo VI "De religiosis",* pp. 198-205. The authors analyse *LG,* 44 and clearly express the importance of the sign of religious life but assert that it "does not have a value because it is a sign; but is a sign because it has a value, and that is a sanctifying and redemptive value", p. 202 (English translation by Sr Mary Paul Ewan).

62 See PAUL VI, "Religious Life: A following of Christ", in J. ALBERIONE et al., *Religious Life in the Light of Vatican II,* Boston, Daughters of St Paul, 1967, p. 412. He states that "man's hope must not be avidly and greedily rooted in time; instead the transcendent hope of the ultimate end must be pursued, in search of that which remains definitively above and beyond the frail and perishable things that pass away." He continues by elaborating on the sign value of religious to all mankind. See also GONZALEZ SILVA, "In the Church and for the Church", p. 51. Here the author claims that consecrated life, transfigured by the spirit and practice of the Beatitudes, becomes a sign for the whole Church, a call addressed to all Christians.

63 F. WULF, "Chapter VI: Religious", in H. VORGRIMLER, *Commentary on the Documents of Vatican II,* vol. 1, p. 273, where the author expresses the need for religious institutes to keep proving the reality of their outward profession "to seek first the kingdom of God and his righteousness" (Matt. 6:33).

64 G. LESAGE, "The Principle of Subsidiarity: A New Way of Governing: A Psycho-Canonical Study", in *Consultations,* 1 (1968), Ottawa, Canadian Religious Conference, p. 10. The author asserts that founders and their followers chose a precise point of spiritual or corporal good works for their goal. Thus, he continues, "a religious institute readily came to be considered as a group of subjects, submitted to authority, in order to attain more effectively their own perfection while working more efficiently in some field of benefaction. The person of the individual was overshadowed and even effaced by the goal pursued and the community body." Concern for the primacy of the dignity of the person was evident throughout the conciliar documents and was supported in *Lumen gentium,* Chapter VI. See HASTINGS, *A Concise Guide to the Documents of the Second Vatican Council,* vol. 2, pp. 203-204. See also K. MCNAMARA, *The Church: A Theological and Pastoral Commentary on the Constitution of the Church,* Dublin, Veritas Publications, 1983, p. 69.

65 See, for example, JOHN PAUL II, "Address to the Catholic Health Care Ministry", September 14, 1987, Phoenix, Arizona, reprinted in *Catholic Health Ministry in Transition: A Handbook for Responsible Leadership,* Silver Spring, MD, National Coalition on Catholic Health Care Ministry, 1995, Section three, Resource 1, pp. 1-3. The Pope reiterates the role of religious in healthcare ministry saying, "Your ministry, therefore, must also reflect the mission of the Church as the teacher of moral truth, especially in regard to the new frontiers of scientific research and technological achievement." He continues, "You have a magnificent opportunity, by your constant witness to moral truth, to contribute to the formation of society's moral vision... you will also be aware of the important contribution you must make to building a society based on truth and justice", p. 2.

66 See especially SECOND VATICAN COUNCIL, "Pastoral Constitution on the Church in the Modern World", *Gaudium et spes* (= GS), 7 December 1965, in *AAS,* 58 (1966), pp. 1025-1115; English translation in FLANNERY 1, pp. 903-1001.

67 For a more detailed discussion see WULF, "Decree on the Appropriate Renewal of the Religious Life", p. 344. For another interesting discussion of what it means to renounce the world, see M.J. SCHNEIDERS, "Religious Death to the World in the Post-Conciliar Church", in *Sisters Today,* 9 (1967), pp. 299-307. See also R. CANTALAMESSA, "The Ideal of Separation from the World in Religious Life Today", in *Consecrated Life,* 17 (1992), pp. 99-115. This author contends that "the religious vows of poverty, chastity and obedience, and more in general

the separation from the world which all three imply, are not the *renunciation of a created good,* or worse the condemnation of them, but they are *the rejection of the evil* which sin has superimposed on those goods. Therefore they are par excellence the proclamation of the original good of creation and of all things", p. 108. For an explanation of the possible origins of withdrawal from the world see W. Scott, *A History of the Early Christian Church,* Nashville, Cokesbury Press, 1936, pp. 349-350, where the author indicates that the development of the concept of Church went hand in hand with its relationship to the secular world of the day. He points out that Jesus not only loved the world but was accused of loving it too much.

68 See Pius XII, Apostolic Constitution *Provida Mater Ecclesia,* 2 February 1947, in *AAS,* 39 (1947), pp. 114-124; English translation in *Canon Law Digest* (=*CLD*), Milwaukee, Bruce Publishing Co., vol. 3, pp. 135-146.

69 Brechter, "Decree on the Church's Missionary Activity", p. 119. This is a specialised use of the concept of "mission" and not to be used in conjunction with ministry in areas or even countries that have become de-christianised. Neither is it to be used for activity with non-Catholic Christians — this is dealt with under ecumenism.

70 See Alexander, p. 37. The author refers to the new "openness" of the Council to the "present state of things which gives rise to a new situation for mankind" (*AG,* Introduction).

71 Brechter, "Decree on the Church's Missionary Activity", p. 120.

72 K. Rahner, *The Church after the Council,* Montreal, Palm Publishers, 1966, p. 25. This author goes on to say that the Church of the future, and by implication, consecrated life will be judged on whether its love for mankind is strong enough, because of its love for God, to show people "the way across the infinite abyss of the divine" (p. 27).

73 See Molinari, "*Perfectae caritatis* – Introduction and Commentary", p. 9 for a discussion on the understanding of "religious" in the document. He suggests that it is a general term for "those who live the life of the evangelical counsels, consecrating themselves to God by vows or other similar bonds, in an institute officially recognised by the Church."

74 See BRECHTER, "Decree on the Church's Missionary Activity", p. 143. See also G. VAN VELSEN, "The Missionary after the Council", in A. FLANNERY (ed.), *Missions and Religions*, pp. 28-33. The author emphasises the need of the Church to take cognisance of the local social, cultural and religious patrimony and to integrate what is possible into the new Church rather than replicating a European situation.

75 See MCDONOUGH, *Religious in the 1983 Code,* pp. 1-7 where the author discusses the relationship of the new law of Christ as seen in St. Paul with the Mosaic law and its implication for religious after the new code. See also F.G. MORRISEY, "Introduction", in J. HITE, S. HOLLAND and D. WARD (eds), *Religious Institutes, Secular Institutes, Societies of Apostolic Life: A Handbook on Canons 573-746* (= *A Handbook of Canons*), revised edition, Collegeville, MN, Liturgical Press, 1990, p. 15.

76 See BATTELLI, *Religious Life in the Light of the New Canon Law,* p. 57.

77 J.T. MARTÍN DE AGAR, *A Handbook on Canon Law,* Montréal, Wilson & Lafleur, 1999, p. 101. See also M. O'REILLY, "The Proper Law of Institutes of Consecrated Life and of Societies of Apostolic Life", in M. THÉRIAULT, and J. THORN (eds), *Unico Ecclesiae servitio: études de droit canonique offertes à Germain Lesage, o.m.i., en l'honneur de son 75e anniversaire de naissance et du 50e anniveraire de son ordination presbytérale,* Ottawa, Faculty of Canon Law, Saint Paul University, 1991, pp. 287- 303.

78 MORRISEY, "Introduction", p. 15.

79 H. BÖHLER, "Consigli evangelici tra teologia e diritto: Dal Codice del 1917 al Codice del 1983", in G. GHIRLANDA (ed), *Punti fondamentali sulla vita consacrata,* Roma, Editrice Pontificia Università Gregoriana, 1994, pp. 189-190. The author indicates that the canons concerning the counsels in the 1983 code are a compendium of the teachings of the conciliar and post-conciliar teachings.

80 For a discussion on what 'patrimony' entails see J. KALLUMKAL, "The Patrimony of an Institute", in *Commentarium pro religiosis,* 70 (1989), pp. 263-303 and see also B.J. SWEENEY, *The Patrimony of an Institute in the Code of Canon Law: A Study of Canon 578,* Roma, Pontificia studiorum Universitas a S. Thomas Aquinas in Urbe, 1995, pp. 161-177. Here the author summarises his understanding of patrimony gained from a study of Conciliar and Post-Conciliar documents.

[81] A vow is public if it is received in the name of the Church by a lawful superior; otherwise, it is private (c 1192, §1).

[82] See O'REILLY, "The Proper Law of Institutes", pp. 293-294 for the elements that must be included in the proper law of an institute. THE CONGREGATION FOR INSTITUTES OF CONSECRATED LIFE AND SOCIETIES OF APOSTOLIC LIFE, *Congregavit nos,* Rome, 1994; English translation, *Fraternal Life in Common,* Médiaspaul, Sherbrooke, QC, 1994, p. 15. This document states that "Vatican II and the new Code insist explicitly on the spiritual dimension and on the bond of fraternity which must unite all members in charity. The new Code has synthesized these two elements in speaking of 'living a fraternal life in common'."

[83] See A. PINHEIRO, "Bishop-Religious Relationship: The 'Apostolic Subjection' of Religious to the Power of the Diocesan Bishop in the Exercise of Apostolic Activities in the Diocese (c.678 §§1&2)", in *Commentarium pro religiosis,* 68 (1987), pp. 35-76.

[84] See O'REILLY, "The Proper Law of Institutes", pp. 293-294. Much emphasis is placed on "the spirit and aims of the founder" and "the institute's sound traditions". There must also be juridical norms to define the character, aims and means employed by the institute to bring its charism to life. The books must be neither too juridical nor too hortatory but a balanced mix of the legal and spiritual incorporating the teachings of the Church documents and other sacred writings. See also E. GAMBARI, *Religious Life: According to Vatican II and the New Code of Canon Law,* trans. Daughters of St. Paul, Boston, St. Paul Editions, 1986, pp. 101-102.

[85] T.E. MOLLOY, "Secular Institutes: Canons 710-730", in HITE, HOLLAND and WARD (eds), *A Handbook on Canons 573-746,* p. 276.

[86] MARTÍN DE AGAR, *A Handbook on Canon Law,* p. 108. See the decree *Perfectae caritatis* no. 11 which states that "while it is true that secular institutes are not religious institutes, at the same time they involve a true and full profession of the evangelical counsels in the world, recognised by the Church... The institutes themselves ought to preserve their own special character— their secular character, that is to say— to the end that they may be able to carry on effectively and everywhere the apostolate in the world and, as it were, from the world, for which they were founded." See also *Provida Mater,* where Pius XII claims that "they could be regarded as a most timely instrument of apostolic endeavour for leavening secular life... Their manifold apostolate and Christian ministry may be turned to good use where even priests and religious are

forbidden or can make no headway." English translation in E.J.B. FRY et al., *Secular Institutes: A Symposium,* London, Blackfriars Publications, 1952, pp. 45-46.

[87] S. HOLLAND, "Secular Institutes, cc. 710-730", in J.A. CORIDEN, T.J. GREEN and D.E. HEINTSCHEL (eds), *The Code of Canon Law: A Text and Commentary;* commissioned by the Canon Law Society of America, New York, Paulist Press, 1985, p. 526.

[88] B.M. OTTINGER and A.S. FISCHER (eds), *Secular Institutes in the 1983 Code: A New Vocation in the Church,* Westminster, MD, Christian Classics, 1988, p. 35. See COUNCIL OF THE GENERAL SECRETARIAT OF THE SYNOD, *De vita consecrata deque eius munere in Ecclesia et in mundo: lineamenta,* Roma, Libreria editrice Vaticana; English translation, *The Consecrated Life and its Role in the Church and in the World, Lineamenta,* Ottawa, Canadian Conference of Catholic Bishops, 1992, p. 25, no. 22. "Secular Institutes are not religious communities but they carry with them in the world a profession of the evangelical counsels which is genuine and total and recognised as such by the Church" (Quoted from *PC,* 11).

[89] COUNCIL OF THE GENERAL SECRETARIAT OF THE SYNOD, *De vita consecrata deque eius munere in Ecclesia et in mundo: Instrumentum laboris,* Roma, Libreria editrice Vaticana; English translation, *The Consecrated Life and Its Role in the Church and in the World, Instrumentum laboris,* Ottawa, Canadian Conference of Catholic Bishops, 1994, no. 13. "Secular Institutes, a form of consecrated life which has arisen in our century, are characterized by their consecration in the world or a 'consecrated secularity' lived in the midst of activities which are typical of lay people."

[90] OTTINGER and FISCHER (eds), *Secular Institutes in the 1983 Code,* p. 35. See K. LAZZATI, "Pluralism Amongst Secular Institutes", in *The Way Supplement,* 12 (1971), p. 78, where the author states, "Pluralism, diversity amongst the various kinds of secular Institutes, has to do with explicit apostolic goals and with communion of life." He goes on to explain that "explicit apostolic goals" does not necessarily imply "works" but is to be seen as "the christian inspiration of temporal realities and through this inspiration as evangelization." See also LAZZATI, "Consacrazione e secolarità", in *Vita consacrata,* 7 (1971), pp. 295-299. See also J. CASTAÑO, "Consécration et séculatité dans les instituts séculiers", in *Dialogue,* 5 (1977), pp. 9-15. "La nature des instituts séculiers consiste dans la simultanéité de la consécration et de la sécularité." S. LEFEBVRE, *Sécularité et instituts séculiers: Bilan et*

perspectives, Montréal, Éditions Paulines & Médiaspaul, 1989, pp. 25-57, gives a thorough analysis of Secularity and Consecration and their relationship.

[91] PAUL VI, "Institutorum Saecularium moderatoribus qui Romae internationali Coetui interfuerunt", 20 September 1972, in *AAS,* 64 (1972) p. 417. "'Secolarità' indica la vostra inserzione nel mondo... come luogo a voi proprio di responsibilità cristiana", (original text in Italian); English translation in *Secular Institutes: The Official Documents,* Rome, Conférence mondiale des Instituts séculiers, 1981, p. 87.

[92] J.R. SHELTON, *The Nature of the Secular Institute: Provida Mater to CIC 83,* Romae, Pontificia studiorum Universitas a S. Thomas Aquinas in Urbe, 1995, p. 122.

[93] J. DE LA CROIX BONADIO, "Notes Toward a Definition of the Secular Institute", in *The Way Supplement,* 12 (1971), p. 23.

[94] PAUL VI, "Apostolic Exhortation", *Evangelii nuntiandi (= EN),* 8 December 1975, in *AAS,* 68 (1976), pp. 5-76; English translation in FLANNERY 2, pp. 711-761.

[95] PAUL VI, "Ad repraesentantes institutorum saecularium", 25 August 1976, in *Commentarium pro religiosis,* 57 (1976), p. 369; English translation, "A Living Presence in the Service of the World and of the Church", in *Secular Institutes: The Official Documents,* pp. 96-97.

[96] JOHN PAUL II, "Allocutio: Iis qui coetui Conferentiae Mundialis Institutorum Secularium Romae habito affuere in Arce Gandulfi coram admissis", 28 August 1980, in *AAS,* 72 (1980), pp. 1018-1024, here at p. 1019, (original text in French): English translation, "To Change the World from the Inside", in *Secular Institutes: The Official Documents,* p. 104.

[97] Ibid., pp. 109-110.

[98] HOLLAND, "Secular Institutes, cc. 710-730", p. 528. Priests, as members of Secular Institutes are secular in the sense of their relationship to the world. They are not religious in the technical sense. Paul VI stated that they have an essential relationship to the world as priests who exercise their responsibility through ministerial action and as educators in the faith. ("On the 25th Anniversary of the Apostolic Constitution *Provida Mater Ecclesia"*, in *Secular Institutes: The Official Documents,* p. 79).

⁹⁹ PAUL VI, "Ad repraesentantes institutorum saecularium", p. 369; English translation in "A Living Presence in the Service of the World and of the Church", in *Secular Institutes: The Official Documents,* pp. 96-97. For a full discussion on apostolate of Secular Institutes see SHELTON, *The Nature of the Secular Institute,* pp. 128-131. See also SACRED CONGREGATION FOR RELIGIOUS AND SECULAR INSTITUTES, "Riflessioni sugli istituti secolari desunte dall'esperienza di vita", in *Informationes SCRIS,* 3 (1977), pp. 178-188; English translation in *Secular Institutes: The Official Documents,* pp. 211-216 for lay members and pp. 251-253 for priest members.

¹⁰⁰ PAUL VI, "Allocutio Die festo Praesentationis Domini, in Basilica Vaticana, tricesimo anno ex quo Pius XII P. M. Constitutionem Apostolicam *Provida Mater* de institutis saecularibus promulgavit", 2 February 1977, in *AAS,* 69 (1977), p. 142, (original text in italian): English translation, "On the 30th Anniversary of the Apostolic Constitution *Provida Mater Ecclesia*", in *Secular Institutes: The Official Documents,* p. 101. "Vogliamo infatti ricordare un anniversario che ricorre oggi: trent'anni fa, il 2 febbraio 1947, la Chiesa riconnobe una forma nuova di vita consacrata, quando Nostro Predecessore Pio XII promulgó la Costituzione Apostolica *Provida Mater*", p. 142.

¹⁰¹ See J. ARRAGAIN, "Est-il canoniquement possible que des Sociétés de vie apostolique soient des Instituts de vie consacrées?", in *Commentarium pro religiosis,* 69 (1988), pp. 31-53, for a discussion on the background of the separation of the Societies of Apostolic Life from Institutes of Consecrated Life in the Code. The crucial point is in the definition of "consecrated" adopted for the revision of this part of the Code. A. SAUVAGE, "Est-il canoniquement possible que des Sociétés de vie apostolique (SVA) soient des Instituts de vie consacrées (IVC)?" in *Commentarium pro religiosis,* 70 (1989), pp. 39-48, replies to Arragain pointing out the vast differences between the male and female origins of the societies and of their purpose for existence. This points to the variety of groups labelled "Societies of Apostolic Life" and the complexity of placing them in categories in the Code.

¹⁰² See the listing of Societies whose members make vows, oaths or other sacred bonds and those who do not in F. MASCARENHAS, *The Identities of Societies of Apostolic Life: An Analysis of c.731,* Rome, Pontificia Universitas Urbaniana, 1990, pp. 64-66.

¹⁰³ Ibid., pp. 13-14. The author traces the preparation of Canon 731 §1, indicating that during the first sixteen sessions the commission "hardly ever kept SAL out of the genus of consecrated life." He links the

apparent change of mind to the fact "that it was not always possible to extend the theological principles in that same measure also in the juridical level." See V. DAMMERTZ, "Gli istituti di vita consacrata nel nuovo Codice di Diritto canonico", in *Vita consacrata,* 19 (1983), pp. 115-116. "Lo Schema del 1977 ha messo queste Società insieme con gli Istituti religiosi e gli Istituti secolari, sotto la denominazione 'Istituti di vita consacrata'", p. 115.

104 Ibid., p. 18. For a full discussion of the problem of identity, see pp. 24-44. See E. SASTRE SANTOS, "Some Suggestions on the Concept of the *Vita apostolica*", in *Commentarium pro religiosis,* 67 (1986), pp. 387-383, for a discussion on the origins and understanding of the concept, *Vita apostolica,* in the Church and of the danger of its being reduced or minimalised if appropriated for a specific purpose as in the naming of a group.

105 L.A. LUNA BARRERA, *Las implicaciones jurídicas en las sociedades de vida apostólica que asumen los consejos evangélicos,* Ottawa, Saint Paul University, 1999, p. 277. "Para ello es necessario la acceptación y aprobación de la autoridad eclesiástica competente, como también la de los miembros que las componen quienes deben manifestar su aprobación por medio de un voto con mayoría cualificada."

106 Ibid., p. 277.

107 H.L. MACDONALD, *Hermits: The Juridical Implications of Canon 603,* Ottawa, Saint Paul University, 1990, pp. 1-56, gives an excellent synthesis of the development of eremitical life in the Church.

108 See COMITÉ CANONIQUE DES RELIGIEUX, *Vie religieuse, érémitisme, consécration des vierges, communautés nouvelles: études canoniques,* Paris, Éditions du Cerf, 1993, p. 165. "Pour la première fois à l'époque moderne, l'Église latine ouvre aux ermites indépendants de tout institut la possibilité d'un statut juridique dans le cadre de la vie consacrée."

109 Ibid., p. 167, and MACDONALD, *Hermits,* pp. 169-176. See T. MANCUSO, "The Urban Hermit: Monastic Life in the City", in *Review for Religious,* 55 (1996), p. 133. The author says that "there is no geography, no time or place, in which monasticism cannot thrive and contemplative life grow", because it is God who makes monks — when and where he pleases.

110 Even in the days of withdrawal to the desert, hermits had contact to collect food, meet with a spiritual director or with those wanting spiritual sustenance from the hermit. See MacDonald, *Hermits,* p. 169. See also Mancuso, "The Urban Hermit: Monastic Life in the City", p. 136, where the author says that work in the real world is not a distraction but a stark and naked reality challenging the monk to deep contemplation.

111 Comité canonique des religieux, *Vie religieuse, érémitisme, consécration des vierges, communautés nouvelles,* p. 172. "Il s'agit donc d'un document personnel, adapté à chaque vocation, tenant compte, pour exprimer mieux les exigences d'une vraie vie érémetique, de la personnalité de l'intéressé (existence antérieure, besoins et possibilités au plan physique, intellectuel, spirituel, etc.)."

112 L. Cada, et al., *Shaping the Coming Age of Religious Life,* New York, Seabury Press, 1979, p. 14. See A. Veilleux, "The Evolution of the Religious Life in its Historical and Spiritual Context", in *Cistercian Studies,* 6 (1971), p. 10. See also M-P Dion, "La virginité", in *Église et Théologie,* 17 (1986), pp. 5-39, where the author discusses the notion of consecrated virginity in contemporary language, in Council documents and in the course of history. See also J. Hourcade, "L'ordre des vierges consacrées", in *Vie consacrée,* 65 (1993), pp. 298-299.

113 M-P. Dion, "Les effets du rite de la consécration des vierges", in *Église et Théologie,* 16 (1985), p. 276.

114 Ibid. See *AAS* 19 (1927), pp. 138-139, where the Sacred Congregation for Religious responded in the negative to a *dubium* seeking clarification on whether women living in the world could be consecrated as virgins.

115 Comité canonique des religieux, *Vie religieuse, érémitisme, consécration des vierges, communautés nouvelles,* p. 185. See Dion, "Les effets du rite de la consécration des vierges", pp. 279-283. As in the case for religious, (discussed in chapter 1), attention is focussed on the understanding of the concept of consecration. The author examines whether it is a gift of self or more a creation of a new sacred state. According to the author, the *Ordo consecrationis virginum, praenotanda, no. 1,* clearly states that the virgin, by her consecration is constituted *persona sacrata,* but this same consecration is not specifically claimed for religious in the *Praenotanda* for the *Ordo Professionis Religiosae,* pp. 283-284.

[116] The revised liturgical rite was promulgated by a decree of the Congregation for Divine Worship on 31 May 1970. See *AAS* 62 (1970), p. 650, for the decree and, for the text, see *Pontificale Romanum, Ordo consecrationis virginum,* Civitate Vaticana, Typis polyglottis Vaticanis, 1970, 64 p. Some questioned if this rite applied to men as well as women. A response came from the Congregation for Divine Worship in 1971 indicating that the rite was for women only (*Notitiae,* 7 (1971), pp. 108-109), including women in secular institutes. The Holy See sometimes gives an indult to women leaving religious institutes to use the rite because of a desire to retain some form of consecration.

[117] E. McDonough, "Hermits and Virgins", in *Review for Religious,* 51 (1992), p. 306.

[118] See S. Holland, "Consecrated Virgins for Today's Church", in *Informationes SCRIS,* 24 (1998), p. 76. The author discusses lengthily the nature of the propositum.

[119] S. Recchi, "Il verbo 'accedere' nei cc. 694 e 731 del Codice di diritto canonico", in *Vita consacrata,* 26 (1990), pp. 950-965, gives a full discussion on the meaning of "accedere" in this context. Consecrated virgins are *like* consecrated life but not equivalent to it. For a different viewpoint, see J. Abbass, "Forms of Consecrated Life Recognized in the Eastern and Latin Codes", in *Commentarium pro religiosis,* 76 (1995), p. 31. The author contends that "by translating *'accedit'* as 'to be added', the order of virgins is added as one of the forms of consecrated life recognized by the Latin Code." He cites the location of the canon as support for his argument.

[120] See R. de Tryon-Montalembert, "La vierge consacrée signe de l'amour de l'Église pour le Christ", in *Vie consacrée,* 61 (1989), p. 232. See also J-M. Hennaux, "Consécration des vierges et hiérarchie", in *Vie consacrée,* 61 (1989), p. 241 where the author supports the idea that the essence of consecration for virgins is not in "doing" but in "being" (which does not exclude service).

[121] E. Gambari, *The Canonical Establishment of a Religious Institute: Process and Procedures,* translated by M.M. Armato, Florence, Artigraf, 1999, p. 137.

[122] Ibid.

[123] Ibid., p. 28.

CHAPTER THREE

CANON 605 AND NEW FORMS OF CONSECRATED LIFE IN THE DOCUMENTS OF THE 1994 SYNOD OF BISHOPS

INTRODUCTION

Through the centuries as the needs of the Church and society changed and became apparent, the Spirit inspired chosen persons to respond. The fruit of the response often culminated in the evolution of new forms of consecrated life. The Church, ever the watchful guardian of all that concerned the faithful, exercised its authority to interpret the manner of living the evangelical counsels, to set parameters for what it understood to be religious life (since that was the most commonly recognised form), and to translate the lived experience into juridical and canonical norms. These codified norms were first promulgated in the 1917 Code of Canon Law. Almost immediately they were in need of revision, not only because new forms had emerged, but because society had changed radically and the theology behind the legislation was also developing apace.

The Fathers of the Second Vatican Council decided that the Council would not concern itself so much with legislation as with a review of the situation of the Church in the modern world, its relationship to that world and with pastoral concerns for the people within the Church. As was seen in Chapter 2, consecrated life was also a subject of this scrutiny with the result that its theological and ecclesiological bases were studied, as were its relationships to the world at large. The ensuing realisation that there was need for updating and renewal led to several determined efforts for a re-definition of consecrated life and its place in the Church. The inclusion of consecrated life as a separate chapter in the Dogmatic Constitution on the Church and the issuing of several conciliar and post-conciliar documents on the subject underscored its importance and opened the way for the new legislation found in the 1983 Code of Canon Law. What was most significant for this study was the recognition that new forms of consecrated life had emerged over time and had been given official Church blessing and that the possibility existed that the Spirit would continue to grace the Church with more new forms. This realisation was concretised in the inclusion of canon 605 in the new Code of Canon Law.

In this chapter we examine c. 605 both in its preparation and in the promulgated text of the canon, then analyse the canon itself, and determine the special role of the diocesan bishop and that of the Apostolic See as expressed in the canon. Part two then studies the further development of the concept of new forms of consecrated life as expressed not only in the *lineamenta* and the *instrumentum laboris* for the 1994 Synod of Bishops on Consecrated Life, but also in some of the Synodal interventions and in the Apostolic Exhortation, *Vita consecrata,* after the Synod.

CANON 605 AND NEW FORMS OF CONSECRATED LIFE

Canon 605 is a new canon in the 1983 Code of Canon Law. It is significant for the recognition that it gives to new forms of consecrated life. We trace its development before proceeding with an analysis of its content.

The Preparation of the Canon and the Promulgated Text

The evolution of c. 605 will be studied in the documents from the Pre-Conciliar and Conciliar preparation periods. Then it will be explored in the Conciliar and Post-Conciliar documents as well as through the process of the actual preparation of the text.

Pre-Council Preparation

Canon 605[1] on new forms of consecrated life did not simply appear in the Code but had a history dating back many years before the Council — in fact, as far back as the dawn of Christianity. The emergence of new forms of religious life, the dominant species of consecrated life until the twentieth century, paralleled the growth and the development of the Latin Church. According to E.J.B. Fry, Pius XII,

> after tracing through the centuries the various forms of the 'life of perfection' — the ascetics and virgins, the desert fathers, the monastic life, the mendicant orders, the societies of Clerks Regular, and finally the Congregations of the nineteenth century and the Institutes of Common Life — speaks of the new Secular Institutes, that he himself has raised to canonical status, as a providential upraising for the needs of our time.[2]

The following year, 1948, he recognised the newness of the secular institutes as a component of the life of perfection, to use the expression then in use.[3] The terminology, "new form", was found in the *Praeparatoria* motions for the Second Vatican Council. Cardinal A. Larraona in an *animadversio* during the debate on *De statibus perfectionis adquirendae,* while speaking of secular institutes, said that "the experience of the Church is not brief; secular institutes already existed in the 16th century and recent new forms are already second generation."[4] After the Second Vatican Council, Paul VI also used the term, "new form", in an address given on the 30th anniversary of the Apostolic Constitution *Provida Mater Ecclesia*, in which Pius XII had recognised a new form of consecrated life, secular institutes. In this statement, the Pope confirmed two facts: one, that the Church has the authority to recognise a new form of consecrated life and, secondly, that it did, in fact, grant official recognition and definition to a new form when the time was ripe and circumstances in the world and the Church demanded it. This was the second time in the 20th century that a new *species* of consecrated life was canonically recognised.[5] The recognition of secular institutes and the accompanying ecclesiastical documents[6] may be said to be the remote *fontes* for c. 605. There was very little indication in the anti-preparatory and preparatory documents of Vatican II that there was any awareness, on the part of Council Fathers, of another spring in the life of the states of perfection.

Of some 1933 submissions from Bishops and Major Superiors of male congregations/orders, there were 202 mentions of religious life on 557 separate aspects.[7] No one of these referred to new forms of consecrated life as such nor gave a sign of a welcoming spirit to the likelihood of new forms. On the contrary, there appeared to be a concern from a small number of bishops that existing foundations with similar goals were merely duplications and should consider aggregating or confederating, but certainly not provide similar or duplicated services in individual dioceses.[8] While there may be a problem of duplication of works, there is little appreciation of an individual charism and the gift that it is to the Church. Five submissions specifically requested that new institutes not be permitted if they have goals similar to those already in existence or have difficulty in forming candidates.[9]

Most of those bishops who mentioned religious life were concerned with rather parochial issues, among which the fact of exemption and its impact on their role as bishop rated highly. Few submissions seemed to exhibit much understanding of the theological basis of religious life or of the broader issues affecting such a vital force in the Church. This may be explained by the bishops' being in their own dioceses when they wrote their submissions. They were very close to immediate concerns without the advantage of the global view and overall perspective that came later in the Council sessions. On the other hand, some missionary bishops appreciated the presence and work of religious in their dioceses and requested the presence of contemplatives, the forming of new local congregations to assist in pastoral work and, even, that each parish have a convent.[10] Judging from the submissions, it does not seem to have reached their consciousness, in this preparatory stage of the Council, that new forms could emerge.

However, the Spirit was at work in their yearnings for their local churches, but it remained for the submission of the Sacred Congregation for Religious to synthesise the call from the bishops and male Superiors General. The Congregation first called for "newness" in the letter to Cardinal D. Tardini accompanying its submission to the Council. It established that there was an unanimous desire for the life of religious institutes to be more authentic and to be renewed so that the life may conform better to the profound needs of the state of perfection itself and be better adapted to the actual needs of the Church.[11]

It was first pointed out that, with the promulgation of the Code of Canon Law in 1917, new forms of the state of perfection in the Church were acknowledged and that the term "religious state" was to be replaced by the term "state of perfection".[12] The report then mentions that various forms of the state of perfection are recognised in the Church.[13] The change of terminology and the recognition of such "various forms" herald an acceptance by the Holy See of the fact that there was no longer just one form. Others have been accepted and still others are in the making.[14] The way was gradually being opened to the possibility that the Church would be endowed with further gifts of new forms of consecrated life.

The Council Preparation

As was discussed in Chapter Two, there was much debate on the understanding and place of consecrated life in the Church. In keeping with the theme of newness introduced by Pope John XXIII, the Council Fathers wished to renew both their understanding of consecrated life and of the very fibre of the life itself. There were many interventions and debates as the nature and place of consecrated life in the Church were considered. The Fathers acknowledged that the life was of divine origin, given to the Church by Jesus himself and recommended by the early Fathers (*LG,* 43).[15] Religious life was the dominant recognised institutional form until the twentieth century when societies of common life[16] and secular institutes[17] were given recognition as states of perfection.

During the Council, Bishop I.P. Zarrantz y Pueyo stated that it was necessary to distinguish between the nature and substance of the state of perfection and its historical and canonical forms. The nature and substance are of divine and apostolic origin, but the concrete forms are human and variable.[18] This insightful statement implies an openness to forms other than those already acknowledged canonically in the Church. It also distinguishes between the essence of consecrated life and its expression. The former does not change, but the latter is incarnated in historical and social settings out of which rise particular concrete expressions. This variety of forms in the Church, as a response to pastoral and spiritual needs, is articulated again in the Council debates and seen as the fruit of the maternal solicitude of the Church.[19] That the way should be left open for other new forms is voiced as an addendum to the proposed document on religious.[20] This view was substantiated by the later request that, while defining and distinguishing religious and other institutes of perfection, the door not be closed to other forms of profession of the evangelical counsels.[21]

This openness must be real, allowing for the work of the Spirit. According to G. Huyghe, speaking on this topic at the Council, neither a preconceived form, such as the monastic model with its particular brand of spirituality, and even cloister, nor "prefabricated" constitutions should be imposed. Rather, active missionary congregations with their own spirituality and apostolic life are called for.[22] In other words, a genuine flexibility to respond to the needs and the call of the times is imperative.

Conciliar and Post-Conciliar Documents

Chapter VI of *Lumen gentium* is foundational for the Church's present understanding of consecrated life. Consecrated life was finally situated as a structure in the Church with all of the implications for its care, supervision, canonical and juridical well-being. However, that the consecrated life was still referred to as "religious life" detracted somewhat from the reality that secular institutes had been recently recognised and that the 1917 Code had included Societies of Common Life without Vows within the states of perfection. "The choice of the term '*de religiosis*' was an unfortunate compromise, since it bred ambiguity once again about the distinct nature of secular institutes."[23] Moreover, it did not sufficiently allude to the fact that the latter new form had been approved fifteen years previously. Despite such shortcomings, Chapter VI definitively established that the role of the Church, through the hierarchy, was to make wise laws for the regulation of the practice of the counsels, to ensure that religious institutes, established all over the world for building up the Body of Christ, may develop and flourish in accordance with the spirit of their founders and that the Church set it forth liturgically as a state of consecration to God (*LG,* 45).

This triple role of the Church, established in *Lumen gentium,* is reinforced in the other conciliar and post-conciliar documents used as the *fontes* for c. 605. The proemium of *Renovationis causam*[24] for example, reiterates these three points quoting *LG,* 45 verbatim. *Mutuae relationes*[25] 9 (c) echoes this teaching, adding to the three listed duties of Bishops, in unison with the Roman Pontiff, the duty of "caring for religious charisms; all the more so because the very indivisibility of the pastoral ministry makes them responsible for the perfection of the entire flock." This firmly places religious institutes in a pastoral relationship to the local Church and very much makes them an integral part of it.

Perfectae caritatis[26] 1 sums up the basis for consecrated life, briefly reviews its historical development, and points again to the responsibility of the Church and its willingness to provide principles for the renewal of consecrated life so that it may be ever more effective in the world. Paragraph 19 of this document underlines the necessity for vigilance in introducing new religious institutes, but also points out that "attention should be paid to the promotion and cultivation of forms of religious life which take into account the character and way of life of the inhabitants, and the local customs and conditions." This adaptation to local circumstances is reiterated in *Ad gentes* 18, where religious institutes are urged to hand on the mystical graces which are part of the Church's religious tradition and give them expression in a manner in keeping with the character and outlook of each nation.[27] The paragraph goes on to request that different forms of religious life be promoted in the new churches (*AG,* 18).

Even at this stage, the Council Fathers did not seem able to envisage any new forms other than religious life despite the many interventions quoted earlier in this chapter. This same attitude prevails in *Mutuae relationes* 51 despite the pleas from the Congregation for an openness to new forms of consecration (See note 14). It speaks only in terms of new religious institutes and then goes on to provide a list of conditions for determining the authenticity of a charism. It also reiterates the responsibility of the bishop to evaluate the genuineness of the founder and the suitability of the foundation.

Code Commission Preparation of Text of Canon 605

As with all the canons of the 1983 Code of Canon Law, canon 605 was to express conciliar doctrine, and adhere to the general principles of revision for the Code[28] and the more particular ones developed for what came to be called "consecrated life".[29] One of the main tasks was to incorporate the doctrinal teachings of the Second Vatican Council, transforming them into juridical norms. From the documents studied thus far it is clear that Bishops, in their dioceses, together with the Apostolic See, have four particular rights, among others, with respect to consecrated life: (i) to interpret the evangelical counsels, (ii) to moderate their practice by suitable laws, (iii) to establish canonically stable forms of living them and, (iv) to take care that the institutes flourish according to the spirit of the founders and sound traditions or patrimony (*LG,* 44-45; *PC,* 1-2; *MR,* 8).

The preparatory work for the new Code began with widespread consultation of bishops and Superiors General of male religious orders/congregations.[30] The Commission on "Religious" prepared three schemata, in 1977, 1980 and 1982,[31] before arriving at the final form of the canons. Canon 605 did not appear as such in the 1977 schema but there was a somewhat similar norm in canon 14, which introduced the section on "Dependence of Institutes upon Ecclesiastical Authority":

> It belongs to the competent ecclesiastical authority, under the guidance of the Holy Spirit, to interpret the evangelical counsels, to moderate their practice by laws, and to constitute by canonical approval stable forms of such living and take care that they may grow and flourish according to the spirit of the Founders.[32]

As J. Beyer states, "No one could doubt the importance of this canon, seeing the number of new foundations arising after the Council and responding to its spirit."[33] He expresses their need for guidance to express in wise laws the gift that they had received, to recognise the fundamentals of their charism and to define the structures that would support it. But the most significant aspect of this canon is its implications for new forms. "The Council had given the possibility of numerous new forms of consecrated life. To be truly new, they would manifest, says the Council, a new aspect of the life of Christ."[34]

The canon, in this form, was subject to revision. A. Neri explains that the canon needed to be examined both in its text and context (cf. c. 17) for a complete understanding. There were the twin situations of the role of the "competent ecclesiastical authority" and the fact of the recognition of secular institutes as a new form of consecrated life.[35] During the meetings of November 1978, the special study group had examined the texts of the schema in light of suggestions received. On 16 November 1978, having reviewed the first and second canons on institutes of consecrated life, they turned their attention to canon 3 of the schema. The relator proposed that canons 3 and 14 of the 1977 schema be combined into one as follows, with the addition of the phrase "for the people of God":

§1. The evangelical counsels based on the teaching and the example of Christ, the Master, are a divine gift which the Church has received from the Lord (for the people of God) and with his grace always preserves.

§2. It belongs to the competent ecclesiastical authorities, under the guidance of the Holy Spirit, to interpret the evangelical counsels (the said counsels), to moderate their practice by laws, and to constitute by canonical approval stable forms of life as well as take care that they grow and flourish according to the spirit of the Founders.[36]

§1 was accepted excluding the added phrase, "pro populo Dei". §2 was examined and, after considerable discussion, was accepted with the addition of the phrase, "pro parte sua"; so that the line would read "…constituere necnon, *pro parte sua, curare…*"[37]

Several other work-sessions were held. As a result canon numbers changed. On 28 May 1979, there was lengthy discussion on canon 37, which was to summarise the recognised forms of consecrated life. Part one read:

> Institutes of consecrated life (adorned with various charisms of the Spirit) which are erected by the competent Ecclesiastical authorities are divided into three classes, namely, Religious Institutes, Institutes of Associated Apostolic Life (Societies of Common Life without vows) and secular institutes.[38]

In the ensuing discussion it was pointed out that including "three classes" did not allow for the inclusion of hermits or consecrated virgins nor did it permit the possibility of new forms as the Bishops had called for.[39] After detailed examination of several possibilities, the following formula was accepted by vote on 29 May 1979:

> Institutes of consecrated life with various charisms of the Spirit, approved by the competent Ecclesiastical authorities, are divided into three kinds, namely: Religious Institutes, Institutes of Associated Apostolic Life (Societies of Common Life without vows) and secular institutes.[40]

On the following day, 30 May 1979, the discussion re-opened with canon 40 on the agenda. The proposed text was:

> With vigilant care the Bishops (the ecclesiastical authorities concerned) strive to discern new gifts (charisms) of consecrated life (constantly) conferred on the Church by the Holy Spirit, to help the promoters (founders) so that they may better express the inspiration received and protect it with suitable statutes (according to the general norms contained in this part).[41]

This session of 30 May was crucial to the development of c. 605. Therefore the text of the discussion, as quoted in Communicationes, will be given in full.[42]

> The first consultor suggested that the words in parentheses be omitted except for the final phrase "adhibitis...contentis".
>
> The second consultor agreed with the first. However, he

wished to add to the beginning of the canon the phrase, "Aliae formae vitae consecratae approbari possunt ab Ecclesia."

The third consultor agreed with the preceding two, but preferred to keep the word, "continuo".

The fourth consultor agreed with the first two.

The fifth consultor agreed with the preceding interventions but wanted to retain "continuo" and "adhibitis...contentis".

The sixth consultor agreed with the proposed text, but suggested that "charismata" be used rather than "dona".

For the seventh consultor it would be sufficient to affirm that other new forms "approbari possunt". The rest – rather exhortative – does not seem necessary from the juridical point of view, and is a little risky, as one can interpret it as an encouragement to recognise just about any initiatives or movements.

The eighth consultor agreed that adding that phrase could create many problems for the bishops.

The ninth consultor was pleased with the text, eliminating all the parentheses except the last one. Better to say "diocesan bishops". The addition, suggested by the second consultor, would add too much weight to the idea presented; it would be better to have just the text of the canon.

The Secretary agreed with the majority. Omit "vigilanti cura", which could put over-emphasis on the text. Eliminate also all the words in parentheses.

The tenth consultor asked to omit "ut inspirationem receptam...", because it could seem to affirm that there was an actual approval by the bishops about the existence of a real gift of the Holy Spirit.

The Secretary doubted whether this was necessary. In fact, in the schema, "De Populo Dei", the legislation on associations is very broad and flexible. If the conditions are right, etc, the bishop can approve the initiative as an association, while waiting for further development. Or, as the seventh consultor suggested, it would be sufficient to add the phrase to canon 37, (now canon 27): "Praeter ea aliae formae possunt a competenti auctoritate ecclesiastica approbari."

The seventh consultor suggested, in canon 37, (now canon 27), already approved, to add, "Praeter eas, novas formas instituere reservatur Apostolicae Sedi." The bishops can encourage/promote new associative forms based on the general law of associations, but the formal constitution of a new type of Institute of consecrated life belongs to the Holy See.

The relator affirmed that this could be the sense of the canon under study.

The Secretary recalled canon 3, §2, already approved, in which it was said, "Competentis Ecclesiae auctoritatis est consilia evangelica interpretari, eorundem praxim legibus moderari atque stabiles inde vivendi formas canonica approbatione constituere..."

The various opinions of the Consultors could be summarised in the following three proposals:

1) Eliminate the canon; 2) transfer to canon 37 (now canon 27) the addition proposed for this canon, that is to say, "Novas formas constituere (approbare) Sanctae Sedi reservatur"; 3) retain the canon under study with the addition of the necessary amendments, such as adding to the initial phrase in number 2: "Novas formas vitae consecratae approbare uni Sedi Apostolicae reservatur. Episcopi diocesani" (11 Consultors were pleased with this third possibility).

They proceeded to vote on the following questions:

To eliminate "Vigilanti cura" (placet 11).

To eliminate "Auctoritates Ecclesiae ad quas spectat"

(placet 11).
To say "dona" (placet 9).
To retain the word "continuo" (placet 1).
To say "promotores" (placet 11).
To keep "adhibitis praesertim generalibus normis in hac parte contentis" (placet 11).
To say "discernere satagant et promotores adiuvent ut proposita quam melius..." (placet 11).

Complete text: "Novas formas vitae consecratae approbare uni Sedi Apostolicae reservatur. Episcopi diocesani autem nova vitae consecratae dona a Spiritu Sancto Ecclesiae concredita discernere satagant et promotores adiuvent ut proposita quam melius exprimant et aptis statutis protegant, adhibitis praesertim generalibus normis in hac parte contentis" (placet 10, abstention 1).[43]

The decision was taken that this was to be an entirely new canon to accommodate new forms. The original (canon 14), was retained and is incorporated into the 1983 Code as canon 576, spelling out the competence of ecclesiastical authority in relation to consecrated life and its interpretation. The approval of new forms was to be the unique prerogative of the Holy See. This session concluded the work on the preparation of the canons on consecrated life. The resulting document was sent to the printer on 9 June 1980 and then forwarded to the Central Commission for distribution.[44] The text, as approved above, appeared in the 1980 schema as canon 532 at the end of the first title, which contained general norms applicable to all institutes of consecrated life.[45] There were only two opinions tabled on c. 532.

1. Reserving to the Holy See the approbation of any new forms whatever of consecrated life, is excessive. Bishops should not be deprived of their prerogatives.

R. The proposal cannot be retained: the canon distinguishes clearly between that which pertains to the Holy See and that which belongs to the diocesan bishops.

2. It would be sufficient for new forms of religious life to be approved by the bishop and, therefore, that this not be reserved to the Holy See.

> R. The canon does not speak of the approval of new
> institutes of religious life, but of new forms of consecrated
> life, which are different from either religious institutes or
> secular institutes. Because of this the reservation is
> maintained.[46]

Some minor adjustments were made to canon 532 and published as canon 606 in the 1982 schema.[47] After final revision, the words "...promotores adiuvent ut proposita meliore quo fieri potest modo exprimant aptisque statutis protegant..." replaced "...promotores adiuvent ut proposita quam melius exprimant et aptis statutis protegant..." This became the final form of canon 605, which was promulgated in the 1983 Code. Appendix 1 gives the sequence of development of the canon.

Analysis of canon 605

1. "Novas formas vitae consecratae...": "New forms of consecrated" life refer to those forms which have not been previously recognised in the Church's law.[48] "Form" refers to the structural expression of the theological life of consecration, which has been given as a divine gift to the Church, regulated by it and protected by juridic norms. While the theological and biblical foundations are probably immutable, the juridical are dependent on history and are, to a large extent, contingent and variable and, therefore, subject to mutation and change.[49] However, the canonical cannot introduce variations that in any way contradict or contravene the theological bases. "New forms" implies the revision of the canonical prescriptions dealing with the structure and the means of the religious life. The structure safeguards and enshrines the charism given to a founder, incorporates it into the overall structure of the Church and permits it to function in the ecclesial setting. New charisms or gifts of the Holy Spirit required new forms at different periods of history in order to safeguard and express adequately their giftedness to the Church and the world. The ruling of the Fourth Lateran Council in 1215 forbidding new institutes, and, by implication, new forms of religious life,[50] could have sounded the deathknell for developing forms of religious life. That new forms emerged points unquestionably to the guidance of the Spirit. The inclusion of c. 605 in the 1983 Code acknowledges both the unfailing influence of the Spirit and the

Church's official acceptance of the possibility of new forms of consecrated life.

2. **"...approbare uni Sedi Apostolicae reservatur"**: "The approval of new forms of consecrated life is reserved to the Holy See." "It is now clear that a life of total consecration according to the evangelical consels can be fulfilled in concretely diverse ways."[51] This new understanding, embodied in c. 605, implies the emergence of new forms whose expression is in conformity with the theological and canonical description in c. 573[52] and whose approval is reserved to the Holy See[53] J. Braux points out that the approval rightly belongs to the Holy See because the particular church exists only in the universal Church and, conversely, the universal Church is present in the particular church. Consecrated life touches the very heart of the Church and, therefore, it is appropriate the the intervention of the Holy See is required to evaluate and safeguard this new gift of the Spirit to the whole Church.[54] This intervention has precedents in the history of consecrated life. In the 20th century, for example, Leo XIII with *Conditae a Christo*, [55] and Pius XII with *Provida Mater*[56] recognised congregations of religious with simple vows and secular institutes respectively.

The approval of either a new institute or a new form of consecrated life is an exercise of the three *munera* of teaching, governing and sanctifying in the Church. The competent authority teaches when it presents to the People of God the new way of sanctity opened up by those who received the gift, thereby increasing the visible patrimony of holiness in the Church. It exercises its office of ruling in determining the juridic state and approving the structural surrounds of the charism in a particular situation. The office of sanctifying is exercised in the visible expression of holiness in the Church, which has discerned the authenticity of the charism. The ecclesial sanctity is expressed more precisely through the proper law where requirements for prayer, norms of charity and penance are delineated.[57] It is to be expected, therefore, that the active involvement of the three *munera* requires the authority of the bishop.

In c. 605, "approval" refers to new forms, not to new

institutes.[58] The approval for new institutes of diocesan right remains the prerogative of the diocesan bishop in his own diocese (c. 579) and for institutes of pontifical right, it belongs to the competent dicastery of the Roman Curia, the Congregation for Institutes of Consecrated Life and Societies of Apostolic Life (=CICLSAL).[59] For new forms, the approval is reserved to the Apostolic See, which has assigned the competence to CICLSAL (*Pastor bonus* Art. 110).[60] However, V. de Paolis would claim that the specific intervention of the Holy Father is required since the competence to approve new forms is beyond the competence of this Congregation.[61] On the other hand, he indicates that the Supreme Pontiff can grant particular competencies to a Congregation "in order to posit acts that would otherwise go beyond its institutional competence."[62] This provision is made in *Pastor bonus* 18: "The dicasteries cannot issue laws or general decrees having the force of law or derogate from the prescriptions of current universal law, unless in individual cases and with the specific approval of the Supreme Pontiff." In practice, it appears that CICLSAL has such competence. The approval of both new forms, that have received pontifical approval under c. 605, appears under the activity of CICLSAL in *L'Attività della Santa Sede.*[63] Since a new form dispenses in some way with one or more requirements of the law which regulates consecrated life, it must be concluded that CICLSAL had the necessary authorisation from the Supreme Pontiff.

3. **"Episcopi diocesani autem nova vitae consecratae dona a Spiritu Sancto Ecclesiae concredita discernere satagant iidemque adiuvent promotores ut proposita meliore quo fieri potest modo exprimant et aptisque statutis protegant":** "Diocesan bishops are to endeavour to discern new gifts of consecrated life, which the Holy Spirit entrusts to the Church. They are also to assist promoters to express their purposes in the best possible way, and to protect these purposes with suitable statutes.

Canon 605 affirms definitively the possibility of the Church's accepting new forms of consecrated life as gifts of the Holy Spirit. This portion of the canon affirms the role of diocesan bishops in their particular churches. It underlines their responsibility for recognising consecrated life in a twofold manner: as individual members of the college of bishops who hold a universal responsibility, together with the Supreme Pontiff, for the gift of consecrated life in the Church and as pastors of a particular Church.[64] In the particular Church, their duties are spelled out in *Christus Dominus,* 15 and in *Mutuae relationes,* 7, 8, 9(c), and 28. The bishops not only have the role of promoting the sanctity of all but have a special responsibility towards consecrated life. Moreover, this canon reminds them of specific competencies in relation to new forms. These twofold competencies — *discernere* and *adiuvare* — to discern and to help, are both rights and duties of the diocesan bishops.

"To discern and interpret the new gifts is first of all a magisterial act, which is the right of the pastors."[65] To discern whether a new gift is of the Holy Spirit is not a simple task. It calls for serious cooperation between those to whom the gift has been allegedly given and the bishop of the diocese.[66] As Sastre Santos says, it is a process of embryogenesis — developing from the first inspiration to possible birth as a fully fledged form or institute.[67] The discernment is not to be a private matter just between the interested parties, but should involve the People of God.[68] It needs to examine both the charism and the interpretation of it by the founder who is to be a person whose proven virtue demonstrates a real docility to the hierarchy and to following the inspiration of the Holy Spirit.[69] It needs to identify the gift, its scope, its spirituality, its goals and its precise identity.[70]

As well as discerning the new gifts of the Spirit, the diocesan bishops are enjoined to help the promoters/founders to express their proposals as well as possible and protect them with suitable statutes (c. 605). This enjoinder implies that there are more persons than the promoter in the group at the time of discernment. Together, these first members and the diocesan bishop gradually begin to formulate the precise ways in which the new gift is to be articulated so that suitable structures for its protection can be put in place. Such fundamental structures include:

> the structure of governance which is bound to the nature, the character and the ends of the institute (c. 587 §1);

the apostolate and proper works (cc. 577, 578), which are tightly bound to the spirituality of the institute and continually nourishing it;

the style of life that gives concrete expression to living the counsels.[71]

These structures, enshrined in the juridic form of the new institute, protect and regulate the authenticity of the gift. "From this felicitous union of spirit and law results the identity and the proper character of the institute. The dialectical fecundity of spirit and law adjust the societal form of the institute through an ordered 'embryogenic process'."[72] The diocesan bishops can participate in the whole process either personally or through a delegate such as the vicar for religious in the diocese.

4. "adhibitis praesertim generalibus normis in hac parte contentis": "consulting especially the general norms contained in this part." While diocesan bishops have the right and the duty to discern new gifts and to help the promoters of such gifts to articulate them and to express them in suitable statutes for their protection, they must consult especially the norms common to all consecrated life. This word, "especially", announces both freedom and flexibility and gives cause for rejoicing to all those persons contemplating beginning a new form of consecrated life. It implies that the general norms be consulted, but it does not impose the norms exclusively. It permits the use of other relevant norms from the Code, for example, those for associations of the faithful (cc. 298-311), for public associations (cc. 312-320), for private associations (cc. 321-326), for juridical persons and acts (cc. 113-128), and others such as those for elections (cc. 164-179) and on temporal goods and their administration.

Such a broad selection of norms permits a refreshing freedom to diocesan bishops in discerning new charisms and translating the charism into statutes. If the bishop and the new group decide, they can incorporate the norms for consecrated life (cc. 573-606), and thus have an institute that corresponds to a canonical institute of consecrated life. They will then have to determine and articulate the "newness" that permits it to be recognised as a new form. If the choice is made to live consecration in an association of the faithful, the members could choose to have a theological consecration (c. 573 §1) without the canonical.[73] The association could, in turn, be a temporary state while awaiting recognition as a new form, or it could be a permanent association in which members of the faithful consecrate themselves according to norms contained in their statutes, which need approval by the competent ecclesiastical authority. The need for definitive and clear terminology is once again obvious and is imperative for a realistic study of what constitutes new forms of consecrated life.

As far as diocesan bishops are concerned, when they discern new gifts and help new forms to attain ecclesial recognition, they may be guided by the general norms for consecrated life as well as many others. Within these general guidelines, they may encourage the promoters of new forms to express their charism in their own proper law and directories. It is in the proper law where the nuances of the charism can be effectively articulated and where the unique gift of the Spirit to the Church and the institute may find a viable expression in the daily life of the members. It is with the proper law and directories that new forms are able to sculpt their unique identity, thus showing a new face of Christ to the world.[74]

NEW FORMS OF CONSECRATED LIFE IN THE DOCUMENTS OF THE 1994 SYNOD OF BISHOPS

The ordinary general assembly of the Synod of Bishops has become a feature of church life since Vatican II. It is described as "an act of episcopal collegiality on aspects of common interest to the Universal Church, a moment of discernment and pastoral animation in favour of the communion and the vitality of the whole people of God."[75] Having set the subject for the ninth ordinary synod, the Holy Father, on 2 February 1992, exhorted the entire Church to assist the bishops through participation in the consultative process. By the time that the bishops convened in Rome for the opening on 2 October 1994, there had been widespread consultation and study to deepen the understanding of the vocation to life, consecrated by the profession of the evangelical counsels.[76] The stage was set for the preparatory discussion with the publishing of the *Lineamenta,*[77] and subsequently the working paper, the *Instrumentum laboris.*[78]

The *Lineamenta* summarise and reinforce the teaching of Vatican II on consecrated life (Part I). They deal with the theological aspects of consecrated life, reviewing the concepts of Vocation, Consecration and Mission (*L,* 6), the import of the evangelical counsels (*L,* 7, 8), the communal and eschatological dimensions (*L,* 9, 10) as well as the values and demands of the spiritual life (*L,* 11-13). In presenting the variety of charisms and plurality of forms in consecrated life and societies of apostolic life (*L,* 14), they examine the concept of charism (*L,* 15) and the historical dimension of foundational charisms (*L,* 16-17), before turning attention to the variety of forms of the consecrated life (*L,* 18). Having dealt with specific forms recognised in the 1983 Code of Canon Law (*L,* 19-23), they introduce a new concept, "New Forms of Evangelical Life"(*L,* 24).

New Forms of Evangelical Life

New forms of evangelical life need to be seen in terms of the new evangelisation, and how it was perceived in the pre-synodal documents, *Lineamenta* and *Instrumentum laboris.*

The New Evangelisation

Because of the very strong link between consecrated life and mission, new forms of evangelical life are meaningful in the Church in terms of the New Evangelisation spoken of by Pope John Paul II.[79] Addressing the bishops of the Latin-American Churches on 9 March 1983, he observed that their next general conference in 1992 would mark the half-millennium of the first evangelisation of the Americas. "This anniversary," he added, "would gain its full meaning with the commitment of the Church in this hemisphere to a new evangelization — 'new in ardor, methods and expression'."[80] He developed his theme in two further documents in 1990. In a letter to the religious of Latin America to prepare for the 1992 anniversary in the Americas, he called attention to the needs of the time.[81] "The new evangelisation must deepen the faith of Christians, forge a new culture open to the gospel message and promote the social transformation of the continent."[82] Later in the year, the Pope issued *Redemptoris missio*,[83] where he set out the principles that he saw as underpinning this new evangelisation. He saw it as a task of the whole Church calling for new means, new attitudes of respect and a commitment from all. It was, however, not a matter of merely passing on doctrine but of a personal and profound meeting with the Saviour (*RM*, 44). It implies conversion, a deep experience of God and a profound witness to one's own faith.

The Pope had given this message clearly in his Apostolic Exhortation after the Synod of Bishops on "Vocation and Mission of the Laity in the Church and in the World 20 Years after the Second Vatican Council", held in Rome in 1987. In his exhortation, *Christifideles laici,* he emphasised the role of lay people in the Church and admonished them saying, "The hour has come for a re-evangelization."[84] However, he continued that it was also at hand for the new evangelization of those who had not yet heard the message of Jesus. Again, he stressed the relationship between the Church and the whole of society and the need for the culture and cultures of humanity (*CL*, 44) to be evangelised. He reminded the lay faithful of the variety of vocations open to them in the heart of the God who goes in search of them. It is a vocation resting on the recognition that the living Christ is, though the Holy Spirit, the chief agent.[85]

The members of the Council of the General Secretariat of the Synod of Bishops, in presenting the *Lineamenta*, remind clergy, religious and the lay faithful that the call to the new evangelisation is central to the misssion of the Church (*L*, 42). They exhort all members of consecrated life to become enthusiastically involved and to be among the first to undertake the task using the best talents and energies coming from their spiritual and apostolic charisms (*L*, 42). They are to express better the fullness and richness of Christ, who is always present with his grace and power in our world (*L*, 46). In the closing message of the Synod the Fathers again reminded members of consecrated life of the challenge presented to them by the new evangelisation.[86]

New Forms of Evangelical Life in the *Lineamenta*

Against this background of the New Evangelisation, it is not altogether surprising that these same members of the Council of the General Secretariat of the Synod of Bishops, in the *Lineamenta*, should speak of new forms of evangelical life. They state that "the Church today, as in other times in her history, is fertile with the stirrings of spiritual and apostolic renewal, and is witnessing the rise of new forms of evangelical life" (*L,* 24). They assert that

> coming about through the power of the Spirit, these new forms are founded on a practice of the counsels of chastity, poverty and obedience and have a specific style of spiritual life — individual and communal — which corresponds to the spiritual aspirations of persons today and the needs of the Church and society (*L,* 24).

Such needs are delineated at greater length in the section entitled, "The Role of Consecrated Life in the World" (*L,* 44). If all forms of apostolic life are, for the purposes of this discussion, subsumed in consecrated life, then it is true to say that the proposals in the *Lineamenta* apply to all consecrated persons involved in apostolic endeavours. They are exhorted to be a specific witness of God's love in the world. They are equally reminded that consecrated life is present in our society through the multiplicity of apostolic services rendered to others, according to diverse charisms, "in one magnificent expression of the charity of Christ."[87] The members of the council of the General Secretariat list such endeavours as the education of children and young people; the care of the sick, the suffering and the elderly; the giving of aid to those with special needs and those emarginated in society (*L,* 44 a). They spell out the dangers to the young who become the unwitting victims of a manipulation, which leads to a lessening of their humanity either through consumerism or extreme poverty (*L,* 44 b). They applaud the preferential option that has been made for the poor but warn against this leading to the temptation to make choices incompatible with the life of faith and the ecclesial community (*L,* 44 c). They affirm the very consequential role that members of consecrated life have played in the preservation and development of culture through the ages and, at the same time, challenge them to establish a vast dialogue between culture and faith (*L,* 44 d). Finally, they reiterate the responsibility of the Church to safeguard, according to the Gospel, the great values of nature and conscience in today's world; to defend life, preserve creation and promote peace and justice. In doing all this, they are to collaborate with the Magisterium of the Church and with the lay faithful to build up the civilisation of love in mutual respect (*L,* 44 e).

What then are the new forms of evangelical life as envisaged by the authors of the *Lineamenta*? If they are defined in terms of function, they seem to be expected to contribute to the Church and society in the same manner as members of consecrated life as outlined above. There are, however, indications that they are not identical in all respects. Some, it is said, are true and proper forms of consecrated life either with Church approval or in the process of attaining it. Some are new forms of consecrated life whose approval is reserved to the Apostolic See, while others are lacking in some elements which preclude them from official recognition as canonically recognised forms of consecrated life. Such groups, for example, may include married persons (*L,* 24) but all enrich the Church through practising an evangelical life according to the counsels. They also manifest the vocation, open to all the disciples of the Lord, to holiness and to basic gospel values.

These indications go no further, in fact, than that which is outlined in the 1983 Code of Canon Law for Associations of the Faithful (cc. 298-311). Such Associations may be public (cc. 312-320) or private (cc. 321-326). It may be concluded, then, that the "new forms of evangelical life" envisaged by the authors of the *Lineamenta* are synonymous with consecrated life either as institutes of consecrated life or as associations without the necessary juridical requirements to be canonically recognised as consecrated life. Further enlightenment may be received from a perusal of the *Instrumentum laboris* (= *IL*), the document prepared for the Synod participants after the worldwide consultation and requests for comments and suggestions through the *Lineamenta*.[88] The necessity of a clear terminology for the components of consecrated life is highlighted here and is expected, particularly, in Church documents, both as a sign of the reality of the variety of forms of consecrated life (already officially recognised) and as a mark of respect for forms other than religious life.

New Forms of Evangelical Life in the *Instrumentum laboris*

What is positive from the discussion on new forms of evangelical life in the *Lineamenta* is a clear recognition of the fact that the response to the call to holiness, given to all the baptised, is being expressed in new forms. Some of these find their niche in canonical forms of consecrated life but others are new and have to stand the test of time and the Church. The *IL* devotes a section (*IL*, 6), to explaining the meaning and terminology used in the documents for the Synod. It acknowledges the confusion and lack of sensitivity in not using the correct terms and, even, the possible inappropriateness of the term "consecrated life". It, however, clarifies that the terms "consecration" and "consecrated life" are taken in their precise theological meaning, indicating a life consecrated by means of the evangelical counsels and recognised as such by the Church (cf. c. 573) (*IL*, 6). The document presents on only one occasion the term, "forms of evangelical life" and this is in a heading entitled, "New communities and revitalised forms of evangelical life" (*IL*, 37). However, the text following refers only to the need to offer some clarification about the new forms of evangelical life which have been springing up (*IL*, 37). It does not offer any such clarification other than the comment that the renewal of the People of God is brought about through re-invigorating forms that already exist and through raising up new ones in the course of history in response to the needs of the Church.

In discussing some of the problems arising from the proliferation of new groups, some characteristics are outlined, which is enlightening. It appears that there should be a continuity of spiritual heritage from the old forms to the new, whose development would bring a gospel freshness and a missionary thrust. There should be a continuity, likewise, with what is essential to the consecrated life through the profession of the evangelical counsels. There should be clarification as to whether the new groups fit into already existing forms or not. It could be a question of new institutes rather than new forms (*IL*, 37).

The description of the problem of the lack of uniformity in composition gives a rare insight into the hallmarks of some of these new groups. There may be men and women in the same groups; there may be groups where some members profess the evangelical counsels while others do not; groups where some live in apostolic communities while others live in monastic ones and still others who live alone in a form of consecration in the world; other groups where there are married couples and even children, some living in family units and others in groups. All of these new groups with a variety in composition have a single president or moderator often with branches having their own person in authority. They are characterised by a strong austerity and prayer life, participation in manual labour, and a limited number of members. Their apostolate consists in a missionary outreach to those who have never received the Gospel, with their ecumenical brethren; involvement in the new evangelisation, with the poor and marginalised and with their local parishes.

The diversity within the group is unified by the gift of its charism but the diverse components need a structural unity as well as a spiritual one. Hence, if there are different branches, they have to choose whether to seek approval from the Church as a new form of consecrated life in conformity with the general norms as set out in cc. 573-602 or as an association of the faithful with their own statutes and official church recognition with different dicasteries because of the variety of membership (*IL*, 38). Whatever the decision for type of recognition, the new forms must be in ecclesial communion (*IL*, 66-85). A whole chapter of *IL* is devoted to the understanding and the practicalities of this communion at different levels of the Church's hierarchical structure.[89] Consecrated life in any form is effective only when lived in and with the Church of Jesus and participating in his mission.

IL acknowledges that many of the traditional apostolates still have needs within the Church and society but there are some new ones needing attention not only in terms of new geographical areas but also in terms of inculturation (*IL,* 98). It is suggested that some new forms of the apostolate could include: participation in ecumenical movements which seek the promotion of Christian unity; dialogue with followers of other religions, especially through presence and community witness; the call to cooperate with various types of local and international groups committed to alleviating suffering of every kind; and sharing with the laity the group's manner of seeing and acting so that the charism could be shared, especially in areas of common interest. Another key role could be in supporting those who are engaged in a spiritual search or who want to commit themselves to the Church's activities (*IL,* 98).

New Forms of Consecrated Life in Synodal Presentations

At the opening Mass for the ninth Ordinary General Assembly of Bishops, John Paul II firmly accredited the phenomenon of new forms of consecrated life. Addressing the congregation in St. Peter's Basilica, he said:

> We are also witnessing the birth of new forms of consecration, particularly within Church movements and associations, which seek to express, in ways appropriate to our contemporary culture, the traditional striving of religious life to contemplate the mystery of God and to fulfil a mission to our brothers and sisters.[90]

The following week at his Wednesday audience, the Pope spoke again of the new charisms given to the Church in our time. He especially mentioned the "movements" or "ecclesial associations", which cover the entire span of the Christian's presence in current society.[91] He stressed again the importance of communion with the Church in mission for all members of movements and of consecrated life. This affirmation of new charisms was continued, albeit *sotto voce,* beginning with the *Relatio ante disceptationem,*[92] delivered by Cardinal Basil Hume. Following him, there were more than three hundred interventions delivered over nineteen general congregations of the ninth assembly of the Synod of Bishops from 2-18 October 1994.[93] Of these, a small number addressed new forms of consecrated life in the Church. While Cardinal Hume did not directly mention new forms of consecrated life, he did speak to the new challenges presented by the mission in today's world and society. The perspective of the new evangelisation,[94] he said, must be the missionary horizon for the whole Church and therefore for consecrated life. He said that each charism must bear in mind the needs of the Church in which it is operative and the new *areopagi* of the same mission. He specifically called attention to the world of communication, of modern culture, human promotion, justice, the new poor and those in search of the sacred.[95] Response to these new needs could imply new charisms being given by the Spirit resulting in new forms of consecrated life.

There were, however, three specific interventions to the Synod on new forms of consecrated life and several mentions in summaries from discussion groups. Bishop S. Fernandes de Araújo of Brazil spoke of new forms of community life that express the continuing fruitfulness of the Gospel and the newness created by the Spirit.[96] He was aware that there are hundreds of such communities in existence and that they do not conform to the institutes of consecrated life already in existence and recognised as such by the Church. They are comprised of virgins, spouses, lay and clerical, who in such diverse states of life, are consecrated to a unique gospel ideal, as equal members of a single body, often having different levels of belonging. Those he referred to as ecclesial families.

According to Fernandes de Araújo, these "ecclesial families" have certain identifiable characteristics:

Unity of work under a single president but with branches having a leader with responsibilities according to the group.

A certain gospel radicality where the Word is the personal and communal basis.

Unity between consecration and the specific mission of the group.

A strong community sense with a clear priority of uniting communion and doing.

The exercise of authority seen in communal lines — not pyramidal.

The desire to avoid the dangers of clericalism by not identifying priests with authority but respecting and promoting lay persons.

A clear accent on poverty depending on Providence, serving the poor and marginalised.

An intense life of personal and communal prayer uniting contemplation and action with the Eucharist as a focal point for the unity of the community. There is also openness to devotion to Mary and the Spirit.

A lived missionary fervour in the sense of Ad gentes and the "new evangelisation".

Cardinal J.C. Turcotte from Canada, in his intervention, presented almost identical characteristics of the new groups from his experience, with the addition of a certain characteristic of joy, cordiality and warm hospitality.[97] Cardinal C. M. Martini of Italy also addressed this subject, saying that he would not repeat the points raised by the previous speakers but that he would not restrict his intervention to ecclesial families but also would include other types such as monastic, apostolic or diaconal groups.[98] He foresaw problems with those groups which did not have internal uniformity, that is, those that included men and women, married and celibate etc. He presented some of the arguments used by spouses with vows of chastity according to their state. These, he said, gave rise to reservations and objections but, despite these, there were many spouses in such groups. On the other hand, there were lay associations of the faithful which imposed the three vows on their members making them virtually the same as institutes of consecrated life. He requested that the Synod, through the small group discussions, provide some guidelines to assist bishops in helping them to discern the validity of new groups.

This request was addressed in part by the inclusion of a special proposition on "New Forms of Consecrated Life" among the final 55 propositions of the synodal Fathers to the Pope for further action.[99] This proposition, no. 13, recognises that there are new forms and that it is imperative to determine whether they have the characteristics of consecrated life according to c. 573 and CCEO c. 410. The question of spouses was raised and declared to be incompatible with consecrated life. It was suggested that a commission be established to research and stabilise criteria that would help discern their authenticity and promote them without hurrying to a definitive juridical and canonical scheme.

The Fathers also proposed that the bishops (1) examine the history of the founder/foundress, the experience of the group, and the authenticity of their doctrine and spiritual life; (2) discern whether the members are fit for the profession of the vows; (3) know the goals and the mission that they are responding to in the Church of now, given the number and the variety that already exist; (4) decide the authority of the competent ecclesiastics. The diocesan bishops have this responsibility.[100]

The passing of proposal 13 signalled the acceptance, by the Synod, of the reality that new forms of consecrated life exist in the Church and that there are also other communities that do not conform to the present canonical norms for consecrated life as described in the 1983 Code of Canon Law.

New Forms of Consecrated Life in Vita Consecrata

The propositions of the Synod were studied over a period of twelve months before John Paul II issued his post-synodal Apostolic Exhortation, *Vita consecrata*.[101] The Pope, in this document, contextualises the work of the Synod, the development of the various forms of consecrated life currently approved in the Church and then gives a rationale for the place of consecrated life in the Church, dwelling at length on communion and its implications. He then links communion with mission, returning once again to his theme of new evangelisation, outlining some new needs. He concludes with exhortations to various groups in the Church and a prayer to the Blessed Virgin Mary.

In all of this lengthy document (112 paragraphs), one of the most significant sections is that on communion in the Church and how consecrated life is a sign of that communion. According to G. Ghirlanda, since consecrated life belongs undeniably to the essence of the Church, it has a unique relationship with bishops in a particular church in their ministry of pastoral charity.[102] It is in the particular church that the institutes are inserted in a concrete fashion, living out the mission determined by their charism. "Since the bishop is not a mere external point of 'authority' with respect to communion, but is essential to it through his apostolic mission, the consecrated life in its different expressions in a particular Church constitutes a charismatic correlation which converges in communion with the bishop."[103] While this is incontestable, Ghirlanda feels that the universal aspect was not sufficiently highlighted in the Synod. The too strong an emphasis on the particular church and on the mission of consecrated life therein could lead to an imbalanced position, where the importance of consecrated life is seen only in terms of contribution to the local church to the detriment of the universal perspective and the inherent value of consecrated life itself.[104] Without a sensitive regard for the autonomy of institutes, it suggests an inordinate control in the hands of the diocesan bishops (*VC*, 48). This delicate balance needs to be kept in mind in dealing with new forms of consecrated life and the role of the bishops in their discernment and first approbation.

Keeping in mind these two significant factors, communion and the relationship with the bishop in a particular church, as highlighted in *Vita consecrata,* we examine the treatment of new forms of consecrated life in the document. Having recalled with gratitude that the Spirit has raised up many different forms of consecrated life throughout history (*VC*, 5), the exhortation revisits those forms already recognised in the Church (*VC*, 5-11), and then addresses "New expressions of consecrated life" (*VC*, 12). This term, new to the synodal documents, seems to embrace both existing forms and new ones. The reference, at this point, is rather negative, in that there is a warning lest there be a proliferation of institutes or forms similar to those in existence, leading to confusion or fragmentation. On a positive note, there is recognition that the ideal of total gift of self to the Lord is still attractive, witnessed by the number of founding charisms drawing the present generation of young people. The document points out that the Spirit is not self contradictory. New forms have not supplanted the old but are in continuity with them, evolving from what has gone before and adding new gifts to the Church. It also points out that, despite such diversity, there is unity in the call to follow Jesus in the pursuit of perfect charity (*VC*, 12).

It is in paragraph 62 that the document treats of "New forms of evangelical life", returning to the phrase used in the *Instrumentum laboris*. Again, there is no definition of terminology, just a presupposition that the context will clarify the meaning sufficiently. The continuity of the gifting of the Spirit over history is reiterated, saying that such gifts foster in already existing institutes a commitment to renewed faithfulness to the founding charism, or encourage men and women to start new institutions[105] to respond to the challenges of the times (*VC*, 62). Such institutions, also referred to as "new foundations", display new characteristics compared to those of traditional ones. Such characteristics include the composition of the groups, men as well as women, married and single, clerics and lay persons all pursuing a particular style of life. Their commitment to the evangelical life takes on different forms but is described as having an intense aspiration to community life, poverty and prayer. All share as equals in governance according to the responsibilities assigned to them, and focus their apostolate on the demands of the new evangelisation (*VC*, 62).

These new institutions need to undergo a discernment regarding their charisms. To be accepted as consecrated life, they must adhere to the fundamental principle that "the specific features of the new communities and their styles of life must be founded on the essential theological and canonical elements proper to the consecrated life" (*VC*, 62). The principle of discernment just enunciated precludes the acceptance of married couples in canonically defined consecrated life. Married spouses may be more easily accommodated in associations.[106] However, the task of discernment must involve both the diocesan bishop and the Apostolic See in accordance with c. 605 discussed above.

Because the details and the richness of the groups are so diverse, there are no accepted established criteria for their approval. Consequently, *Vita consecrata* suggests that a commission be convened to research and set such criteria as an aid to the bishops and the groups themselves. Meanwhile, older established groups are exhorted to dialogue with the new ones to share experiences and partake of each other's vitality.

That *Vita consecrata* does not attempt to define terminology in a definitive manner, or to set forth criteria for recognition of new groups, or place boundaries for their development is one of the greatest gifts to these new groups. It exhibits a welcoming of the gifts with which the Spirit wishes to endow the Church. It also acknowledges that the groups are still in a state of fluidity so that legislation would not only be premature but stifling at this time.

CONCLUSION

The inclusion of c. 605 in the 1983 Code of Canon Law is the response on the part of the Church to the burgeoning of a new phenomenon in recent decades, namely, the appearance of new forms of living a consecrated life. That all these new forms are not eligible to be called institutes of consecrated life devolves on the fact that all the requirements of consecrated life in canonical terms have not been met. Some groups include married couples whose promises/vows/bonds of conjugal chastity are not congruent with the understanding of c. 573 of the Code which requires perfect continence. Other members do not profess all of the three counsels or in a public manner, while some take the three traditional counsels and live life in common.

The mixture of those belonging in various ways, as well as the inclusion of both men and women in the same group, challenges the existing laws. The possibility that the Spirit is breathing anew on the Church and granting new charisms for its life at this moment in history led to the formulation of c. 605 during the process of the revision of the Code. The impetus coming from the then Sacred Congregation for Religious gave momentum to the need for study. Despite some claims that it was unnecessary, the code commission members felt that there were sufficient reasons for its inclusion. Canon 86 would demand that none other than the Supreme Legislator could change the constitutive requirements for consecrated life. However, the new canon clarifies both the role of the Holy See and that of diocesan bishops in the approval of new forms of consecrated life. It does, nonetheless, leave some problems.

There are the questions of terminology. What exactly is consecrated life? Are the defining canons now found in the Code the definitive word? What is the relation to a developing theology of consecrated life? How is the historical development integrated into the present understanding?

Some of these questions were presented to the Synod of Bishops on consecrated life in 1994. The study and world wide consultations clarified some issues but raised equally as many. The material relevant to new forms was scarce in the interventions. However, the ensuing document, *Vita consecrata,* recognised the reality that there were new forms. It did not add to the clarity of terminology (rather introduced some confusion), but it did genuinely seek to address the present needs in terms of the new evangelisation and how these groups may be a response to these needs. Its positive acceptance of the need for further study augurs well for the future, as did the recommendation to set up a commission for determining criteria for the approval of new forms.

There could be some cause for concern regarding the very strong emphasis on the role of the diocesan bishop in the approval process. If a local perspective were to be followed too stringently at the expense of a more universal view of the Church and the world, in which it is situated, and at the expense of the development of a genuine charism expressed in a new form, this would be cause for a re-examination of the delicate balances of local and universal authority with respect to consecrated life. It would also demand a real attention to the history and theology of consecrated life remembering that they are ever evolving. The possible application of c. 605 in concrete circumstances is treated in the next chapter.

NOTES

¹ *Codex iuris canonici auctoritate Ioannis Pauli PP. II promulgatus,* Libreria editrice Vaticana, 1983, xxx, 317 p.; British commonwealth version of English-language translation: *The Code of Canon Law in English Translation,* new revised edition prepared by THE CANON LAW SOCIETY OF GREAT BRITAIN AND IRELAND, in association with THE CANON LAW SOCIETY OF AUSTRALIA AND NEW ZEALAND and THE CANADIAN CANON LAW SOCIETY, London, Collins: Ottawa, Canadian Conference of Catholic Bishops, 1997, xvi, 509 p. This translation will be used for subsequent quotation of canons, unless the official Latin text is quoted.

² E.J.B. FRY et al., *Secular Institutes: A Symposium,* London, Blackfriars Publications, 1952, pp. 9-10.

³ PIUS XII, Motu proprio *Primo feliciter,* In Praise of Secular Institutes and in Confirmation Thereof, in *AAS,* 40 (1948), pp. 283-286; English translation in *Canon Law Digest* (= CLD), vol. 3, pp. 147-151.

⁴ A. LARRAONA, Comment on Caput VIII: "De institutibus saecularibus" of "De statibus perfectionis adquirendae", in *Acta et documenta Concilio oecumenico Vaticano II apparando,* Series II, Vol. II, Part II, Roma, Typis polyglottis vaticanis, 1967, p. 670. "Ceterum experientia Ecclesia non est brevis; instituta saecularia iam a saec. XVI habentur et, nova forma recentiore, iam fere a duobus saeculis".

⁵ G. BATTELLI, *Religious Life in the Light of the New Canon Law,* Nairobi, Kenya, St. Paul Publications – Africa, 1990, p. 47 makes the case that secular institutes "were the first form of consecrated life in the Church. [It] had the ascetics and virgins leading a consecrated life at home, given to prayer and works of mercy."

⁶ PIUS XII, Apostolic Constitution *Provida Mater Ecclesia,* 2 February 1947, in *AAS,* 39 (1947), pp. 114-124; Motu proprio *Primo feliciter,* 12 March 1948, in *AAS,* 40 (1948), pp. 283-286 and SACRED CONGREGATION FOR RELIGIOUS, Instruction on Secular Institutes *Cum sanctissimus,* 19 March 1948, in *AAS,* 40 (1948), pp. 293-297; English translations for the three documents in *Canon Law Digest,* Milwaukee, Bruce Publishing Co., vol. 3, pp. 135-146; 147-151 and 151-157.

⁷ Data gleaned from an analysis of the submissions as recorded in *Acta et documenta Concilio oecumenico Vaticano II apparando,*

Series I, (*Antepraeparatoria*), Roma, Typis polyglottis vaticanis, 1960-1961, 4 vols, 8 Parts.

⁸ *Acta et documenta Concilio oecumenico Vaticano II apparando,* Series I, (*Antepraeparatoria*), Volumen II, *Consilia et vota episcoporum ac praelotorum,* Part I, Roma, Typis polyglottis, 1960, p. 348; "Permultae minores Congregationes religiosarum iuris dioecesani ab hoc saeculo conditae sunt et ex sororum parvo numero constant qui inter duodecim et quinquaginta includitur et raro maior est". Part II, p. 260; "Cum fines plurimarum Congregationum sint paralleli, immo et frequenter identici...nonne conveniens foret ut inutilis multiplicatio Congregationum aliquatenus compesceretur, et illae, quae fines similes vel identicos prosequuntur, ad *quandum formam superioris unitatis* reducerentur?"

⁹ *Acta et documenta Concilio oecumenico Vaticano II apparando,* Series I, (*Antepraeparatoria*), appendix voluminis II, *Analyticus conspectus consiliorum et votorum quae ab episcopis et praelatis data sunt,* Part I, Roma, Typis polyglottis, 1961, pp. 693, 695. "Non expedit multiplicare varia Instituta religiosa et saecularia identici finis et similis indolis" (Sup. Gen. Soc. Iesu, p. 693).

"Non facile admittantur novae Congregationes quae finem specialissimum non habeant, (Circesien, Polyboten, Sup. Gen. Ord. Carm. Disc.).

Impediantur novae fundationes quorum fines iam ab aliis Fundatoribus praevidentur, (Montisvidei, Risinitan, Medellen, Papantlen, Reconquisten).

Ne multiplicentur Instituta sive vivorum sive mulierum, (Nepten, Andropolitan).

Solutio inveniatur pro parvis Congregationibus quae difficultates habent in efformandis candidatis, (Montisvidei, Reconquisten).

Ne erigantur canonice novae fundationes cum eodem fine, (Acheruntin, Venetiarum)," p. 695.

¹⁰ *Acta et documenta Concilio oecumenico Vaticano II apparando,* Series I, (*Antepraeparatoria*), Volumen II, Part V. F.C. DE LANGAVANT, "Numerosae sunt Congregationes religiosarum... tamen fundatio aliqua in locis missionum ita difficillima est ut saepe

necessarium erit instituere aliquam novam Congregationem localem", p. 245. J. COLLINS, "More and more Convents should be established throughout the Missions the ideal being that every Parish and Quasi-Parish should have a Convent of even a few Sisters", p. 271.

[11] *Acta et documenta Concilio oecumenico Vaticano II apparando,* Series I, (*Antepraeparatoria*), Volumen III. P. PHILIPPE, "Questo Sacro Dicastero ha costatato, con piacere, che i voti degli Ecc.mi Vescovi e dei Rev.mi Superiori Generali sono unanimi nel chiedere al Concilio Ecumenico di prendere le eventuali disposizioni perchè la vita degli Istituti religiosi sia sempre più 'autentica' e più 'aggiornata', più conforme alle esigenze profonde dello stato di perfezione evangelica o maggiormente adatta ai bisogni attuali della Chiesa", p. 217.

[12] *Acta et documenta Concilio oecumenico Vaticano II apparando,* Series I, (*Antepraeparatoria*), Volumen III. *Propositiones ad concilium oecumenicum,* "Cum a promulgatione *Cod. Iur. Can.* Novae formae status perfectionis in Ecclesia sint exortae, deinceps loco termini 'status religiosus' convenientius terminus 'status perfectionis' uti generalis adhibeatur", p. 219. The document indicates that the "state of perfection is divided into three generic forms – the religious state, the state of common life without vows and the state of secular perfection."

[13] Ibid. "Nostris autem diebus, variae sunt formae status perfectionis ab Ecclesia recognitae, ita ut christifideles statum perfectionis facilius ingredi valeant, remanendo etiam in saeculo sicut fit in Institutis saecularibus", p. 220.

[14] See NERI, A., *Nuove forme di vita consacrata (can. 605 C.I.C.),* Roma, Editrice Pontificia Università Lateranense, p. 19.

[15] See SECOND VATICAN COUNCIL, Dogmatic Constitution on the Church, *Lumen gentium* (=*LG*), 21 November 1964, in *Acta Apostolicae Sedis* (= *AAS*), 57 (1965), pp. 5-75; English translation of this and other conciliar documents in A. FLANNERY (ed.), vol. 1, *Vatican Council II: The Conciliar and Post Conciliar Documents,* new revised edition, Northport, NY, Costello, 1992, (= FLANNERY 1), pp. 402-407. Here at p. 402.

[16] *Codex iuris canonici Pii X Pontificis Maximi iussu digestus, Benedicti Papae XV auctoritate promulgatus,* Romae, Typis Polyglottis Vaticanis, 1917, cc. 673-681.

17 See *Provida Mater* in which official status was conferred on secular institutes.

18 *Acta synodalia sacrosancti Concilii oecumenici Vaticani II,* Volumen II, Periodus secunda, Pars IV, Congregationes generales LIX-LXIV, Roma, Typis polyglottis Vaticanis, 1972. I.O. ZARRANZ Y PUEYO, "Nam bene distinguendum est *inter rem et substantiam status perfectionis* et eius *formas historicas et canonicas.* Res et substantia est originis divinae et apostolicae; formae concretae sunt variabiles et humanae", p. 345. See L. BOISVERT, "Conseils et voeux", in *La vie des communautés religieuses,* 57 (1999), pp. 72-73.

19 Ibid., A. DUTIL, "Status professionis consiliorum evangelicorum, in suis variis formis, fructus est maternae sollicitudinis Ecclesia erga filios suos qui vocatione divina attracti, plene Deo sese consecrare intendunt", p. 170.

20 Ibid., C. HEILIGERS, "Ut via aperta pateat ulterioribus formis vitae perfectionis, bonum esset commemorari quod praxis consiliorum evangelicorum varietatem graduum intensitatis et extensionis admittit, sive quoad characterem officialem seu publicum, sive quoad effectus, sive quoad stabilitatem etc", p. 213.

21 Ibid., Volumen III, *Periodus tertia,* Pars VII, *Congregationes generales CXIX-CXXII,* "Quatuor Patres rogant ne in definitionibus et in divisionibus religionum aliorumque institutorum perfectionis porta claudatur ulterioribus formis professionis consiliorum evangelicorum.

Response — Suggestio est omnino fundata; sed cum schema loquatur de 'iure vigenti', nulla porta clauditur iuri condendo", p. 110.

22 Ibid., Volumen II, Pars III, G. HUYGHE, "Multae congregationes religiosae virorum ac mulierum novissimis saeculis exortae sunt, ad apostolatum activum vel missionarium. Sed vi coactiva iuris canonici et traditionum, imposita sunt eis tria vota religionis e vita cenobitica orta, et constitutiones quasi 'praefabricatae', ubi praevalent consuetudines monasticae ut, exempli gratia, clausura. Et praesertim spiritualitas data est alumnis, similis spiritualitati contemplativae, ubi non apparet character missionarium, et in qua anima in duplici directione divisa est...Volumus praesertim congregationes activas adiuvare ad inveniendam spiritualitatem propriam et unificatam, et a vita eorum apostolica inspiratam", p. 649.

23 V.L. BARTOLAC, *The Practice of the Evangelical Counsels in Secular Institutes,* Ann Arbor, Michigan, UMI, 1991, p. 83.

24 SACRED CONGREGATION FOR RELIGIOUS AND SECULAR INSTITUTES, Instruction on the Renewal of Religious Life *Renovationis causam,* (= *RC*), 6 January 1969, in *AAS,* 61 (1969), pp. 103-120; English translation in FLANNERY 1, pp. 634-655. Here at p. 634.

25 SACRED CONGREGATION FOR BISHOPS and SACRED CONGREGATION FOR RELIGIOUS AND SECULAR INSTITUTES, Directives for Mutual Relations Between Bishops and Religious in the Church,*Mutuae relationes,* (= *MR*), 14 May 1978, in *AAS,* 70 (1978), pp. 473-506; English translation in FLANNERY 2, pp. 209-243.

26 SECOND VATICAN COUNCIL, Decree on the Up-to-date Renewal of Religious Life, *Perfectae caritatis* (= *PC*), 28 October 1965, in *AAS,* 58 (1966), pp. 702-712; English translation in Flannery 1, pp. 611-623.

27 SECOND VATICAN COUNCIL, Decree on the Church's Missionary Activity, *Ad gentes,*(= *AG*), 7 December 1965, in *AAS,* 58 (1966), pp. 947-990; English translation in Flannery 1, pp. 813-856.

28 PONTIFICIA COMMISSIO CODICI IURIS CANONICI RECOGNOSCENDO, *Communicationes:* Romae, 1 (1969), pp. 78-85. Here are outlined the ten general principles for the revision of the Code.

29 *Communicationes,* 2 (1970), pp. 170-173. See F. G. MORRISEY, "Introduction", in J. HITE, S. HOLLAND and D. WARD (eds), *Religious Institutes, Secular Institutes, Societies of Apostolic Life: A Handbook on Canons 573-746* (= *A Handbook of Canons*), revised edition, Collegeville, MN, Liturgical Press, 1990, pp. 15-20. When these principles were enunciated the title of the Schema was "De Religiosis". Since it was to include secular institutes which were declared in *Perfectae caritatis* 11 not to be religious institutes, the title was changed to "De Institutis Perfectionis", (*Communicationes,* 2 (1970), p. 174. By 1975 when consecrated life was defined in terms of consecration to God by profession of the evangelical counsels (*LG*, 45), the title changed again to "De institutis vitae consecratae per professionem consiliorum evangelicorum", (*Communicationes,* 7 (1975), p. 63. This was abbreviated to "De institutis vitae consecratae", (Ibid., p. 90). The change of title flowing from the choice of basic definition had significant repercussions for those societies to be known later as societies of apostolic life.

[30] See E. Mc Donough, *Religious in the 1983 Code: New Approaches to the New Law,* Chicago, Franciscan Herald Press, 1985 p. 14.

[31] Neri, *Nuove forme di vita consacrata (can. 605 C.I.C.),* p. 36.

[32] Pontificia Commissio Codici Iuris Canonici recognoscendo, *Schema canonum de institutis vitae consecratae per professionem consiliorum evangelicorum,* English translation, *Schema of Canons on Institutes of Life Consecrated by Profession of the Evangelical Counsels; Draft,* Washington, DC, Publications Office, United States Catholic Conference, 1977, p. 10. "Competentis Ecclesiae Auctoritatis est, duce Spiritu Sancto, consilia evangelica interpretari, eorumdem praxim legibus moderari atque stabiles inde vivende formas canonica approbatione constituere necnon curare ut secundum spiritum fundatorum crescant et floreant", p. 11.

[33] J. Beyer, *Le droit de la vie consacrée,* Paris, Tardy, 1988, vol. 2, p. 165. "Personne ne doute de l'importance de ce canon, vu le nombre de fondations nouvelles suscitées par le Concile et répondant à son esprit." See E. Sastre Santos, "Las nuevas formas de vida consagrada. Variaciones sobre el canon 605", in *Claretianum,* 35 (1995), p. 37. The author noted that, after the Council, there was born "a new Church", with a "new moral", with a "new hierarchy" and with a "new religious life" that excluded the evangelical counsels. New religious foundations "were seen to be getting out of hand" and some of the renewal undertaken by congregations seemed to be destructive of the old ways and of consecrated life in general. The situation worried the 1977 Synod of Bishops so that the 1977 schema, *De institutis vitae consecratae per professionem consiliorum evangelicorum,* was suspended (ibid., p. 39) and a new one called for. The Code Commission responded accordingly.

[34] Beyer, *Le droit de la vie consacrée,* p. 166. "Le Concile a donné la possibilité de nombreuses formes nouvelles de vie consacrée. Pour être vraiment nouvelles, elles manifesteront, comme dit le Concile, un nouvel aspect de la vie du Christ."

[35] See Neri, *Nuove forme di vita consacrata (can. 605 C.I.C.),* pp. 37-38 for a fuller discussion of the issues involved.

[36] *Schema of Canons on Institutes of Life Consecrated by Profession of the Evangelical Counsels; Draft,* pp. 3, 11. "§1. Consilia evangelica in Christi Magistri doctrina et exemplis fundata, donum sunt divinum (pro populo Dei) quod Ecclesia a Domino accepit et gratia Eius

semper conservat.

§2. Competentis Ecclesiae auctoritatis est, duce Spiritu Sancto, consilia evangelica (eadem consilia) interpretari, eorumdem praxim legibus moderari atque stabiles inde vivendi formas canonica approbatione constituere necnon curare ut secundum spiritum fundatorum crescant et floreant", *Communicationes,* 11 (1979), p. 36.

[37] *Communicationes,* 11 (1979), p. 37. This canon was eventually accepted into the 1983 Code of Canon Law as two separate canons, numbers 575 and 576.

[38] *Communicationes,* 11 (1979), p. 325. "§1. Instituta vitae consecratae (variis Spiritus charismatibus ornata) quae a competenti Ecclesiae auctoritate erecta sunt in tres dividuntur classes, nempe: Instituta religiosa, Instituta vitae apostolicae consociatae (Societates vitae communis sine votis) et Instituta saecularia."

[39] *Communicationes,* 11 (1979), p. 327.

[40] *Communicationes,* 11 (1979), p. 328. "Instituta vitae consecratae, pro variis Spiritus charismatibus a competenti Ecclesiae auctoritate approbata in tria dividuntur genera, nempe: Instituta religiosa, Instituta vitae apostolicae consociatae (Societates vitae communis absque votis) et Instituta saecularia."

[41] *Communicationes,* 11 (1979), p. 334, "Vigilanti cura Episcopi (Auctoritates Ecclesiae ad quas spectat) nova vitae consecratae dona (charismata) a Spiritu Sancto Ecclesiae (continuo) concredita discernere satagant et promotores (fundatores) adiuvare ut inspirationem receptam quam melius exprimant et aptis statutis protegant (adhibitis praesertim generalibus normis in hac parte contentis."

[42] *Communicationes,* 11 (1979), p. 334-336.

[43] *Communicationes,* 11 (1979), p. 336. "It is reserved to the Apostolic See alone to approve new forms of consecrated life. Diocesan Bishops should strive to discern new gifts of consecrated life given to the Church by the Holy Spirit; they should help promoters to express their proposal better and to protect it by appropriate statutes in accordance with the general norms contained in this section."

[44] See *Communicationes,* 15 (1983), p. 55 for the list of those

individuals and groups that were consulted and *Communicationes,* 14 (1982), pp. 116- 119 for the list of those who received and examined the opinions offered. A synthesis was presented to the Commission in August 1981. The Commission then met in plenary session from 20-28 October 1981 to examine and debate the results. See also J.BEYER, "Le deuxième projet de droit pour la vie consacrée", in *Studia canonica,* 15 (1981), p. 87.

45 PONTIFICIA COMMISSIO CODICI IURIS CANONICI RECOGNOSCENDO, *Schema Codicis iuris canonici. schema Patribus Commissionis reservatum,* Romae, Libreria editrice Vaticana, 1980, p. 129.

46 *Communicationes,* 15 (1983), p. 67. "1. Nimia est centralizatio quod approbatio S. Sedis exigatur pro qualibet nova forma vitae consecratae. Ne priventur Episcopi suis praerogativis (Quidam Pater).

R. Animadversio admitti nequit: quae Sanctae Sedi et Episcoporum dioecesanorum respective sunt apte in canone distinguuntur.

2. Sufficit ut novae formae vitae religiosae approbentur ab Episcopo, et ideo ne fiat reservatio ad Sedem Apostolicam (Aliquis Pater).

R. Agitur in canone de approbandis non novis Institutis, sed novis formis vitae consecratae, quae differant tum ab Institutis religiosis tum ab Institutis saecularibus. Propter hoc fit reservatio."

47 PONTIFICIA COMMISSIO CODICI IURIS CANONICI RECOGNOSCENDO, *Schema Codicis iuris canonici. schema novissimum iuxta placita Patrum Commissionis emendatum atque Summo Pontifici praesentatum,* Romae, Typis polyglottis Vaticanis, 1982, p. 112. See SASTRE SANTOS, "Las nuevas formas de vida consagrada", pp. 42-43.

48 V. DE PAOLIS, "The New Forms of Consecrated Life, (according to the norm of c. 605)", in *Consecrated Life,* 19 (1996), p. 68. This author defines "new forms" from a negative perspective saying that forms are new "precisely because they do not possess the elements required by the legislator to be able to be defined forms of consecrated life." See J. PFAB, "Neue Formen des geweihten Lebens", in S. HAERING, (ed.), *In unum congregati: Festgabe für Augustinus Kardinal Mayer OSB zur Vollendung des 80. Lebensjahres,* Metten, Abtei-Verlag, 1991, p. 468.

49 V. DE PAOLIS, *La vita consacrata nella Chiesa,* Bologna, Dehoniane, 1991, p. 74. The author distinguishes between consecrated life as a theological entity, defined in c. 573 §1, and as an institute of consecrated life, defined in c. 573 §2. He points out that both parts of the canon need to be embraced to give members of consecrated life both theological and juridical standing in the Church. Canons 607 and 710 further define religious and secular institutes.

50 MANSI, vol. 22, col. 1002: "Ne nimia religionum diversitas gravem in ecclesia Dei confusionem inducat, firmiter prohibemus, ne quis de cetero novam religionem inveniat: sed quicumque voluerit ad religionem converti, unam de approbatis assumat. Similiter qui voluerit religiosam domum fundare de novo, regulam & institutionem accipiat de religionibus approbatis." English translation in TANNER, p. 242. See R. SEBOTT, *Ordensrecht: Kommentar zu den Kanones 573-746 des Codex Iuris Canonici,* Frankfurt am Main, Verlag Josef Knecht, 1995, p. 80.

51 S. HOLLAND, "Norms Common to all Institutes of Consecrated Life, (cc. 573-606)", in J.A. CORIDEN, T.J. GREEN and D.E. HEINTSCHEL (eds), *The Code of Canon Law: A Text and Commentary;* commissioned by the Canon Law Society of America, New York, Paulist Press, 1985, p. 469.

52 E. GAMBARI, *I religiosi nel Codice: commento ai singoli canoni,* Milano, Ancora, 1986, p. 102. The author says that it is possible to have forms with a diverse content, but including consecration coupled with a determined apostolate or activity of christian life which many people live to-day, even spouses. See DE PAOLIS, "The New Forms of Consecrated Life", pp. 72-73. The author sets out his understanding of the constitutive elements of consecrated life. He would claim that married couples cannot be members of institutes of consecrated life. This opinion contrasts with that of E. GAMBARI and J. BRAUX.

53 For a historical analysis of the involvement of Church authorities in the approbation of religious institutes see E. SASTRE SANTOS, "On Church Approbation of Religious Institutes and of their Rules and Constitutions: (*Historical excursus*)", in *Consecrated Life,* 21 (1999), pp. 127-157.

54 J. BRAUX, "Les formes nouvelles de la vie consacrée (can. 605), in AA VV, *Questions juridiques et canoniques: Hommage au R.P.P.-E Bouchet,* Toulouse, Institut Catholique de Toulouse, Faculté de Droit canonique, 1987, p. 32. See G. ROCCA, "Le nuova comunità", in *Quaderni di diritto ecclesiale,* 5 (1992), pp. 168-169.

[55] LEO XIII, Apostolic Constitution Conditae a Christo, in Acta Leonis XIII Pontificis Maximi, Romae, ex Typographica Vaticana, 1881-1905, vol. 20, pp. 317-327; English translation in D.I. LANSLOTS, Handbook of Canon Law for Congregations of Women Under Simple Vows, 9th edition revised and enlarged to conform with the new Code of Canon Law, New York, F. Pustet Co., Inc., 1920, pp. 246-258.

[56] See footnote 5.

[57] See E. SASTRE SANTOS, "The Diocesan and Pontifical Approval of an Institute of Consecrated Life", in *Consecrated Life,* 15 (1990), pp. 48-51.

[58] See PFAB, "Neue Formen des geweihten Lebens", p. 469; T. Rincon-Pérez, "Comentario – c. 605", in A. MARZOA, J. MIRAS Y R. RODRIGUEZ-OCAÑA, *Comentario exegético de derecho canónico,* Pamplona, Ediciones Universidad de Navarra, 1997, vol. II/2, p. 1498 and De Paolis, *La vita consacrata nella Chiesa,* p. 81. Several other commentators emphasise that it is not a question of new institutes but of new forms of consecrated life. A bishop may still approve a new institute in a diocese after consultation with the Holy See. This indicates that his role in his diocese is not undermined as was feared during discussions on the formulation of the canon.

[59] See E. GAMBARI, *The Canonical Establishment of a Religious Institute: Process and Procedures,* translated by M.M. ARMATO and T. BLESSIN, Florence, Artigraf, 1999, pp. 159-216. See also SASTRE SANTOS "The Diocesan and Pontifical Approval of an Institute of Consecrated Life", pp. 41-63.

[60] JOHN PAUL II, "Apostolic Constitution on the Roman Curia", *Pastor bonus,* 28 June 1988, in *AAS,* 80 (1988), pp. 841-924; English translation in *Code of Canon Law,* Latin-English edition, prepared under the auspices of THE CANON LAW SOCIETY OF AMERICA, Washington, DC, Canon Law Society of America, 1999, pp. 681-751.

[61] DE PAOLIS, *La vita consacrata nella Chiesa,* pp. 81-82. "Precisiamo che 'Sede Apostolica' in questo caso si intende solo il romano pontefice, mentre sono esclusi i dicasteri della Curia romana, a meno che non abbiano un mandato specifico da parte del santo padre. L'approvazione infatti di nuove forme nel senso inteso, va al di là delle competenze che spettano ai dicasteri della Curia romana, e in particolare alla Congregazione per gli istituti di vita consacrata e le società di vita apostolica." See DE PAOLIS, "The New Forms of

Consecrated Life", pp. 73-74, where the author again asserts that the authority to give approval for new forms is the Pontiff since CICLSAL enjoys only executive power. G. ROCCA, "Le nuova comunità", p. 169 concurs with this view. NERI, *Nuove forme di vita consacrata (can. 605 C.I.C.)*, pp. 95-97, would disagree with this viewpoint while acknowledging that this is a minority option (p. 95). He points out that, if "Apostolic See" meant "Roman Pontiff", there would be no need for the canon. He goes on to cite from the discussion of 30 May 1979 where, he claims, it is evident that the Commission meant the Apostolic See rather than the Pontiff, (*Communicationes* (1979), pp. 334-336). For a general overview of the competence of CICLSAL see J. TORRES, "Sacra Congregazione per i religiosi e gli istituti secolari (1908)", in G. PELLICIA, and G. ROCCA, (eds), *Dizionario degli istituti di perfezione* (= *DIP*), Romae, Edizione Paoline, 8 (1988), pp. 234-251.

62 DE PAOLIS, "The New Forms of Consecrated Life", footnote 43, p. 83.

63 *L'Attività della Santa Sede; Pubblicazione non ufficiale* (= *ASS*), Città del Vaticano, Libreria editrice Vaticana, 1990, p. 1173, which lists as approved *Opera della Chiesa,* (Madrid) under the heading "erezione di una famiglia ecclesiale di vita consacrata". An article by G. FEDELE, "L'Opera della Chiesa: una famiglia ecclesiale nuovo e profetico dono di vita consacrata", in the Italian edition of *L'Osservatore romano,* 16 November 1990, n. 264, p. 5, reports the approval, saying that CICLSAL "authorised" Cardinal A. Suquìa of Madrid to recognise *Opera della Chiesa* as an ecclesial family of diocesan right. The text indicates that c. 605 reserves such approval to the Apostolic See. This ecclesial family received pontifical recognition in 1997 and is listed in *ASS* for that year on p. 906; *ASS,* 1993, p. 1234 lists as approved with pontifical recognition *Società di Cristo Signore* (Montreal, Canada). It is interesting to note that this is the only "new form" listed in the *Annuario Pontificio per l'anno 1995,* Città del Vaticano, Tipografia Poliglotta Vaticana, 1995, p. 1446 under c. 605. The previous year (p. 1444) the canon was not included. In subsequent years *Società di Cristo Signore* continues to be the only "*altri istituti di vita consacrata*" with c. 605 specified.

64 See BRAUX, "Les formes nouvelles de la vie consacrée (can. 605)", p. 32; and also PFAB, "Neue Formen des geweihten Lebens", pp. 469-470.

65 DE PAOLIS, *La vita consacrata nella Chiesa,* p. 83. See COUNCIL OF THE GENERAL SECRETARIAT OF THE SYNOD OF BISHOPS, *De vita consecrata deque eius munere in Ecclesia et in mundo: Instrumentum*

laboris, (= *IL*), Roma, Libreria editrice Vaticana; English trans, *The Consecrated Life and Its Role in the Church and in the World, Instrumentum laboris,* Ottawa, Canadian Conference of Catholic Bishops, 1994, n. 75.

[66] See *MR,* 12, where "some signs of a genuine charism" are outlined and *MR,* 51 which states the conditions to be fulfilled in order to pass judgement on the authenticity of a charism. See also A. POGGI, "New Institutes", in *Consecrated Life,* 11 (1986), p. 264; PFAB, "Neue Formen des geweihten Lebens", pp. 470-471 and J. A. GALANTE, "Consecrated Life: New Forms and New Institutes", in *CLSA Proceedings,* 48 (1986), pp. 121-124.

[67] SASTRE SANTOS, "The Diocesan and Pontifical Approval of an Institute of Consecrated Life", p. 49.

[68] RINCON-PÉREZ, "Comentario − c. 605", p. 1500. "Muchas de estas experiencias, que a veces se desarrollan con gran dinamismo, merecen que se les acompañe con un discernimiento iluminado y una guía válida, para que puedan alcanzar una situación clara y orgánica en el conjunto del Pueblo de Dios."

[69] POGGI, "New Institutes", p. 264.

[70] DE PAOLIS, *La vita consacrata nella Chiesa,* p. 84.

[71] G. GHIRLANDA, "La vita consacrata nel Codice di Diritto canonico", in *Credere oggi,* 66 (1991), p. 96.

[72] SASTRE SANTOS, "The Diocesan and Pontifical Approval of an Institute of Consecrated Life", p. 46. For the stages of approval see GALANTE, "Consecrated Life: New Forms and New Institutes", pp. 124-125 and GAMBARI, *The Canonical Establishment of a Religious Institute,* pp. 49-216, where the author discusses the various phases in the development of an institute from beginnings to final approval. See also J. TORRES, "Approvazione delle religione", in *DIP,* 1, cols. 768-773 and CONGREGATION FOR RELIGIOUS AND SECULAR INSTITUTES, "Documents and Information to be Sent to the Holy See in View of Canonical Erection of an Institute of Diocesan Right". This document, available from the Congregation, lists the basic requirements for determining if an institute can be approved. It assumes that the discernment of the new gift has taken place prior to statutes being formulated.

73 See V. DE PAOLIS, "Associations Founded with the Intent of Becoming Religious Institutes", in *Consecrated Life,* 21 (1999), pp. 159-160.

74 See MORRISEY, "Introduction", pp. 17-19. The author explains the term "proper law".

75 G.B. HUME, "Relatio ante disceptationem", in *Consecrated Life,* 20-21 (1999) (combined edition), pp. 61-62. The author outlined the process for the Synod. The Holy Father assigned the theme, *"De vita consecrata deque eius munere in Ecclesia et in mundo",* on 30 December 1991. This was followed by the discussion paper, *Lineamenta,* on November 24, 1992, "which served as a stimulus toward reflection by the episcopal conferences, and in particular by the consecrated people and their national and international organisms." The fruit of the studies was published as *Instrumentum laboris,* which became the reference point for the Synodal exchanges and interventions.

76 See R. MCDERMOTT, "The Ninth Ordinary Session of the Synod of Bishops: Four Moments and Six Canonical Issues", in *Commentarium pro religiosis,* 77 (1996), pp. 262, 269.

77 COUNCIL OF THE GENERAL SECRETARIAT OF THE SYNOD OF BISHOPS, *De vita consecrata deque eius munere in Ecclesia et in mundo: lineamenta,* (= L), Roma, Libreria editrice Vaticana; English trans, *The Consecrated Life and its Role in the Church and in the World, Lineamenta,* Ottawa, Canadian Conference of Catholic Bishops, 1992, 71 p. This document was prepared after consultation with the Oriental Churches, the Episcopal Conferences, the Heads of the Departments of the Roman Curia and the Union of Superiors General (preface, p. 3). Curiously, at this stage, there seems to have been no consultation with members of consecrated life who are women, whose numbers far exceed those of male members of consecrated life in the Church. Responses were to be sought from as wide a source as possible and sent to the General Secretariat of the Synod of Bishops for final collation and drafting into the *Instrumentum laboris.*

78 *Instrumentum laboris,* Introduction. The authors set out the aim of the synod and, hence, the basis for working. It is called "to reflect on the consecrated life in the light of God's plan, returning to the sources of grace from which it arises, the great wealth of its historical expressions and the legacy of its saints. At the same time, however, the synod is intended to discern the challenges and expectations of the

contemporary world" (n. 2).

[79] JOHN PAUL II, "The Task of the Latin American Bishop", in *Origins,* 12 (1982-1983), pp. 569-662. The Pope was greatly influenced by PAUL VI, "Apostolic Exhortation", *Evangelii nuntiandi,* 8 December 1975 in *AAS,* 68 (1976), pp. 5-76; English translation in FLANNERY 2, pp. 711-761. For development of the concept see H. CARRIER, "Nuova evangelizzazione", in R. LATOURELLE e R. FISICHELLA (eds), *Dizionario di Teologia fondamentale,* Assisi, Cittadella editrice, 1990, pp. 421-426 and C. CHAMPAGNE, "La nouvelle évangélisation: la pensée de Jean-Paul II", in *Kerygma,* 26 (1992), pp. 247-270. For the relationship between consecrated life and the new evangelisation as discussed in the Ninth Ordinary Synod of Bishops, see P.G. CABRA, "La nuova evangelizzazione", in *Informationes SCRIS,* 21 (1995), pp. 164-173.

[80] See A. DULLES, "John Paul II and the New Evangelization", in *America,* 166 (1992), p. 55. The Pope, in his missionary journeys to several countries, continues to facilitate this evangelisation, which should generate hope in the future civilisation of love. See also D.L. SCHINDLER, "Reorienting the Church on the Eve of the Millennium: John Paul II's 'New Evangelization'", in *Communio,* 24 (1997), pp. 728-779.

[81] JOHN PAUL II, "Toward the Fifth Centenary of New World Evangelization", in *Origins,* 20 (1990-1991), pp. 208-216. The Pope develops the themes of incarnation, inculturation and the role of consecrated life.

[82] Ibid., p. 56.

[83] JOHN PAUL II, Encyclical letter, *Redemptoris missio* (= *RM*), 7 December 1990, in *AAS,* 83 (1991), pp. 249-340; English translation in *Origins,* 20 (1990-1991), pp. 541, 543-568. In this document the Pope distinguished between those who had never heard the good news of Jesus (n. 33) and those who needed re-evangelisation. The two groups are not necessarily geographically distinct.

[84] JOHN PAUL II, "Apostolic Exhortation", *Christifideles laici,* 30 December 1988, in *AAS,* 81 (1989), pp. 393-521; English translation in *Origins,* 18 (1988-1989), pp. 561, 563-595.

[85] See DULLES, "John Paul II and the New Evangelization", p. 57. See also J. O'DONOHUE, "To Awaken the Divinity Within: Towards a New Theory of Evangelization", in *The Way,* 34 (1994), pp. 265-272. The

author presents evangelisation as "an inherent and ongoing activity in every act of faith; a non-linear journey from presence to awareness" (p. 268).

[86] NINTH ORDINARY SESSION OF THE SYNOD OF BISHOPS, "Message of the Synod on Consecrated Life", in *L'Osservatore romano,* (English edition), 2 November 1994, p. 7. The Fathers say that the Church is called to a new evangelisation and that "consecrated persons are uniquely apt for playing a leading role in this providential task."

[87] See S. RECCHI, "La missione della vita consacrata nella Chiesa missione", in *Quaderni di diritto ecclesiale,* 6 (1993), p. 405. Here the author emphasises that "the mission of Christ is rooted in the mystery of the mission-consecration of Christ. Christ is eminently the missionary of the Father, and is also the consecrated of the Father. All consecration and mission find their reference essentially in Christ."

[88] See P.G. CABRA, "A Reflection for the Synod on the Consecrated Life", in *Consecrated Life,* 19 (1995), pp. 48-49, where the author portrays the *Lineamenta* as a "martyr" document. He sees it as needing to be "pierced" through, perfected and discussed.

[89] For further understanding of the concept and its necessary integration in consecrated life see JOHN PAUL II, " The Value and Efficacy of Religious Life Always Depend on Ecclesial Communion", in *Consecrated Life,* 15 (1990), pp. 17-19; E. SASTRE SANTOS, "Communio institutorum vitae consecratae cum Sede Apostolica", in *Commentarium pro religiosis,* 66 (1985), pp. 5-41; J. BEYER, *Communione ecclesiale e strutture di corresponsabilità: dal Vaticano II al nuovo Codice di diritto canonico,* Roma, Pontificia Università Gregoriana, 1990, 80 p; CONFERENCE OF RELIGIOUS, INDIA, *Consecrated Life - A Call to Communion in the Light of "Vita consecrata" for the Third Millennium,* New Delhi, CRI House, 1997, 90 p; A. BANDERA, "L'identità ecclesiale della vita religiosa", in *Vita consacrata,* 33 (1997), pp. 372-389 and C. LAUDAZI, "La vita consacrata nella dimensione ecclesiale", in *Vita consacrata,* 33 (1997), pp. 170-191. These authors and others underline the necessity for real and earnest endeavours to understand the doctrine of communion and live it. For the importance of this section of *IL* see R. McDERMOTT, "The Ninth Ordinary Session of the Synod of Bishops: Four Moments and Six Canonical Issues", pp. 261-294.

[90] JOHN PAUL II, "Christ Invites Us: 'Come, follow me'", in *L'Osservatore romano,* (English edition), 5 October 1994, p. 1.

[91] JOHN PAUL II, "Spirit Continues Giving New Charisms", in *L'Osservatore romano,* (English edition), 12 October 1994, p. 15.

[92] G.B. HUME, "Relatio ante disceptationem", in *Consecrated Life,* 20-21 (1999) (combined edition), pp. 61-85; original in Latin from archival ms.

[93] See MCDERMOTT, "The Ninth Ordinary Session of the Synod of Bishops", p. 270. See G.F. POLI, "Bibliografia sul sinodo", in *Vita consacrata,* 31 (1995), pp. 9-51; pp. 196-200; p. 276. Of 843 articles listed on the synod — before, during and after — only two have titles on New Communities and one titled "Towards New Forms of Consecrated Life". Despite the topicality of the subject, not many examined it then.

[94] For further discussion on the relationship between consecrated life and the new evangelisation, see CABRA, "La nuova evangelizzazione", pp. 164 – 173.

[95] See HUME, "Relatio ante disceptationem", p. 81. See also G.B.HUME, *Relatio post disceptationem,* Rome, E. Civitate Vaticana, 1994, p. 20.

[96] S. FERNANDES DE ARAÚJO, "Le 'Nuove comunità' o 'Famiglie ecclesiali'", in archival ms, p. 1; Summary and translation in *L'Osservatore romano,* (English edition), 2 November 1994, p. 20.

[97] J.C. TURCOTTE, "Les communautés nouvelles: en lien avec *l'Instrumentum laboris,* par. 37, 38, 40 et 87", archival ms., pp. 1-4; English translation from the CCCB.

[98] C.M. MARTINI, "Verso nuove forme di vita consacrata? *I.L.* 37 e 38", in archival ms, pp. 1-2; Summary and translation in *L'Osservatore romano,* (English edition), 16 November 1994, p. 7.

[99] NONA ASSEMBLEA GENERALE ORDINARIA DEL SINODO DEI VESCOVI, "*Propositiones* del sinodo al papa: Identità, comunione, missione", in *Il regno-documenti,* 21 (1994), pp. 665.

[100] Ibid., Proposition 13 was voted on and carried by 212 votes to 14.

[101] JOHN PAUL II, Post-synodal Apostolic Exhortation *Vita consecrata,* (= *VC*), 25 March 1996, in *AAS* 88 (1996), pp.377-486;

English translation, *Consecrated Life,* Sherbrooke, QC, Médiaspaul, 1996, 208 p.

[102] G. GHIRLANDA, "The Consecrated Life in the Church", in *Consecrated Life,* 20-21 (1999), (combined edition), p. 95.

[103] Ibid., p. 97. See H. BÖHLER, "Vita consacrata e Chiesa particolare", in *Quaderni di diritto ecclesiale,* 10 (1997), pp. 360-362.

[104] See HUME, "Relatio post disceptationem", p. 20 where the author treats the relationship of consecrated life to the universal Church through the petrine office. He refers to the practice of exemption as a special service to the Church by some institutes.

[105] The term "institution" is used rather than "institute" which has canonical and juridical connotations.

[106] See H. LEROY, "Chronique du droit de la vie consacrée", in *L'Année canonique,* 40 (1998), p. 272.

CHAPTER FOUR

THE APPLICABILITY OF CANON 605

INTRODUCTION

Just as canon 605 did not come to birth in a vacuum, it cannot be applied in a vacuum. It must be interpreted and applied in the context of an ecclesiology and in a world characterised by definable trends and motivations, with human beings who are conditioned both by Church and world experiences in a global, local and personal manner. In this chapter we examine some of these key factors, and establish some basic criteria to assist bishops in discerning new charisms and new forms of consecrated life. We explore the characteristics of some of the new forms that have arisen at this moment in history and, finally, explore the possibilities for the application of c. 605 in the future.

CONTEXTUAL BACKGROUND FOR THE APPLICATION OF CANON 605

New forms of consecrated life arise in a particular moment of history that is defined in the Church and in society by specific theological, ecclesiological and socio-cultural conditions. During the Second Vatican Council, the ecclesiology of *communio* was presented as a basis for understanding the Church in modern times, and relationships between all peoples within it. The Church was no longer envisaged as a perfect society, with an emphasis on a hierarchical structure, but as a communion of the People of God with all the inter-relationships that this implies, and at all levels. We see it as a key element of the ecclesiology which must underpin the emergence of new forms of consecrated life. This ecclesiology comes to life in a world where the understanding of God has changed over time and where the new insights into the dignity of peoples and the human person demand attention to inculturation in the Church's approach to its mission. Moreover, the world itself is changing at an unprecedented rate. Therefore, the applicability of c. 605 demands that there is an understanding of *communio,* the postmodern concept of God and inculturation against the backdrop of some of the characteristics of the modern world. The next part of the chapter endeavours to provide such a background, so that the applicability of c. 605 can be examined in context, and the criteria for discerning new forms can be established in a framework that is not merely theoretical but also related to the Church and the world in which the new forms are lived and experienced.

The Ecclesiology of Communio and Consecrated Life

Since canon law is a derived science, one that flows from the doctrine of the Church, it is appropriate that the ecclesiology of *communio* be examined in order to set c. 605 in a broad ecclesiological framework. The concept of *communio* was given new impetus over the period of the Council and in the conciliar and postconciliar documents. "The word *communio* refers to the essential 'concern' from which the Church comes and for which it lives. *Communio* does not designate the structure of the Church but its essence, or as the Council says: its mystery."[1] This approach sets the mystery element in an understanding of the Church in the focal position rather than within the visible and hierarchical configuration — or the perfect society model prevalent prior to the Council. Consecrated life, according to *LG,* 43, is situated in the Church and, therefore shares in its mystery, and actively participates in the lived experience of *communio.*

Lumen gentium presents the Church as a sacrament — a sign and instrument of communion with God and of unity among all men.[2] Its mystery is presented under three aspects. First, *LG,* 2 states that God, "with the utterly gratuitous and mysterious design of his wisdom and goodness, created the whole universe, and chose to raise up humanity to share in his own divine life." It is this sharing with God that gives persons dignity.[3] Second, *LG,* 2 adds that salvation was accomplished in and through Christ in a unique way in a historical moment. God entered human history "to establish a relationship of peace and communion with himself, and in order to bring about brotherly union among persons."[4] Christ became not only the mediator between God and humankind but took all to himself in a mysterious union. Third, Christ, having being lifted up from the earth, has drawn all to himself. Having risen from the dead, he sent the Holy Spirit and, through him, set up his Body, which is the Church, to be the sacrament of salvation. Therefore, united with Christ in the Church and marked with the Holy Spirit, we are called and are truly the children of God (*LG,* 48). This community with God, realised through the Spirit, is the foundation of the community of the Church. Thus, the Spirit gives access to the Father through Christ and the members are united one with the other and drawn into the Trinitarian mystery.[5]

This *communio* is nourished through the Word of God and through the sacraments, especially the Eucharist. Through the Eucharist the faithful participate with Christ in the redeeming act and are part of the ecclesial communion. In the final *relatio* of the 1985 extraordinary synod of bishops, the Fathers say that, "for this reason, the ecclesiology of communion cannot be reduced to purely organisational questions or to problems that simply relate to powers. Still, the ecclesiology of communion is also the foundation for order in the Church, and especially for a correct relationship between unity and pluriformity in the Church."[6] They go on to say that the sacraments point to the ecclesial communion with the successor of Peter and the Church. The Catholic Church consists of and abides in local Churches (*LG,* 23). Thus is established the links between diocesan bishops, the particular churches and the universal Church. Such links, forged between diocesan bishops and the petrine successor, account for the collegiality of the bishops with the head and with one another.[7] "The simultaneously episcopal and papal *communio* is the essential organic expression of the essential structure of the Church, of its unity in catholicity and its catholicity in unity."[8] Above all, it is the expression of unity between people and peoples.

This unity extends to the desire for ecumenical *communio*. "The wound of disunity still existing between believers in Christ and the urgent need to pray and work for the promotion of

Christian unity were deeply felt at the Synod (on consecrated life)" (*VC*, 100). Members are urged to participate in dialogue of friendship and charity, to exchange the gifts of mutual knowledge, and to cooperate in common undertakings of service and of witness (*VC*, 101).[9]

The union expressed in genuine *communio* holds true in the expression of unity between members of consecrated life.[10] Here, fraternal life seeks to reflect the depth and richness of this mystery, taking shape as a human community in which the Trinity dwells, in order to extend in history the gifts of communion proper to the three divine Persons (*VC*, 41). The fraternal life, whatever its mode of expression, plays a fundamental role in the spiritual journey of consecrated persons both for their constant renewal and for the full accomplishment of their mission in the world (*VC*, 45).[11]

The essence of *communio* is linked to consecrated life through the charism. The charism is that unique, living gift given to founders to be expressed in a particular manner within the institutional Church. It is reduced to canonical terms in c. 578 which describes the patrimony of an institute. The patrimony, it says, is comprised of the mind of the founders, their intent, together with their understanding of the nature, purpose, spirit and character of the institute as well as sound traditions, all approved by the competent ecclesiastical authority. This canon is a static, juridical reduction of what is a vivifying, changing and evolving gift of the Spirit. Cardinal Hume, in the *relatio* for the opening of the 1994 Synod on Consecrated Life, emphasised this fact, drawing on the work of the *Instumentum laboris*.[12] Continuing to draw on the *IL,* he affirms that the charism has a special relationship with the Church. It is a new way of living the organic communion of the Church, collaborating with the bishops, other institutes, the secular clergy and the laity in a special service for the growth of the Body of Christ. Because the communion itself is living, it is open to growth and change. Consecrated persons promote communion in the Church through their witness to the universality of the gospel message, which goes beyond differences of any kind and, through their solidarity and availability to all, especially the very poor. In such a manner, they create bonds within the

Church as well as between the Church and marginalised groups in the world.[13]

Mission in the World

Gaudium et spes attempted to express the relationship of the Church to the world. Instead of seeing it as a separate society, the Council Fathers came to see the Church as living and active in the world — a world created by God, redeemed by his Son and blessed by the Holy Spirit. Nothing that is genuinely human fails to find an echo in the hearts of the followers of Christ (*GS*, 1). Therefore, the world that the Council has in mind is the whole human family seen in the context of everything that engages it: it is the world as the theatre of human history, bearing the marks of its travail, its triumphs and failures (*GS*, 2). No part of the human condition is too small or insignificant to be of concern to the Church and its members in communion with it. For the purposes of the eventual application of c. 605, the following are considered briefly: the changing concept of God, inculturation and its relevance to consecrated life, and some aspects of the world situation, such as the major trends in technology, science and communications. These are examined in order to glean some understanding of their affect on the mission of consecrated persons and their institutes.

The Changing Concept of God

The idea of God is central to the call to consecrated life.[14] While seeking God is a universal human quest,[15] E. Johnson claims that the fascination with the mystery of God is endemic to consecrated life, everywhere and at all times.[16] Consequently the prevailing idea of God sustains the life-search for intimate union with the Godhead and gives meaning to lifelong commitment in consecrated life.

Classically, the notion of God was modelled on that of an earthly monarch who ruled over his subjects and had dominion over his creatures.17 This God was unknowable, was a mystery. Modernity tended to objectify God, reducing infinite mystery to an independently existing Supreme Being alongside other beings.[18]

This concept of a distant, uninvolved God is no longer tenable in a postmodern world. The God, who is now perceived, is enmeshed in history and its sufferings and is sought through

> any created good: male, female, animal, cosmic. This mystery does not dwell in isolation from the world but encompasses it as the Matrix of its being and becoming. God in the world and the world in God... is a God of pathos who participates in the suffering of the world in order to transform it from within. Divine power is the strength of love, rather than raw, monarchical omnipotence. Passionate for justice and peace and compassionate over pain, holy Wisdom typically self-reveals in the fragmentary breakthroughs of well-being that come about through human partnership with divine purpose.[19]

This God is neither self-sufficient nor changeless. He weeps with those who weep and suffers with those who suffer and weeps for them through us.[20] This is the God whom Jesus preached and embodied: the God of life (cf. John 10:10). He is present in life and in the living, seeking to be known and to transform (cf. Matt. 11:14). He is the God who "meets us to-day among the godless, among the corpses, as the victim of torture and of ethnic cleansing; as the disappeared and the not-looked for; as the refugee, the migrant, the homeless; as the hungry, the beggar, the outcast; the lonely, the unpopular, the unattractive."[21] He is the God present to and in his people and very much part of life. Such a view of God will have immeasurable influence in the spirituality and approach to mission in any new form of consecrated life.

Inculturation

After the Second Vatican Council, the word *inculturation* became widely accepted to describe bringing the gospel into a culture.[22] The Church realised that people can hear the good news only in terms of their own culture and experiences. "Not only can no human being enter this world without simultaneously being born into a culture, but also the mind of every person can understand, judge and decide only through a culture."[23] The fundamental event of inculturation is the Incarnation when God took on the human condition as a Jew in the Jewish culture with all that it implies. Every culture builds a home in which the Gospel may be welcomed.[24] For those members of consecrated life sharing in evangelisation, their charism, too, must be inculturated so that it can respond to the concrete situation in which the Gospel is preached. This does not refer to professional competence alone but to the saving action which is directed to the whole person in his existential situation. It allows others to experience the loving kindness of God and the influence of the Spirit in their lives.[25] The Spirit is like yeast that transforms what it meets.

This theme was taken up in the *Instrumentum laboris,* 93 and again in *Vita consecrata,* 80. Inculturation involves the whole of the consecrated life: charism, life-style, formation and forms of apostolate, prayer and community organisation and administration. It is not merely a question of adapting certain customs but rather of a profound transformation of mentalities and ways of living, affecting both the cultures of the younger churches and those of western civilisations (*IL,* 93). Consecrated life must be inculturated so that it can, in turn, perfect and challenge the culture it meets. The process demands a freedom of the children of God who can choose, in dialogue and healthy experimentation, what leads to the Truth. Consecrated life in no way makes its members useless for human society (*LG,* 46). On the contrary, it permits them to have their sisters and brothers present with them in the heart of Christ so that human society may be renewed according to the Gospel (*IL,* 103) and in harmony with the culture of the peoples to whom service is offered. Culture is not static but in a constant state of change, creating new meaning. Inculturation is a painful process as it brings the newness to birth, demanding great mutual trust and a welcoming of the stranger.[26]

Some Aspects of the World on the Eve of the Third Millennium

New forms of consecrated life come into existence at an historical moment in a world governed by definite ideologies, politics, concerns and social realities. It is not the intention to analyse or even list all such contingencies but a few that are deemed to be particularly relevant will be granted a passing acknowledgement. There is a host of problems or needs — homelessness, ignorance, ill health, violence, social unrest — which make claims on people of the Gospel. These problems exist within a culture tainted by materialism, consumerism, transitoriness, promiscuity, loneliness, xenophobia, alienation, and so on.[27] There is the isolation of minorities, the rejection of homosexuals, lesbians in the Church and society.[28] There is a continuing debate on the role of women in society and in the Church.[29] Some even speak of "woman-Church" as if it were separate from the Catholic Church, where women still do not have their true role recognised.[30] There is the overwhelming burden of third world debt for some poor countries which have no means of emerging from the morass of grinding poverty without the help of their first world neighbours.[31] There is exploitation of the body in all conceivable forms through the sex trade and promiscuity in real life and in the virtual, through the internet.[32] There is violence to persons and to nature. There are thousands of examples: "ozone depletion, climate change, land degradation, water pollution, deforestation, habitat destruction, species extinction, use and misuse of biotechnology."[33] In addition, there are the effects of racism, of a search for reconciliation among peoples and religions, and, above all, the new phenomenon, globalisation.[34]

The world of today is seeing a revolution in communication. It has various names: cyberspace, the Internet, the Web, computer-mediated communication.[35] It makes for an information overload, for a rapidity of change that was unthinkable five years ago, for connections that span the world in seconds, that make immediacy the norm, for a new understanding of science and for the development of a new understanding and category of poor.[36] While this insight has implications for new forms of evangelisation and new approaches to mission, its most profound effect will be in the search for a new spirituality for this postmodern age where the quantity and quality of information is both humbling and overwhelming.[37] The persons developing and maturing in this environment are not accustomed to lifelong commitment. The change potential and the flexibility of the information culture as well as the increased longevity and concern for quality of life strain long term commitments.[38]

The phenomenon of the instant and constant change in modern life has repercussions for taking vows for life in any form of consecrated life. People expect to change lifestyle many times in the course of a lifetime. Individualism is promoted and institutions levelled so that people no longer have a sense of belonging. The alienation and isolation demand that new forms of consecrated life establish community which fosters the interconnections of human compassion and interweaves high energy networks of relationships. The good of the planet and all that is created demands a commitment to fashioning a global communion committed to interdependence, mutuality and authority and a strong focus on the Gospel.[39] None of these aspirations can be achieved without some understanding of the stages of development of individuals and communities, including the Church.[40] Such studies assist in putting into perspective some of the present day happenings and dreamings on a personal, national and global scale.

This brief study of the ecclesiology of *communio*, of the changing understanding of God, of the need for a realistic sense of inculturation and of an awareness of the present realities of the world community, provides some of the contextual material which must be utilised in establishing criteria for the discernment of a charism and of a new form of consecrated life. These elements constitute some of what came to be called "the signs of the times"(GS, 4). No new form can stand on its own but must be integrated into the Church and the world, having taken cognisance of "the signs" for the sake of the mission of Jesus. It is the task of the Church, and, more particularly, of the diocesan bishop, to discern charisms and new forms. Since no definitive norms are yet determined, the following criteria are suggested. They are based on the above study, selected documents of the Church and the norms of the Code of Canon Law.

SUGGESTED PRINCIPLES FOR THE APPROVAL OF NEW FORMS

Charisms are given to individuals or groups as a manifestation of the absolute freedom of the Spirit. The charisms are bound to the Church in a communion fostered by the bishops as pastors of the Church, for the service of the people and the world. Before charisms can be incorporated into an institutional form they must be discerned as genuine (*CL,* 24; *VC,* 62). Canon 605 assigns responsibility to the diocesan bishop to assist founders of new forms of consecrated life in discerning their charism and protecting it in suitable statutes.

Discernment of a Charism

The directives, *Mutuae relationes,* give criteria to pass judgement on the authenticity of a charism.[41] Since these emanate from the Congregations for Bishops and for Religious and Secular Institutes, they are recommended as basic to any discernment.[42] Though these criteria were set for the discernment of a charism for a new institute of consecrated life, they have relevance also for a discernment of the charism for a new form. In addition, the following principles are presented, based on the study of the relevant conciliar and post-conciliar documents, on discussions by various authors and on the contextual study just outlined. The principles are in two groups — one for the discernment of the charism *per se* and one for the discernment of the new form which enshrines the charism and which seeks to be acknowledged as new. The principles are broad and need to be utilised against a sound biblical and theological background. They are not definitive but, together with the ensuing questions, are offered in order to assist a diocesan bishop discern both the charism and the new form. This he does together with the founder, the members of the new group and the portion of the People of God with whom the new group interacts in the local Church.[43]

The new charism:

reflects a new face of Christ to the world (cf. LG, 46).
Is the new charism already in existence in the diocese or in nearby dioceses? Even if it is similar, in what does its newness consist and does it constitute a gift for this diocese? How does the essence of the gift contribute to the holiness and mission of the local Church?

is grounded in the Gospel, its values and spirit, on Tradition

and on the teachings of the Second Vatican Council.
Are genuine Gospel values expressed? What is the ecclesiology
that inspires this new charism? What concept of God shines
through? A classical, modern or postmodern concept of God?

**reflects a current understanding of the world and its needs,
while taking root in a particular church or series of particular
churches.**
How relevant is the new charism to current needs? Does its
expression reflect an awareness of the present world situation? Is
it merely a reversion to an old mode more suitable for a long gone
era?

**is enshrined in an institute that gives it concrete expression
in a form that meets the juridic and canonical requirements
for eventual recognition as a new form of consecrated life.** [44]
How do the statutes express the charism? Are they flexible
enough to allow for development and change as the institute
evolves?

**is articulated by the group and evaluated by it, together with
the diocesan bishop and the portion of the People of God
with whom the new group interacts.**
Does the articulation of the charism truly reflect the nature of the
new gift offered by the Spirit to the Church at this moment? While
the charism is not contained in mere words, do the words express
the culture, living and spirit of the charism?

The institutional structures and the way of life of the
members embody the charism, protect it and provide an
environment where it can grow, flower and flourish so that it may
be incorporated into the structure of the Church. The charism,
structures and way of life are articulated in suitable constitutions
and statutes. Such structures must be flexible in the birthing years
and reflect the principles developed in the next section.

Principles to Assist in Discerning a New Form of Consecrated Life

The principles presented below are to aid in discerning new forms of consecrated life.

i) The governance structures of the institute reflect the ecclesiology of communio.

Governance structures — Do they reflect the equality of each person consecrated in baptism? Is there a hierarchy of positions reserved to particular members? For example, in an institute of mixed membership, is the role of supreme moderator reserved to clerical members only or is it open equally to all definitively incorporated members, men and women, cleric or lay?

Decision-making — Do the structures allow for maximum participation of the members in making decisions that affect the lives of all members? How do the structures enshrine the profession of evangelical obedience? Is there genuine respect for the role of leadership exercised in a spirit of service?

Conflict resolution — What processes are in place for a gospel-based resolution of conflicts?

Daily life — Is the daily horarium respectful of the maturity appropriate to the age of the members? Their sense of responsibility, commitment and personal integrity? Does it reflect a balanced approach between the needs of members, community and the ministry?

Relationship to the Church — Are the lines of communication with ecclesiastical authorities open and mutually respectful? Might there be so-called "total" loyalty to the Holy Father, implying a bypassing of the diocesan bishop?

ii) The spirituality of the members of the institute expresses the charism, is based on Gospel values, the teachings of the Second Vatican Council and sound theology.

Is the spirituality that is expressed in prayer forms, rituals, reading materials in accord with contemporary theology and understanding of God or is it more suitable for another era? Is it healthy with respect to liturgy or are there simply pious devotions without sound theological foundation? Is it connected to visions? Apparitions? Or other paranormal experiences? Are the members free to choose confessors?

iii) The formation of the members has a high priority so that there is ample time to integrate the riches of the charism, the Gospel and the teachings of the Second Vatican Council.

Is the formation adapted to show the newness in the institute, to reflect the maturity of the candidates, the flexibility required at a beginning stage? Does it focus on mission rather than being preoccupied with self? Does it reflect awareness of how adults learn? Of the psychological stages of development? Of the stages of faith development? What are the criteria for acceptance to formation and, thus, to membership? Is there respect for individuality, reflecting the life of the Trinity where differences are cherished within a loving unity?

iv) The institute adapts symbols which reflect its charism, concept of God, its role in the Mission of Christ and its understanding of the world.

How is the commitment to consecrated life made visible? If there is a habit, is it a reversion to a style that is more suitable to bygone eras? Does the style have value as a symbol of dignity and simplicity (*VC*, 25) in the modern world or is merely an object for comedy situations? Is the style of dress congruent with the written expressions of the charism? Does it reflect a simplicity that speaks of poverty rather than of fashions favoured by a consumer-oriented society?

v) The lifestyle of the members is congruent with the profession of the evangelical counsels.

How do buildings, means of transport, clothing,

recreational pursuits, food and general standard of living reflect the charism and the commitment to the poor? And to the Mission of Jesus? Is there an over-eagerness to divest of property or finance and place all in common? Is there room for healthy interaction with people, to have friendships, to have free time? Is there a code of secrecy imposed on members or is there a genuine spirit of openness to each other and to the Church?

vi) The documents of the institute, practices and approaches to ministry indicate a healthy awareness of and sensitivity to inculturation?

How is this principle verbalised? How is it put into practice in daily life, decision making, rituals, liturgies, ministry? In policies on acceptance and formation of new members?

vii) The documents and practice reflect an engagement with the Church's call to ecumenism.

How are the invitation of the Second Vatican Council and the repeated call of the present Pope to engage in ecumenism, heeded? Is there prayer and action to achieve the unity that Jesus prayed for at the Last Supper? Are there opportunities for involvement in interreligious dialogue?

viii) The institute is inserted into a particular Church and is in communion with the diocesan bishop and with the universal Church.

Is there a suggestion of independence from the Church? (with due respect for the autonomy proper to the institute in its internal affairs). Is there active collaboration in the discernment of the charism, the expression of it in suitable statutes and in the ministry undertaken? Is there mutual respect and concern for the whole People of God? Does the fraternal life symbolise *communio* to the world?

ix) The institute can articulate, however inadequately, the essence of the newness of its form and its claim to approval under c. 605.

What new face of Christ is it showing to the world? Is it merely a re-arranging of elements of already existing forms without anything new? Are there some genuinely new insights into the living of consecrated life and its contribution to the Mission of Jesus?

x) The institute is in accord with the theological, canonical and juridical requirements as set out in the common norms for all institutes of consecrated life (cc. 573-602), the relevant general norms of canon law and those relating to associations.

The norms, from the Code of Canon Law, were agreed upon during the formulation of c. 605 as the basis for any new forms of consecrated life

While these principles are not exhaustive, they supplement those given in *Mutuae relationes,* and provide some food for reflection for those engaged in the discernment of new charisms and new forms of consecrated life.[45] *Vita consecrata* enjoined that a commission be set up in Rome to deal with questions relating to such new forms, to determine criteria of authenticity to help in discernment and decision-making. The Commission was also to have the task of evaluating, "in the light of experience of recent decades, which new forms of consecration can, with pastoral prudence and to the advantage of all, be officially approved by Church authority, in order to be proposed to the faithful who are seeking a more perfect Christian life" (*VC,* 62). A personal interview with the under-secretary of CICLSAL confirmed that such a commission had been formed, that it met several times and then disbanded because the members could not reach accord at this point in time.[46] While this outcome may be viewed negatively by those waiting for directives, it is, nevertheless, a heartening result. The members of the commission felt that it was too soon in the history of groups aspiring to be recognised as new forms to develop definitive criteria. There were no clear-cut indications at this stage to delineate in what the newness consisted. The members believed that the Spirit was guiding the Church and giving gifts where he willed. They considered that it would be wiser, for the present, to examine each request on its merits and make a decision on whether the new institute could be recognised or not. After all, the Church has never hurried in this regard.[47] The Holy Father affirmed this slow, careful approach in his message for the World Congress of Ecclesial Movements and New Communities. He appreciated that they represent a new springtime in the Church, foretold by the Second Vatican Council, and that they are something new waiting to be properly accepted and appreciated.[48] Hurry and impatience cannot be permitted to stifle the prodigality of the Spirit in giving new gifts to the Church. These gifts cannot be constrained for the sake of categorisation and the tidiness that comes with formalisation.

THE PRINCIPLES AS FOUND IN NEW FORMS OF CONSECRATED LIFE

In recent decades there has been a proliferation of new groups in the Church. Some of these groups have emerged from charismatic or other movements, some have arisen as associations of the faithful and some have formed as ecclesial families. To illustrate the variety of forms, we will give a brief profile of one "new form"in Canada, pontifically approved as an ecclesial family; we will also examine a pontifically approved Pious Union in Australia, and a diocesan public association of the faithful, in the USA, aspiring to pontifical recognition as a new form.

Profile of a Pontifically Approved Ecclesial Family in Canada

On 11 February 1993 Cardinal Eduardo Martinez Somalo, Prefect, and Fr. Jesús Torres, Under-Secretary of CICLSAL co-signed the decree approving the constitutions of the *Société du Christ Seigneur*. At the same time, the decree confirmed approbation, which was already granted to the society as an institute of consecrated life on 15 December 1958.[49] It is of interest to note that the original approbation of the society was prior to the new code and was granted to it as "a state of perfection". In 1993, the approbation was given as a new form of consecrated life according to c. 605 of the new Code of Canon Law. This is the only "other form" to appear consistently since 1993 in the *Annuario pontificio* as being approved according to c. 605.

A study of the approved constitutions indicates that the *Société du Christ Seigneur* is indeed an example of an ecclesial family. "The society, in the image of the Church which constitutes the People of God, is a spiritual family open to all the faithful: lay persons and clerics, men and women, celibates and couples, widowers and widows" (Art. 4).[50] The ecclesial family receives members in any one of five levels according to commitment:

Permanent Members — these are the full time members (20 women currently) who are totally at the disposal of the society to minister in any designated apostolate without personal remuneration.

Associates — these, (2 women currently), have a full-time commitment to the Society but are able to work in their chosen profession and receive a salary which they freely give to the society receiving only what they need for living expenses. These members live in community with the Permanent ones. The society is responsible for the lives and living conditions of both these groups.

Auxiliaries — the Society admits men and women who desire to participate in the life. The Society does not have any responsibility for their lives in terms of finance or related issues. They live at home and work in the regular manner. All three of these groups profess the three vows of chastity, poverty and obedience and make the same consecration in the Society, using the phrase, "I consecrate myself to you" within the context of a longer dedication.

Affiliates — are a cross section of the community at large. They live chastity according to their state, married or single, and poverty and obedience in the spirit of the Society. They are responsible for all that pertains to their lives but contribute to the Society as far as their means permit. This group also uses the phrase, "I consecrate myself to you", but they do not profess the evangelical counsels. They promise to cooperate with the goals and works of the society to the best of their ability.[51]

Aggregates — are the numerous people who are attracted to the charism, follow it as a life perspective, pray for the Society and help wherever and however their lives and means permit. There is no formal consecration in the Society for these persons.[52]

The Society is governed by a *Responsable générale,* assisted by a general Council, all chosen from the Permanent members with perpetual profession. The General Assembly is attended by the Leader and Council, regional and local leaders of the Permanent and Associate members, as well as elected delegates from the members with perpetual profession. A third of the Assembly may be composed of Auxiliaries and Affiliates with definitive consecration. This method of governance seems to be consistent with that of other ecclesial families and new communities.

The *Société du Christ Seigneur* is now a section of a wider group, *Mater Christi,* which includes two fraternities, *Fraternités Foi et Vie* and *Équipes Pierres Vivantes.* These fraternities are for members of differing ages who follow the Ignatian spirituality and grow in the understanding of their faith and commitment to God.[53] The whole ecclesial family has a programme of prayer, liturgy, daily recollection and regular retreats and meetings to enable them to plumb the depths of the charism and live the Ignatian spirit that is their heritage. The commitment of the permanent members to the Mission of Jesus is through retreat work, counselling, catechesis and parish work, all in communion with the bishops of the five dioceses and the priests of the parishes where they minister.[54]

Profile of a Pious Union of Pontifical Right in Australia

"The Christian Community for the Social Apostolate" is currently a Pious Union (since approval was granted prior to the 1983 Code of Canon Law). The community has male and female members who have full time, definitive commitment through the three vows, professed privately, and a large number of associates who work and pray with and for the community in their ministry to the poor. These spiritual associates are the catalyst between the group and the wider community, enjoying a dynamic role in a social context. The community members are committed to "alleviating personal poverty, whether it be moral, emotional or psychological, and by so doing, to help persons enter into a proper relationship with God and with one another."[55]

The members live in small groups in ordinary houses among the poor with whom they work. The dispossessed and needy often find refuge in the homes of the community for short periods. Because members are not received until they have "demonstrated in attitudes, values, religious convictions and behaviour, that there has been acquired a level of psychological and emotional maturity commensurate with the responsibilities of the commitment", there is not a tight governance structure. There is a guardian of the constitutions and, since the community is still small in numbers, decisions that affect the community are taken in common. Day to day decisions are entrusted to the judgement of the members in an adult fashion showing respect for their personal autonomy and integrity. Each member has co-responsibility for the Community and its life (Art. 33). The members have a responsibility to acquire professional qualifications as needed for their ministry and to contribute to the upkeep of the community. They do not wear a distinguishing habit, dressing in simple clothing appropriate to the work, climate and occasion. This Pious Union (now an association of the faithful), sees two options for the future, namely, that it remains as is, given the flexibility it enjoys in the Church, or seeks to become a new form of consecrated life when numbers grow and other conditions are right.

Profile of a Public Association of the Faithful of Diocesan Right in the United States

The Institute of St. Joseph is a public association of the Faithful since 1998 in the diocese of La Crosse, WI.[56] In terms of membership the profile is similar to that described above, but it has a monastic focus. The institute describes itself as an ecclesial family of secular priests, monastic brothers and sisters, single and married laity committed to the consecrated, contemplative life proper to each respective state in life.[57] Each category of person belongs in a fraternity appropriate to his state. There are four fraternities, one for secular priests, one for men and women following a consecrated life in the monastic tradition, one for single men and women living in the world dedicated to an evangelical life as leaven in society and one for married couples.

In terms of governance, they have a supreme moderator with a council (which includes representatives of each state in life) for the whole institute, a moderator for the monastic fraternity and a superior for each monastic house, as well as a chapter consisting of all temporarily and definitively incorporated members. It is of interest that the supreme moderator shall be a priest and that there appears to be no formal governance policies for the lay fraternities.

In contrast to the two previous groups, which have no formal habit, the members of the monastic fraternity have chosen to wear a formal style of habit. The concept may need to be evaluated in the light of their aspiration "to live in the context of history and the ordinary circumstances of daily life."[58] This institute aspires to pontifical recognition as a new form of consecrated life according to c. 605.

These three groups represent a small sample of the groups appearing as new forms in the Church. They illustrate the enfleshment of the criteria for new forms in varying ways but a detailed critique is outside the scope of this paper and is impossible without all the documentation found in the proper law. Each institute has a particular set of gospel values that they live by, and that are expressed in their forms of prayer, ministry and structures for governance. Each group has a defined outreach in mission and, in a general way, reflects the tenets of ecclesial communion.

POSSIBILITIES FOR FUTURE APPLICATION OF C. 605

Numerous new institutes have arisen in the Church in recent years and many are awaiting further development so that the bishops may discern their individual charisms.[59]

Assistance to Bishops in Discerning New Forms

The principles given above, based on relevant Conciliar and Post-Conciliar documents, the Code of Canon Law and the post-synodal Apostolic Exhortation, *Vita consecrata,* are designed to assist bishops in the arduous task of discernment. Many of the new groups present themselves as movements or ecclesial families, for each of which we will give a brief description.

Movements

A movement is a collective attempt to bring about changes in institutions. It is often equated with revolution or disturbance in order to change the established order.[60] In a spiritual sense, it may be the means of bringing the members closer to God while serving society and endeavouring to change it.[61] The new movements in the Church are a continuation of the associations that have always been present throughout the Church's history, either as confraternities, third orders and sodalities (CL, 29). Pope John Paul II affirmed that "alongside the traditional forming of associations and at times coming from their very roots, movements and new sodalities have sprouted, with a specific feature and purpose."[62]

These new movements may involve full-time or part-time voluntary membership and may include members of religious congregations, clerics, lay people, married and single. Members may belong to more than one movement, provided that there is no conflict of interest. Some movements, however, see themselves not as fluid groupings in the sociological sense, but as recognised entities with special structures, formal membership and approved statutes. Many, such as the *Focolare* movement, are recognised as associations of the faithful, either private or public.[63] Some are known as ecclesial families.

Ecclesial Families

An ecclesial family includes members belonging to each of the states of life recognised in the Church, that is, clerical, lay and members consecrated by living the evangelical counsels through vow or other sacred promise. With such inclusiveness, these families represent a microcosm of the whole Church. Many of the new groups begin as ecclesial families. Some seek recognition as associations of the faithful, public or private or else as new forms of consecrated life.

There is a certain amount of confusion between the use of terminology and what it represents with respect to many of the new groups. The term "ecclesial movement" includes both movements, as such, and ecclesial families, both of which may have recognition as associations of the faithful. For example, more than half a million members from 56 groups around the world crowded into St. Peter's Square on the eve of Pentecost, 1998, for a meeting with the Pope during the World Congress of Ecclesial Movements, which had 350 formal delegates. This Congress was the fourth international one for ecclesial movements but it differed from the previous ones in that it was the first to have been sponsored directly by the Holy See through the Pontifical Council for the Laity.[64] Since this Council has been given responsibility for those groups that intend to remain as associations of the faithful, it may be presumed that those 56 groups in attendance were associations that intend to remain so. This situation raises some questions about the incardination and ministry of priests and about the living of the evangelical counsels by vow in these associations. Present canonical legislation does not cover either of these exigencies. Hence, there are two significant areas that require the attention of canon law and that of the bishops seeking to discern the canonical status of new groups in the Church.

The bishops have a choice at the outset. They may suggest three options to those wishing to begin new institutes. They may direct them to choose to become one of the already canonically recognised institutes or societies, or a new form of consecrated life according to c. 605, or an association of the faithful on a permanent basis. The first option, namely, a canonically recognised institute, is based on the general norms for such institutes (cc. 573-606), in addition to the norms for either religious (cc. 607-704), or secular institutes (cc. 710-730), or societies of apostolic life (cc. 731-736).

The second option, associations of the faithful, may include persons who undertake the evangelical counsels by binding themselves with vows or other sacred bonds, the living of which is described in the statutes. These associations will be governed by the statutes of the association and the canons on associations of the faithful (cc. 298-311, and either cc. 312-320 for public associations or cc. 321-326 for private associations). Such associations will not be recognised as institutes of consecrated life according to the present Code, because the status of the members as lay persons has not changed. The persons taking vows in these associations will live "life consecrated" in contradistinction to "consecrated life". That is, they are living consecrated life in a theological sense without it being so in a canonical sense.[65] Such an association can remain so permanently or can foresee eventual movement towards seeking recognition either as one of the canonically established institutes of consecrated life or as a new form (c. 605).[66]

The third option, new forms (c. 605) has not yet had its specifics defined but such groups are to be guided especially by the norms common to institutes of consecrated life, though not exclusively. They need to refer, for example, to the canons on public associations of the faithful, cc. 298-320 and to the general norms, especially cc. 94-95 on statutes and ordinances, cc. 113-128 on juridical persons and acts and cc. 164-179 on elections.[67]

In addition to assisting the founder to choose the type of consecrated life in which members make a commitment, the bishop needs to take cognisance of c. 578 which concerns the patrimony of an institute. At the beginning stage there will obviously be no patrimony. However, it is here that it begins and the canon alerts those involved to the need to describe the intent of the founder, the nature, purpose, spirit and character of the institute. This first attempt will be moderated and developed as the institute comes to life, since this is a dynamic, organic process. The elaboration of these elements will determine the contents and spirit of the statutes and set the stage for the development of sound traditions.

Finally, a bishop assisting founders will consult the Apostolic See for the *nihil obstat,* before erecting a new institute whether it be one of the already existing forms or a new form. If it is one of the former, the process is already in place with the directives from CICLSAL. If it is the latter, only the Apostolic See can approve a new form. The communication between diocesan bishops and the Apostolic See not only gives witness to *communio* in the Church but safeguards against the proliferation of new institutes or new forms without good canonical and theological bases.

Re-interpreting the Expression of the Evangelical Counsels

The Fathers of the Second Vatican Council stated in *Lumen gentium* that the teaching and example of Christ provide the foundation for the evangelical counsels of chaste self-dedication to God, of poverty and of obedience (*LG,* 45). In making chastity the primary counsel, they reversed a long-standing tradition of placing poverty first. This decision was "canonised" by the 1983 Code of Canon Law in c. 573 §2. Jesus was chaste for the sake of the Kingdom, which was so overwhelming in its presence to him that it became the overriding determinant of his life. There was no room for marriage. His life of chastity, and celibacy, is nothing else but the existential consequence which flows out of his prior experience of the urgent presence of the Kingdom of God.[68] It reflects the total love that Jesus had for the Father and the reciprocity of that love.

When Jesus called the first four disciples, the Gospel tells us that they left their boats behind and went with him and he preached throughout the whole of Galilee, proclaiming the good news, healing the sick and curing all kinds of disease (Matt. 4: 19-25). Jesus combined the call to poverty with an active mission to the poor. The focal story for poverty in religious life has been that

of the rich young man invited by Jesus to sell all and follow him
(Mark, 10:17-22, Matt., 19:16-22, Luke, 18:18-23). The call, even
in new forms of consecrated life, is still the same but must be
interpreted in the light of the exigencies of today. The poor take on
many faces and not always just that of material poverty.

The obedience of Jesus to his Father and to the will of the
Spirit in an outpouring of love, led him to the Cross and, ultimately,
to the Resurrection. This obedience to the Father remains the
ideal. It is an active listening to the voice of God manifested
through the world, the Church, the community and interaction with
the leaders of the particular form of consecrated life. It is not a
blind exercise doing violence to the dignity of any human being.

The expression of the evangelical counsels in canonical
terms requires that it deal with the external forum only. The
resulting formalisation of the counsels and their incorporation into
legal structures has resulted in their presentation in a negative
fashion in the Code of Canon Law. The person **renounces**
marriage and family, material possessions (or, at least, their use),
and control over one's own future.[69] The choice of professing the
evangelical counsels is often deemed an impoverishment of
values that are truly human or a denial of the values inherent in
sexuality, in the legitimate desire to possess material goods and
to make one's own decisions (*VC*, 87).[70] What is needed for a
meaningful expression of the vows in contemporary settings is a
positive formulation that calls a person to holiness, that signifies a
true development of his humanity, and that highlights and
witnesses to the profound anthropological meaning of the
counsels.

One possibility could be the return to poverty as the basic
counsel, with chastity and obedience as the adjuncts.[71] M. Himes
claims that to be human is to be poor and that celibacy and
obedience are other ways of being poor.[72] The expression of
poverty reaches its zenith in the cry of Jesus on the cross, "My
God, my God, why have you abandoned me?" (Matt. 27:46). To
have lost all is nothing in comparison to the feeling of
abandonment by God — an experience of the ultimate poverty of
man as a created being.

Whatever the starting point, the object is not the vows or the counsels in themselves but the love of God, who loved all people first and demands this love in return in a great act of intimacy and creativity. In fact, there are not really three counsels, but one, nor are there three vows, but only one vow, that of love.[73] The counsels, professed through vows, are simply expressions of this love, this commitment to Christ crucified in union with the Father through the Spirit. For new forms of consecrated life, the Church, through its theologians, needs to explore the meaning of the evangelical counsels in these times and present a credible, theological basis, while being very honest about the motivations for the origins of perfect chastity in the early Church.[74] Whether the primary vow is seen as chastity or poverty is not vital. What is vital is the consecration of the person who seeks the perfection of love of God.

In addition, there is need to examine the time-frame for the profession of the evangelical counsels, either as vows or other sacred bonds. If the purpose of their profession is to direct the individual towards a greater love of God, then the professing of the vows or other sacred bonds must take cognisance of the realities of everyday life and culture. According to J. M. R. Tillard, fidelity is experienced as being very fragile in today's society.[75] In relation to the gift of oneself, he asks whether one opts for successive fidelity or for fidelity in portions? Could the vows be taken for fixed periods and then renewed? Is it conceivable that a person could commit himself for a number of years and then decide to continue life in another state of being? This question of temporary commitment in forms of consecrated life needs study and sensitivity. Does God demand more than a person, immersed in a particular culture, can give? Is a temporary commitment merely canonising instability or is it acknowledging a reality of modern existence? Does a temporary commitment, through vows, imply that consecration to God is not permanent or does it mean that the expression of that consecration can change? In other words, are the vows one mode of expression of the consecration or are they perceived to be the consecration?[76] Such questions emerge as bishops consider new forms of consecrated life and attempt to discern their genuineness.[77] New forms should be able to incorporate a core of people with life-long commitment as well as those who wish to express their consecration to God by taking vows for shorter periods, and then to be either renewed or concluded at the end of the relevant period.

In addition to reflecting deeply on the overall meaning of the profession of the evangelical counsels, either through vows or other sacred bonds, there is need to examine the canonical expression of the vow of poverty. The conditions must be attuned to the demands of the civil and social requirements of the wider community. Even in monastic times, the religious were expected to support themselves by the work of their hands, but fellow monks cared for them in sickness and old age. In western society in particular, the reality of superannuation, costly healthcare packages and support in declining years is vastly different from that of earlier years when such necessities were covered by the religious community and the catholic community at large. What does commitment to poverty really mean today? Is it to contribute to the burden on society? Or is it to contribute to the well-being of those to whom the consecrated person ministers? What are the responsibilities of consecrated persons to the families that they have left? Is there a responsibility to care for ageing parents, sick or distressed family members? How can such situations be responded to with charity and compassion without compromising or overburdening the institute? Therefore, the practicalities of the living of poverty must be in tune with the reality of life and should be expressed adequately in the proper law of each new form. It should not be governed by mere traditionalism which is already ossified, dead and a counter witness to what is being re-interpreted in new forms meant for present situations.

Similarly, the expression of obedience calls for on-going interpretation so that a genuine respect and mutual cooperation can interplay with rightful authority, be it ecclesial or communitarian. Obedience must not give way to authoritism,[78] which exercises control in a legalistic, stultifying manner, disrespectful of the integrity and maturity of the persons.[79] It calls for a genuine appreciation of the goodness of the other, the good faith and the sharing in the mission of Christ in a responsible authority that is life giving and life producing.[80] The expression of obedience in proper law must attempt to reincarnate and represent in a contemporary situation, the words, message and demands of Jesus. This means that the law verbalises the call to total love — a love which will render each consecrated person more authentically human.[81] It implies the need to have both leaders and those accepting of genuine leadership for the sake of the Kingdom. The invitation of c. 605 to approve new forms of consecrated life concomitantly invites the Church to re-interpret the living of the counsels in contemporary terms.

Married Persons and Consecrated Life

John Paul II, in *Vita consecrata,* reiterates what he calls "the fundamental principle, when speaking of the consecrated life." He confirms that new communities and their styles of life must be founded on the essential theological and canonical elements proper to consecrated life (*VC,* 62). Such fundamental elements are expressed in c. 573 of the 1983 Code of Canon Law and refer to canonical institutes of consecrated life. The Pope recommends and praises married couples who, in some of the newer communities, assume commitment to the obligation of chastity proper to the married state, often by means of a vow. He continues, "They do so with the intention of bringing to the perfection of charity their love, already 'consecrated' in the sacrament of Matrimony" (*VC,* 62). This sentiment echoes that expressed during the Second Vatican Council in *Gaudium et spes,* 48. However, he states, that the theological and canonical principles enunciated in c. 573 preclude such couples and their form of commitment from being included in the specific, canonical category called consecrated life.

Such exclusion is based on the definitive understanding of canonical consecrated life as presented in the 1983 Code. Consecration is described in terms of commitment to God, expressed through profession of the evangelical counsels either by vows or other sacred bonds. The counsel of chastity must be lived in perfect continence. This choice of definition of consecrated life was made as a result of the study of "religious life" at the Second Vatican Council (*LG,* chapter 6). However, another Council document, *Perfectae caritatis,* describes the purpose of consecrated life as the experience, expression, and mission of "perfect love" — a love which emerges from and exists within the inner Trinitarian love.[82]

All Christians are called to live the evangelical counsels and that includes chastity — living a chaste love. The total gift of such love in marriage is a reflection of the total love within the Trinity, a sign of the Church and a concrete expression of the creative love of God. The commitment in marriage was blessed by the presence of Jesus at Cana, the scene of his first miracle. Such approbation and acceptance surely indicate his reverence for the partners in their love, mirroring the Incarnation whereby God's love burst forth to the world in visible presence.[83] The Church is referred to as the bride of Christ and the image of marriage is a symbol of the Church. It mirrors God's loving self-giving in space and time so that the Christian community can have tangible witness of such love. Therefore, marriage in itself is good and holy and manifests a particular sacramental "consecration" of the couple who shares in the creative intimacy of the Trinity.

That two of the newly recognised pontifical ecclesial families include married couples infers that married consecration is accepted in these new forms. However, it could be interpreted that an institute does not have to include only consecrated celibates to be recognised as a form of consecrated life.[84] An institute could be recognised as a new form with the newness being that the institute itself meets the canonical requirements but not all members do.

It is clear that married couples do not conform to the current canonical requirements for belonging to religious life, secular institutes or societies of apostolic life.[85] However, if their families are respectfully cared for, they should be able to give their lives totally to the God who calls them to a life of the perfection of love. The commission set up after *Vita consecrata* to determine criteria for approving new forms of consecrated life, decided that it is too early to make definitive judgements on the call of the Spirit. Hundreds of thousands of men and women, married and single, priest and lay, have responded to this call in recent decades.[86] The status of married couples in the new movements may be clarified as the definition of consecration and the applicability of c. 605 become more encompassing and inclusive of the gifts being offered to the Church today.

Ecumenical Communities of Consecrated Life

Canon 597 of the Code of Canon Law states that every Catholic with the right intention and the qualities required by universal law and the institute's own law and who is without impediment, may be admitted to an institute of consecrated life. Canon 205 gives the conditions for being considered in full communion with the Church but does not speak of membership of the Church *per se*.[87] These canons would seem to exclude non-Catholic Christians from membership in the same institutes of consecrated life. This situation contradicts practice[88] and the numerous calls to ecumenical dialogue made by many recent popes and especially Pope John Paul II.[89] Certainly, the question of the reception of the Eucharist could pose problems, as well as the understanding of certain doctrinal elements.

One of the most widely known ecumenical communities is that of Taizé, founded by Roger Louis Schutz-Marsauche in 1949 in the Burgundy region of France.[90] During the war years, the devastation and despair were obvious everywhere in Europe and Roger dreamed of a house where the discouraged could be offered a place of silence and work. By 1950 he had the nucleus of his community — himself who was Lutheran, another brother and a Catholic priest. When numbers increased he wrote a rule, *The Parable of Community,* in which he stated that the life of the brothers was to be a parable, a living sign of the Unity of the Church. The brothers, now numbering over 100 from 25 countries and all five continents, are to be men of the present, aware of the social, political and cultural realities around them.[91] They are not to ignore their differences but endeavour to transcend them. The community welcomes all to come and pray with them and the centre has become a haven for youth who gather in very large numbers for prayer, community singing, liturgy and sharing the word of God. As the community has grown, members have gone to the poorest nations in Asia, Africa and Latin America to share with the poor. The pivotal aim of the community is that of reconciliation. Their spirituality is firmly rooted in the great

Christian tradition and yet is open to the contemporary world. Although it has not asked for nor received any official Catholic recognition, it is a known fact that Pope John Paul II is a friend of Roger Schutz-Marsauche and refers to the community as "that little springtime." The Pope visited there in 1986.

While such communities do not meet the Code of Canon Law requirements, they are performing a necessary function in the Church, torn by division and lack of trust. They heed the prayer of Jesus, "That all may be one" (Jn. 17:11), and attempt to live it. Such communities, after appropriate discernment could well wish to seek approval under c. 605. On the other hand, they may consider that ecclesiastical independence could give them more flexibility to determine how they can live, work and pray in the world. However, any "work" carried out in the name of the Church needs the approval of the bishop. Such cooperation in common undertakings of service and of witness are among the many forms of ecumenical dialogue (*VC,* 101).

Consecrated Widows

In the early days of the Church, there were three groups of widows: "true" or enrolled widows, widows (usually older) who were not enrolled and younger widows.[92] The divisions were based on need. The "true" widows were officials in the Church and performed ministries. B. Thurston claims that there was a promise made on enrollment and that the widows were to be alone, that is, dependent on God; must be continually faithful and chaste.[93] The faithfulness and chastity reflect the preoccupation of the non-Christian world with continence. The widow had to be over sixty years of age, the wife of one husband and the doer of good deeds of domesticity, hospitality, humility and compassion. She was also enjoined to pray constantly. This author goes on to state that the "order" of widows continued into the fourth century and was the forerunner of women's monastic orders. Deaconesses, who took over the roles and functions of widows in the Church, eventually replaced them in ministry. The edict of Constantine (313 AD) also contributed to their decline. As a result of this edict, the Church became institutionalised and the order of widows fell victim. The move to institutionalisation led to the formalisation of ministry.

What had been a response to a charism, the work of widows, now became incorporated into a ministry and led to the constriction of the leadership roles available to women in the church. The equality of men and women in ministry, characteristic of the early Church (Gal. 3:28), gave way to the development of "offices" and the regularisation of ministries. The offices were held by males — bishop, priest, and deacon. With this shift of focus from "charism" to ministry through an office, the order of widows was diminished and ultimately faded from the life of the Church. [94]

In the twentieth century, during World War II, many young women lost their husbands. They came together for support and to find a way to live their Christianity as widows, and to educate their children in the faith. Gradually, they formed a group that wished to live a consecrated life as widows. A ritual of blessing was devised, approved by the archbishop of Paris and by the Congregation for Divine Worship on 2 February 1984. [95] This ritual is reserved for those widows who have formed the *Fraternité Notre Dame de la Résurrection.* These women pledge themselves to prayer, to total self-giving to God and fidelity to the spouse they loved in marriage. This fraternity is exclusive to those women validly married in the Church. There is no provision for this form of consecrated life in the 1983 Code of Canon Law, but the omission has been rectified in the Eastern Code which provides for the situation in c. 570.[96] Here the canon recognises widows who live on their own in the world. The way is now open for widows to continue as individuals or to form an association or request the erection of an institute of consecrated life under c. 605, thus becoming a new form. A similar move has been entertained for widowers wishing to consecrate themselves to God.[97]

The Meaning of the Term "Consecrated Life" in canon 605

If the term "consecrated life" has at least two meanings as understood in the Code of Canon Law, what is its meaning in c. 605? The fact that the canon is positioned in the Code at the end of Title I: Norms Common to all Institutes of Consecrated Life, suggests strongly that the canon is considered in terms of institutes of consecrated life. That implies that new forms are governed by these same norms and must comply with them to be canonically recognised as institutes. However, the canon says that the bishop, in helping new founders to draw up statutes to protect the new charism, is to utilise/employ/consult especially the norms in this part, namely, the common norms. Such phraseology does not impose the strict use of the norms nor does it exclude the use of other norms contained in the Code or in other teachings of the Church. Thus, a bishop may guide the founders using, also, some of the norms chosen from those governing associations of the faithful. This flexibility and freedom of choice gives immense scope for the development of new charisms in the Church.

What is clear, however, is that the theological requirements for a consecrated life must be met. Canon 573 §1 pinpoints the theological basis for consecrated life in a norm that is dense in its content and rich in its biblical and ecclesiologcal foundations. Theologically defined consecrated life is based on the profession of the evangelical counsels, in a stable form of living for the purpose of following Christ more closely. The second paragraph details the requirements for the concrete canonical expression of the counsels of chastity, poverty and obedience. They must be assumed by vow or other sacred bonds, in institutes of consecrated life established by the competent ecclesiastical authority. Canons 607 and 710 specify the canonical requirements for religious life and secular institutes respectively, while c. 731 outlines the basis for societies of apostolic life. These three canons, together with c. 573, set the parameters for canonical institutes of consecrated life and societies of apostolic life.

Consecrated life in a theological sense, without canonical recognition, may be assumed in an association of the faithful where the living of the evangelical counsels is regulated by the statutes of the association. To the extent that the bishop must approve the statutes, it can be said that the competent ecclesiastical authority regulates the concrete living of the counsels. However, there is a *lacuna* in the Code of Canon Law. Although it does not exclude the possibility, the Code does not make specific provision for the formal living of the evangelical counsels other than in institutes of consecrated life or societies of apostolic life or as a consequence of private vows. The recognition of new forms with their attendant canons in a revised or amended code would attend to this situation.

The position of c. 605 in the Code would seem to indicate that "consecrated life" in the canon referred only to that lived in canonical institutes. This opinion would be supported by the analysis of A. Neri, judging by his contention that possible new forms could arise from permutations and combinations of the elements in the canonically recognised forms.[98] He does, however, treat three suggestions made by V. De Paolis.[99]

In the first hypothesis, De Paolis foresees that there could be institutes where not all the members are consecrated according to c. 573 §1. Some members may have full consecration but others would not. He sees that this could be a new form and Neri concurs but adds that the different types of membership should be in different branches, each with its own statutes, melded as one with some norms common to all members. G. Rocca disagrees and says that such a proposition should be rejected.[100] However, both groups that have received pontifical approval as ecclesial families include members with full consecration and others without.[101] Praxis supports the proposition that there can be an institute of consecrated life without every member being consecrated in a theological and canonical manner. For there to be true *communio* and equality of dignity, it should be possible to have new forms where members with different forms of consecration are all included in a single institute with a common form of governance, without the need for separate branches.

The second proposal of De Paolis is that there be a form of consecrated life which did not explicitly contain the three evangelical counsels. Neri says that, at least, the evangelical counsel of chastity should be explicit.[102] Rocca concurs with this opinion.

The third proposal of De Paolis is that there be the requirement of the three evangelical counsels but not through vows or other sacred bonds. According to Rocca who is in agreement with Neri, this suggestion is already incorporated in the provisions for societies of apostolic life, by c. 731 §2. This option, Neri says, would best be left with societies of apostolic life and utilise c. 605 for new situations.

The re-ordering of compositional elements of institutes may lead to the approval of new forms, but it does not elaborate on the meaning of "consecration". The theological definition in c. 573 §1 is based on the public profession, by vow or other sacred bond, of the evangelical counsels, (that is, received in the name of the Church by an approved representative, usually the Congregational Superior or delegate), and lived in a stable manner. The "faithful" (interpreted as "catholics" in c. 597) are called to follow Christ in total dedication to God, for the mission of Jesus and as a sign of the Kingdom. This form of dedication constitutes canonical consecrated life, lived either in institutes, the associative form, or by individuals, the personal or individual form.

Many members of associations of the faithful profess the evangelical counsels either by vow, oath or promise and concretise their expression in the statutes. Can such an undertaking be considered "consecration"? According to S. Recchi, the answer is yes. She states that the profession of the vows is largely theological and implies a stable and effective practice of the counsels. She quotes c. 207 §2 which says that those professing the evangelical counsels through vows or other sacred bonds recognised and approved by the Church, are consecrated to God in their own special way and promote the salvific mission of the Church.[103] The undertaking of the evangelical counsels through sacred bonds, rather than vows, is also to be deemed consecration. The nature of the bonds must be determined in the statutes of the association. What is of importance is that all the members dedicate themselves totally to God in a radical way to follow Christ more closely. They lived a life consecrated rather than a consecrated life.

Thus there is, in the Church, consecrated life and life consecrated. What is the meaning ascribed to "consecration"?[104] Consecration is a dance of the Spirit. It includes the call of God to an individual, (a vocation), a response from the one chosen and acceptance on the part of God who receives and blesses the response, often through a minister of the Church.[105] The one called and responding commits himself/herself to God in an irrevocable manner, making visible the loving and saving presence of Christ, the one consecrated by the Father and sent on mission (*VC,* 76). Consecration is an extension of the baptismal consecration whereby the person is invited in a special way into the ineffable life of the Trinity to be caught up in it, revivified and then emerge in a new creativity, expressed in mission to the Church and the world. This consecration invites the consecrated one into a closer following of Christ in a manner that is not a necessary consequence of baptismal consecration and that goes beyond the consecration received in confirmation (*VC,* 30). It demands the commitment to living the evangelical counsels in a form not required by baptism. It presupposes a particular gift not given to everyone (*VC,* 30) but it is not a matter of saying that it is a better or more perfect way of life than that of other Christians. Consecration expresses in a deeper way the following of Christ, in the search for the perfection of love.[106]

The consecrated person is a manifestation of the love of the Triune God, a sign of God's fidelity to humankind, a symbol of communion and a pointer to the world to come. The dance is not a once off occurrence — the invitation is continually being extended so that the person grows in the perfection of love in a human, dynamic way through the course of life. In c. 605, consecration may take the traditional meaning of life consecrated to God through the profession of the evangelical counsels through vows, or other sacred bonds (c. 573). It may also be broadened to encompass the dedication to God in response to a call, made by a baptised person who wishes to live his life totally and in a visible manner, in the spirit of the counsels, according to his state in life for the perfection of love. Both of these meanings of consecration (and other differently nuanced ones) could be encompassed in c. 605. The unity of the different interpretations comes from Christ. Each person is animated by the same vocation, the call to perfect love, and each strives appropriately to reveal the form of Christ in and to the world.[107] Therefore, it may be said, finally, that there is only one consecration, with multiple concrete expressions. When the variety of concrete expressions are incorporated into canon law, there will be no need for the distinction between life consecrated and consecrated life.

Canon 605, in opening the vistas to include new forms of consecrated life, is an imaginative response, on the part of the Code Commission, to the exigencies of the post-Vatican II period. The broad possibilities of the canon give scope for the new infusions of the Spirit, witnessed in the prodigality of new groups in the world of our times. That so many of these new groups, either in associations of the faithful or in new forms, include a wide spectrum of lay people committed in varying ways and at different levels, indicates the dawning of a new age of the laity. It is a particular fruit of the Second Vatican Council, a fruit recognised and encouraged greatly by the present Holy Father. Truly c. 605 is a gift to the Church. Its task is to pose the question or questions for consecrated life taking shape under the historical and social impact of this moment in the Church. The search for answers will become part of the fruits of development of new forms. Such fruits will have to be expressed eventually in canonical terms for their adequate systemisation and the good of the whole Church.

CONCLUSION

The interpretation and application of c. 605 are enmeshed in the socio-cultural fabric of today's Church and society. Any bishop discerning a new charism needs to take cognisance of these factors, out of which has blossomed the charism and in which it must grow, develop and mature. A new institute or form of consecrated life must enflesh the new charism in such a way that it is structured and visible but not risible. The symbols chosen and the way of life must reflect present day realities. The fundamental tenets must be based on the Gospel, the teachings of the Church, especially those of the Second Vatican Council and sound Catholic tradition. They must be formulated in language that is clear and doctrinally sound without having recourse to sentimentality, visions or other paranormal activities. And they must conform to the guidelines from the appropriate ecclesiastical authority, with due attention to the Code of Canon Law. Canon law provides the structures that protect and nourish the charism which is encapsulated in the symbols that put the human spirit in touch with deeper realities.

It is the duty of the diocesan bishop to assist the founders to discern the charism, to formulate suitable statutes and to express them in a way that will enhance the charism. While the bishop watches over and assists the new institute on its way, in both a pastoral and canonical capacity, he must keep a delicate balance between permitting the gift of the Spirit to become fully fledged in its own way and between exercising an undue control that would stifle the Spirit. There must not be an undue emphasis on "works" because the life of an institute is a gift in itself for the growth of holiness in the individuals, the institute and the Church. It is not purely for ministry, however important this may be in a diocese. The ecclesiology of *communio* points the way to unity in Jesus, who is the Way to union with the Father in the Spirit — not even he claimed to be an endpoint.

The expression of new charisms, given as gifts to the Church of today, will find their place in new forms of consecrated life. There is considerable confusion in the use of the terminology and in its meaning. What consecration means in theological and canonical terms is not identical and it is possible to have the first without the latter. However, both are needed to have an institute of consecrated life according to the norms common to institutes of consecrated life in the Code of Canon Law. That there are other forms of consecration is without dispute and when such forms are clarified it will bring some order to the prevailing creative chaos. A new form of consecrated life will be different in structure and components from those already canonically recognised. It will, however, point to the holiness of the Church, lead people to an intimate union with the Trinity while promoting a civilisation of love.

The following are possibilities for new forms:

a) the ecclesial family in which there are clergy, lay persons, married and single as well as consecrated persons professing the evangelical counsels through vows, promises or other sacred bonds. This family form is a microcosm of the Church and could include variations such as the following:

(i) The distinct groups could have different levels of commitment. They could also be in distinct branches with each branch having its own statutes and governance structure and all branches having an overall president.

(ii) There could be one group with all equal, that is, not in branches, with a single governance structure. The statutes would spell out the differences in responsibility and commitment.

(iii) There would be a core of consecrated persons but not all persons would need to have consecration according to the evangelical counsels. Other persons could commit to living the charism for a time.

(iv) There could be a core of members with life-time commitment and other members who would commit for a period with the possibility of completing the commitment in a given time or renewing it.

b) **ecumenical communities** where persons of different Christian denominations live a charism in a consecrated lifestyle. These could even include members of other religious faiths.

c) **communities of persons living the traditional consecrated life.** They could include religious, other members living according to the norms of secular institutes or societies of apostolic life with hermits, and groups of virgins and widows or combinations of the above.

Whatever the structure of the new forms of consecrated life, the emphasis needs to be on inclusivity, openness and flexibility. Communities in the third millennium will have persons of different races, cultures and creeds, of different ages and states of life, of different terms of commitment. [108] The unity of the communities will stem from the overriding love of a God who is present with them in all the exigencies of life. They will live life in a missionary spirit so that the good news of Jesus is brought to all. Otherwise there is no *raison d'être* for any such forms.

All such new forms will present themselves for approval to the Apostolic See whose prerogative it is to signal the birth of a new form of consecrated life in the Church. The Apostolic See will endorse the constitutions and statutes, realising that the new form is an organic entity subject to growth and change. Each new form, and each new institute therein, will present a new face of Christ to the world, a sign of the immutable love of the Father.

NOTES

¹ W. KASPER, "Church as *Communio*", in *Communio: International Catholic Review,* 13 (1986), p. 103.

² SECOND VATICAN COUNCIL, "Dogmatic Constitution on the Church", *Lumen gentium (=LG),* 21 November 1964, in *Acta Apostolicae Sedis (= AAS),* 57 (1965), pp. 5-75; English translation of this and other conciliar documents in A. FLANNERY (ed.), vol. 1, *Vatican Council II: The Conciliar and Post Conciliar Documents,* (= FLANNERY 1), new revised edition, Dublin, Dominican Publications, 1992, pp. 350-426. Here at p. 350.

³ See SECOND VATICAN COUNCIL, "Pastoral Constitution on the Church in the Modern World", *Gaudium et spes (=GS),* 7 December 1965, in *AAS,* 58 (1966), pp. 1025-1115: English translation in FLANNERY 1, pp. 903-1001, here at *GS,* 12, 14.

⁴ SECOND VATICAN COUNCIL, "Decree on the Church's Missionary Activity", *Ad gentes (= AG),* 7 December 1965, in *AAS,* 58 (1966), pp. 947-990; English translation in FLANNERY 1, pp. 813-856. Here at p. 814.

⁵ See KASPER, "Church as *Communio,*" pp. 104-105. See also J. RENKEN, "The Ecclesiology of *Communio* as Hermeneutic for Canon Law", in Glasmacher Lecture presented at Saint Paul University, 14 February 2000, p. 6.

⁶ THE SECOND EXTRAORDINARY GENERAL ASSEMBLY OF THE SYNOD OF BISHOPS, "Final *Relatio*: The Church in the Word of God Celebrates the Mysteries of Christ for the Salvation of the World", in *L'Osservatore romano,* (English edition), 16 December 1985, p. 7.

⁷ See Y. CONGAR, "De la communion des Églises à une ecclésiologie de l'Église universelle", in Y. CONGAR et B. D. DUPUY (eds), *L'Épiscopat et l'Église universelle,* (Unam Sanctam, 39), Paris, Cerf, 1962, pp. 229-260. There are numerous articles on the topic but an in-depth study is not appropriate here. See JOHN PAUL II, Post-synodal Apostolic Exhortation *Vita consecrata,* (= VC), 25 March 1996, in *AAS* 88 (1996), pp. 377-486; English translation, *Consecrated Life,* Sherbrooke, QC, Médiaspaul, 1996, 208 p. See Chapter 2 where consecrated life is presented as a sign of communion in the Church.

⁸ KASPER, "Church as *Communio,*" p. 113.

⁹ See J. D. WEISENBECK, "Ecumenism a Scripture Mandate for Religious", in *Review for Religious,* 54 (1995), pp. 675-680. The author points out that Jesus came so that we may have life and have it to the full. The Church, fragmented into thousands of denominations, lacks wholeness. To achieve wholeness is a challenge to all, but to consecrated people in particular.

¹⁰ See B. MALVAUX, "La vie consacrée, signe de communion dans l'Église", in *Vie consacrée,* 69 (1997), pp. 162-163. See JOHN PAUL II, "The Value and Efficacy of Religious Life Always Depend on Ecclesial Communion", in *Consecrated Life,* 15 (1990), p. 18, where the Pope affirms that the "value of the consecration of men and women religious and the supernatural efficacy of their apostolic activity always depend on their communion with the Church." See also E. ROSANNA, "The Synod's Discussion of the Consecrated Life of Women", in *Consecrated Life,* 20-21 (1999), p. 196, where the author points out that the theme of ecclesial communion in the Synod on Consecrated Life was the foundation for other themes such as the exchange of gifts within the Church, the relationships between consecrated life and the Magisterium, collaboration among institutes, the knowledge of the theology of the particular Church in order to situate charism and the relationship between communion and mission.

¹¹ For other implications of living the ecclesiology of *communio* in consecrated life, see *VC,* 46-56. The Pope expresses the urgent need for members of consecrated life to *sentire cum Ecclesia,* to be the expression of *communio* in the Church, amongst institutes, with the clergy and with the laity both in the particular and universal Church.

¹² G.B. HUME, "Relatio ante disceptationem", in *Consecrated Life,* 20-21 (1999) (combined edition), pp. 72-73; original in Latin from archival ms.

¹³ See HUME, "Relatio ante disceptationem", p. 73, and COUNCIL OF THE GENERAL SECRETARIAT OF THE SYNOD OF BISHOPS, *De vita consecrata deque eius munere in Ecclesia et in mundo: Instrumentum laboris,* (= *IL*), Roma, Libreria editrice Vaticana; English translation, The *Consecrated Life and Its Role in the Church and in the World, Instrumentum laboris,* Ottawa, Canadian Conference of Catholic Bishops, 1994, n. 73.

¹⁴ C. LEAVEY and R. O'NEILL, *Gathered in God's Name: New Horizons in Australian Religious Life,* Sydney, Crossing Press, 1996, p. 15.

¹⁵ J. CHITTISTER, *The Fire in These Ashes: A Spirituality of Contemporary Religious Life,* Kansas City, Sheed and Ward, 1996, p. 46.

¹⁶ E. JOHNSON, "Between the Times: Religious Life and the Postmodern Experience of God", in *Review for Religious,* 53 (1994), p. 16.

¹⁷ LEAVEY and O'NEILL, *Gathered in God's Name,* p. 10.

¹⁸ See JOHNSON, "Between the Times", p. 20.

¹⁹ JOHNSON, "Between the Times", p. 21. For another view of God's intervention in the world see A. PEACOCKE, *Theology for a Scientific Age,* Oxford, Basil Blackwell, 1990, pp. 135-183. The author discusses the relation between God as seen and exemplified in the natural sciences.

²⁰ See B. FIAND, *Wrestling with God: Religious Life in Search of Its Soul,* New York, The Crossroad Publishing Co., 1997, p. 46. See also CONFERENCE OF RELIGIOUS, INDIA, *Consecrated Life - A Call to Communion in the Light of "Vita consecrata" for the Third Millennium,* New Delhi, CRI House, 1997, p. 7 where M. AMALADOSS says that Jesus announces his good news of freedom, fellowship and justice, revealing God's love in the context of the "poor... economically exploited, politically oppressed, socially marginalised, psychologically victimised, culturally dominated and religiously alienated with legalism and ritualism."

²¹ FIAND, *Wrestling with God,* p. 48. See J. M. R TILLARD, *Dilemmas of Modern Religious Life,* Wilmington, DE, Glazier, 1984, p. 68. The author says that "the incarnation is the mystery of God himself in the mystery of one poor man. Jesus is made poor, because ...he made the condition of mankind in its most tragic aspects his own." See also N. H. GREGERSEN, "The Idea of Creation and the Theory of Autopoietic Processes", in *Zygon: Journal of Religion and Science,* 33 (1998), pp. 353-358. The author presents his theory arguing that God is very involved in nature, is a compassionate co-sufferer of the trials and errors, accomplishments and breakdowns of creatures. This view substantiates that presented by J. POLKINGHORNE, *Serious Talk: Science and Religion in Dialogue,* Valley Forge, Trinity Press International, 1995, p. 85.

[22] See J.J. MUELLER, "Second-Stage Inculturation: Six Principles of the American Mind", in *Review for Religious,* 53 (1994), p. 658.

[23] Ibid., p. 659.

[24] T. RADCLIFFE, "Inculturation", in *Review for Religious,* 53 (1994), pp. 647-648. See W. KASPER, "The Church as Sacrament of Unity", in *Communio: International Catholic Review,* 14 (1987), p. 7, where the author states that the Church "must realise herself in the various local churches, according to the givens of history and culture, in diverse forms of proclamation, liturgy, piety, theology, canon law, societal and political engagement, social service, customs and traditions."

[25] See P. PUTHANANGADY, "The Call to Communion: A Spirituality for the Religious of our Time", in CONFERENCE OF RELIGIOUS, INDIA, *Consecrated Life - A Call to Communion in the Light of "Vita consecrata" for the Third Millennium,* New Delhi, CRI House, 1997, p. 73.

[26] See T. RADCLIFFE, *Sing a New Song: the Christian Vocation,* Springfield, IL, Templegate Publishers, 1999, p. 252.

[27] See D. GOTTEMOELLER, "Religious Life: Where Does It fit in Today's Church?" in *Review for Religious,* 57 (1998), p. 159.

[28] See G.B. HUME, "Note on Church Teaching Concerning Homosexual People", in *Origins,* 24 (1994-1995), p. 767. See also, EDITORIAL COMMENT, "East of Eden", in *The Month,* 247 (1986), p. 317, where the editor of the Jesuit periodical pleads for "a more truly authoritative theology and anthropology which can address ... the reality of homosexuals in their living of Christian discipleship."

[29] As an example of exclusion of women in Church, see L.N. LORENZONI, "The *Annuario Pontificio:* The Vatican's 'Pontifical Yearbook' and a Recent Editorial Decision", in *Review for Religious,* 58 (1999), pp. 261-265. The author documents the fact that women's religious orders were not included in the year book until 102 years after the listings for male counterparts but it took another 56 years for the names of the female leaders to be included (p. 265). On the more positive side, *VC,* 97-98 presents the special role of consecrated women in the Church.

[30] See *IL,* 88. See also JOHN PAUL II, "Apostolic Exhortation", *Christifideles laici (= CL),* 30 December 1988, in *AAS,* 81 (1989), pp. 393-521. The synod fathers (from the synod on the laity), when

confronted with the various forms of discrimination and marginality of women just because they are women, affirmed the urgency to defend and promote the personal dignity of woman and consequently, her equality with man.

31 See T. AMBROGI, "Goal for 2000: Unchaining Slaves of National Debt", in *National Catholic Reporter,* 26 March 1999, 35 (1999), pp. 3-5. The author summarises the financial situation of the poorest countries: 32 in Africa with a total debt of $156 billion, 4 in Latin America with a total debt of $17 billion, 3 in Asia with a total debt of $34 billion and 1 in the Middle East with a debt of $6 billion. Most of these countries pay excessive interest each year and can never hope to defray the debts. It is hoped that, for the Jubilee year, the debts can be forgiven or reduced to a sustainable level. See also K. COATES, "Speaking out for the World's Poorest People", in *The Month,* 259 (1998), pp. 219-221.

32 See M. KÄSSMANN, "Covenant, Praise and Justice in Creation", in D.G. HALLMAN, *Ecotheology: Voices from South and North,* Geneva, WCC Publications, 1994, pp. 37-41.

33 Ibid., p. 48.

34 See É. HERR, "La mondialisation: pour une évaluation éthique?", in *Nouvelle revue théologique,* 122 (2000), pp. 51-53. The author describes the phenomenon of globalisation. The author describes the phenomenon and outlines a proposed ethical approach. See also INTERNATIONAL LABOUR ORGANIZATION: WORKING PARTY ON THE SOCIAL DIMENSIONS OF THE LIBERALIZATION OF INTERNATIONAL TRADE, "Final Report: Globalization: Perceptions, Definition and Measurement", November 1999,<http://www.ilo.org/public/english/standards/relm/gb/docs/gb276/s dl-1.htm> (3 May 2000), for the definition of globalisation and its impact on society.

35 J. FREUND, "From Parchment to Cyberspace: New Technologies Can Serve Charisms", in *Review for Religious,* 56 (1997), p. 492.

36 See ibid. p. 497. See F. MOLONEY, "Religious Life Beyond 2000", private ms, lecture given in Perth, Australia, September 1998, p. 1. The author states that the icon of the postmodern world is the personal computer, in fact, it is almost sacramental. It represents the vastness of the information network, the rapidity of change, the flexibility of the possibilities available to people and the ephemeral nature of life. See also S. SCHNEIDERS, "Congregational Leadership and Spirituality in

the Postmodern Era", in *Review for Religious,* 57 (1998), pp. 6-33. This author links the postmodern world-view with the autopoietic view that living systems renew themselves continually and regulate the process in a way that the integrity of their structure is maintained. Change is inevitable but it is the return to equilibrium that is important — but always at a new point.

[37] For more discussion on spirituality for today, see R. SCHREITER, "Reflecting upon Religious Life's Future", in *Origins,* 28 (1998-1999), pp. 165-166. See SCHNEIDERS, "Congregational Leadership and Spirituality in the Postmodern Era", pp. 18-25. See also W.C. ROOF, *A Generation of Seekers: The Spiritual Journeys of the Baby Boom Generation,* San Francisco, Harper Collins, 1993, x, 294 p. and M. DOWNEY, "In the Ache of Absence: Spirituality at the Juncture of Modernity and Postmodernity", in *Liturgical Ministry,* 3 (1994), p. 96. For further development, see S.D. SAMMON, "Last Call for Religious Life", in *Human Development,* 20 (1999), p. 17. This author moves from baby boomers to generation X, after the baby boomers, to examine the factors that affect their spirituality.

[38] SCHREITER, "Reflecting upon Religious Life's Future", p. 166.

[39] See D. MARKHAM, "Religious Life To-morrow", in *Human Development,* 18 (1997), p. 6. See also JOHNSON, "Between the Times", p. 19.

[40] See LEAVEY and O'NEILL, *Gathered in God's Name,* pp. 21-34 and D. MURPHY, *The Death and Rebirth of Religious Life,* Alexandria, N.S.W., E.J. Dwyer, 1995, pp. 34-53. See also D. MURPHY, *A Return to Spirit: After the Mythic Church,* Alexandria, N.S.W., E.J. Dwyer, 1997, pp. 137-154. For another view see B. PIERCE, "The Vatican II Generation and Religious Life", in *Review for Religious,* 56 (1997), pp. 15-24.

[41] SACRED CONGREGATION FOR BISHOPS and SACRED CONGREGATION FOR RELIGIOUS AND SECULAR INSTITUTES, "Directives for Mutual Relations Between Bishops and Religious in the Church, *Mutuae relationes*" (= *MR*), 14 May 1978, in *AAS,* 70 (1978), pp. 473-506; English translation in A. FLANNERY, (ed.), *Vatican Council II: More Post Conciliar Documents,* (=FLANNERY 2), Northport, NY, Costello Publishing Co., p. 237.

[42] See *MR,* 51 for the four criteria and *MR,* 12 where the true marks of an authentic charism are described. There are many books and articles on this process, which may include some steps described as

secular. However, discernment must incorporate a faith and God dimension because it is the interaction of the human and divine that is the essence of discernment. See B. O'LEARY, "Discernment and Decision Making", in *Review for Religious,* 51 (1992), p. 62.

43 These principles do not pre-empt those steps to be taken during the process required by CICLSAL for the approval of new institutes nor do they substitute for the guidelines provided by the Congregation. Other useful information is to be found in E. GAMBARI, *The Canonical Establishment of a Religious Institute: Process and Procedures,* translated from Italian by M.M. ARMATO and T. BLESSIN, Florence, Artigraf, 1999, 220 p.

44 BRAUX, J., "Pour les communautés nouvelles, quel statut?", in *Les cahiers du droit ecclésial,* 4 (1987), pp. 124-126.

45 The criteria in *Mutuae relationes* are more than twenty years old and need revising in the light of more recent developments. A list of criteria developed by CICLSAL for the approval of new forms of consecrated life according to c. 605 was approved in a *congresso* of the Congregation for Religious on 26 January 1990 and published in G. ROCCA, "Le nuova comunità", in *Quaderni di diritto ecclesiale,* 5 (1992), pp. 171-172, footnote 25. For a translation, see Appendix 2. See also list provided by S. FERNANDES DE ARAÚJO, "Le 'Nuove comunità' o 'Famiglie ecclesiali'", in archival ms, p. 1; Summary and translation in *L'Osservatore romano,* (English edition), 2 November 1994, p. 20. FERNANDES DE ARAÚJO identifies the following characteristics: a) unity of the ministry/work and of the presidency of the institute; b) a certain evangelical radicalism; c) unity between consecration and the specific mission inspired by the charism; d) a strong sense of community which has priority over work; e) the exercise of authority is based on *communio* rather than being pyramidal; f) a desire to avoid clericalism by not identifying authority with priesthood but respecting and promoting the laity; g) a strong emphasis on poverty, dependence on Providence and commitment to the poor of today; h) a life of intense personal and corporate prayer; i) a missionary fervour *ad gentes* and to the new evangelisation. See PFAB, J., "Neue Formen des geweihten Lebens", in S. HAERING, (ed.), *In unum congregati: Festgabe für Augustinus Kardinal Mayer OSB zur Vollendung des 80. Lebensjahres,* Metten, Abtei-Verlag, 1991, pp. 470-475, where the author gives some criteria that he considers necessary for the approbation of new forms of consecrated life. He does not concede that any institute, which included married couples or non-Catholics, would meet the necessary criteria. He points out that solemn vows, as well as simple vows, are possible in such new

forms. See also M. WEISENBECK, "Emerging Expressions of Consecrated Life in the United States: Pastoral and Canonical Implications", in *CLSA Proceedings*, 58 (1996), pp. 380-381, where the author discusses some of the problems associated with new forms and, especially, some signs of contradiction where the stated aims are not borne out by structures and practices — often unhealthy from theological and psychological vantage points.

[46] Interview graciously granted by Fr. J. TORRES CMF, Undersecretary, CICLSAL, to the author on 24 June 1999.

[47] Angela Merici had attempted, in the 16th century, to establish a company of women who would dedicate themselves totally to God but remain in the world so that they could care for the poor of the time. Her band of women was forced to accept cloister and become true religious. It was not until 350 years later, in 1967, that the Sacred Congregation for Religious gave the original institute founded by St. Angela official recognition as "the Secular Institute of the Daughters of Saint Angela Merici, called the Company of Saint Ursula." Information taken from *Report of the Congress of the Large Family of the Daughters of Saint Angela Merici,* Rome, privately printed, 1968, p. 40.

[48] JOHN PAUL II, "You Express the Church's Fruitful Vitality: Message for the World Congress of Ecclesial Movements and New Communities", in *L'Osservatore romano,* (English edition), 10 June 1998, p. 2.

[49] L. RACICOT, *La Société du Christ Seigneur: une forme de vie consacrée pour les laïcs,* Montréal, Centre Leunis, 1994, p. 5. Another pontifically recognised new form, *Opera della Chiesa,* simply appears on the list of "other forms" despite being publicised as new according to c. 605 in *L'Osservatore romano,* 16 November 1990, n. 264, p. 5. The text reported the approval, saying that CICLSAL "authorised" Cardinal A. Suquía Goicoechea of Madrid to recognise *Opera della Chiesa* as an ecclesial family of diocesan right. The text also indicated that c. 605 reserves such approval to the Apostolic See, implying that this was such a case. Pontifical approval was granted in 1997 and the institute appears in subsequent *Annuarii* as an "other institute" but with no reference to c. 605. However, a personal interview with a spokesperson indicated that the approval was for the institute in accord with c. 605 and, therefore, it was considered a new form. A third family, *Famiglia monastica di Betlemme, dell'Assunzione della beata Vergine Maria e di S. Bruno,* is listed in the 2000 *Annuario pontificio,* p. 1802, as a new form of consecrated life. However, information received on 2 May 2000,

indicates that it is not a new form and is not approved under c. 605 but is an ancient form according to the rule of St. Bruno. It has a male branch and a female branch with separate superiors. It received approval in 1998.

50 *Société du Christ Seigneur, Constitutions,* Montréal, Centre Leunis, 1997, p. 8.

51 Ibid., p. 24. The words used are "Souverain Seigneur et Sauveur des hommes, qui m'as aimé le premier et m'appelles à collaborer au salut du monde, moi, N., je me consacre à toi dans la Société du Christ Seigneur..." The final article states that no member changes canonical status from clerical or lay.

52 For a history of the development of the Society see, L. RACICOT, *La Société du Christ Seigneur,* pp. 1-25 and also, L. RACICOT, "La Société du Christ Seigneur: Une nouvelle forme de vie consacrée", in *La vie des communautés religieuses,* 57 (1999), pp. 78-93. The author presents an interesting sequence in the unfolding of the story of approval. The Society began as a Marian sodality, of which a group wished to live a more dedicated life while remaining seculars. The members of this group, under the guidance of L. Brien, the founder, took the three vows. In 1956, while in Rome at the world congress of Young Catholic Women, two members presented a petition to Pius XII outlining the plans. They did not wish to be a secular institute but asked if a similar lifestyle could be presented as a true vocation and if they could receive Church approval (p. 82). They received a reply from the Sacred Congregation of Religious recognising the *Société Leunis,* (as it was then known), as an Association which had all the ascetic and apostolic requirements of a true secular institute. The juridic form of the secular institute was not imposed and the founder was left free to follow his inspiration. In 1976, the Society was recognised as a section of the Christian Life Community (as the Marian sodalities were then known) and accorded a distinct canonical form as a Pious Union of diocesan right. The author says this was an error as the Society already had pontifical approval. In 1993, Pontifical approval was granted by decree to the Society as a new form of consecrated life.

53 RACICOT, "La Société du Christ Seigneur: Une nouvelle forme de vie consacrée", p. 91. It was envisaged that it would be possible to do a profile of the second pontifically approved ecclesial family, *Opera della Chiesa,* from the European context. However, several approaches through mail, phone and a personal visit failed to elicit a copy of the constitutions. From the *Annuario pontificio 2000* and a brief face to face

interview with a spokesperson at their headquarters in Rome, in June 1999, it was determined that the family has three branches: a branch for priests who live in community, a branch for lay persons — male, female, single and married, and children — and a third branch for consecrated women. The members of the first two groups may work together in ministry. There are also priest "adherents" who do not live in community. The family has an overall president and each branch has a superior. The foundress is the current president.

54 This particular ecclesial family mirrors the Order of Malta, which is more than 900 years old. The Order has three classes of members; those who profess the three vows, those men and women who make the Promise and a third class whose members support the Order financially and through living its spirit. In this ancient Order the main positions of governance are held preferably by the Professed members. Their structure is very similar to that which is now found in many of the new ecclesial communities and associations of the faithful. As a form of consecrated life, it is very old in the Church but is a model that seems to meet the needs of the faithful in the Church of these decades.

55 *Christian Community for the Social Apostolate Constitutions and Statutes,* Perth, privately published, 1981, p. 2. Because of the governance structure and the method of decision-making, the constitutions provide that there will be no more that 12 members in a community. When the number is exceeded, a new community, autonomous with respect to governance, ministry and civil incorporation, will be formed. The constitutions and charism remain the common bond.

56 *Constitutions of the Institute of Saint Joseph,* La Crosse, Privately published, 1998.

57 INSTITUTE OF ST. JOSEPH, *To Make God Present to the World, and the World Present to God,* Chippewa Falls, Institute of St. Joseph, 1987, p. 4.

58 Ibid.

59 Figures from the Chancellery of Baie Comeau, Quebec, 1997, show that there are 9 new groups while those from the US indicate that there are several hundred though the number changes constantly. Many of these wish to become new institutes of consecrated life according to the 1983 Code of Canon Law, while some are aspiring to be recognised as new forms. The data, at present, does not distinguish between the

categories. See M. WEISENBECK, "Emerging Expressions of Consecrated Life in the United States", pp. 375-376, where the author outlines the characteristics of some of the groups which she studied and emphasises the need for thorough formation.

60 See D.L. SILLS (ed.), *International Encyclopedia of the Social Sciences,* New York, Macmillan Co. and the Free Press, 1968, vol. 14, pp. 438-441. A movement is deemed to have a loose aggregation of persons who follow a particular way of life or spirituality without very formal structures. These may evolve later depending on the goals of the movement. Cf. J. WILKINS, "My Three Dreams: An Interview with Cardinal Martini", in *The Tablet,* 253 (1999), p. 1489, where the Cardinal says that movements, as such, are made to disappear. They bring their values to the centre of the Church and after that their task is done to some extent. At one point, he says, the movement divides into two parts: one is absorbed into the Church, the other will constitute itself as a society or as a religious order, and continue as a canonical reality.

61 For a definition on this type of movement see ZENIT REPORT ON ROME ENCOUNTER, "World Congress of Ecclesial Movements Held in Rome", <http://www.its.caltech.edu./~bwilson/movememt/ zw980531-3> (6 March 2000). The Holy Father gives as his definition of ecclesial movement: "A concrete ecclesial entity, in which primarily lay people participate, with an itinerary of faith and Christian testimony that founds its own pedagogical method on a charism given to the person of the founder in determined circumstances and modes." See A. BORRAS, "Le droit canonique et la vitalité des communautés nouvelles", in *Nouvelle revue théologique,* 118 (1996), p. 201. The author explains that in Italy and Spain one speaks of "ecclesial movements" while in France and Belgium, the term "les communautés nouvelles" is used. For another interesting use of terminology see J. RATZINGER, "The Theological Locus of Ecclesial Movements", in *Communio: International Catholic Review,* 25 (1998), pp. 500-501. Here, the cardinal proposes that there are movements, currents and actions. A "current" is exemplified by the liturgical and Marian movements in the first half of the 20th century. Petitions for the proclamation of a dogma or for changes in the Church would constitute "actions". Some currents solidify into movements, which have a common essence in the midst of great diversities. They take shape in concrete communities that live the whole Gospel anew from this origin and recognise the Church as the ground of their life.

62 JOHN PAUL II, *Angelus* address, "Associazioni e movimenti come fattori di arricchimento della communione e della missione della Chiesa", 23 August 1987, in *Insegnamenti di Giovanni Paoli II, X/3,*

1987, Roma, Libreria editrice Vaticana, 1988, p. 240. Accanto all'associazionismo tradizionale, e talvolta dalle sue stesse radici, sono germogliati movimenti e sodalizi nuovi, con fisionomia e finalità specifiche."

[63] For the differences between public and private associations, see cc. 312-369. See also BORRAS, "Le droit canonique et la vitalité des communautés nouvelles", p. 205. The author indicates that recognition by the competent authority gives a *canonical* value to the goals of the association as assigned by the members. It protects the members, objectifies the rapport of the members with each other, with the association, with other groups of the faithful and with ecclesial institutions. The canonical recognition shows that "life precedes law." The statutes indicate what the association is and what it may become at a future date.

[64] See CONGRESS OF MOVEMENTS, "The Ecclesial Movements: Communion and Mission on the Threshold of the Third Millennium, Rome 27-29 May 1998",<http://www.newevng.org/mov/english/congreso.html, (8 March 2000).

[65] See V. DE PAOLIS, "Associations Founded with the Intent of Becoming Religious Institutes", in *Consecrated Life,* 20-21 (1999) (combined edition), pp. 159-161.

[66] E. GAMBARI, *The Canonical Establishment of a Religious Institute,* pp. 140-150.

[67] See *CL,* 30 for "Criteria of Ecclesiality" for lay groups. A key underpinning in these criteria is the importance of *communio* — in which the lay faithful both participate as individuals and groups to promote the Kingdom. The living of these criteria in everyday life will produce the eight fruits delineated at the end of § 30. See also R. PAGÉ, "Note sur les 'critères d'ecclésialité pour les associations de laïcs'", in *Studia canonica,* 24 (1990), pp. 455-463. *VC,* 62 gives guidance on what a bishop should examine: witness of life; orthodoxy of the founder's spirituality; ecclesial awareness in carrying out mission; methods of formation; manner of incorporation into the community; suitability of persons who wish to receive holy orders. In addition, the bishop is exhorted to determine if the new communities are founded on the essential theological and canonical elements proper to consecrated life.

[68] See F. MOLONEY, *Disciples and Prophets: A Biblical Model for the Religious Life,* London, Darton, Longman and Todd, 1980, pp. 111-

115. The author asserts that the decision for chastity is intelligible only within the context of a major religious experience, just as the decision for marriage comes about within the context of a major religious experience. (Religious experiences he defines as those which all men and women have and which are somehow greater than them eg. falling in love).

⁶⁹ See W. REISER, "Reformulating the Religious Vows", in *Review for Religious,* 54 (1995), p. 595. See also M. HIMES, "Returning to Our Ancestral Lands", in *Review for Religious,* 59 (2000), pp. 6-25. This author views religious life, after the writings of E. Troeltsch, as a sect community where membership is acquired. The members have experienced a dramatic conversion or call, the community sees itself as specially commissioned, and set to contrast with the larger community, and frequently has a radical vision of what needs to be done in the larger community. Under normal circumstances, the sect community would disintegrate in a few generations. In contrast, the church community has a varied membership, into which most are born. There are a variety of motivations, a building of bridges to the world and other groups and a lifelong process of nurture. In the Catholic Church, sect communities survive because they have been incorporated as "religious life" and have a history dating to the early centuries. For further discussion, see E. TROELTSCH, *The Social Teaching of the Christian Churches,* translated by O. WYON, Kentucky, Westminster/John Knox Press, reprinted 1992, pp. 328-343.

⁷⁰ See J. GALOT, "Challenges and Obligations", in *Consecrated Life,* 22 (1999), p. 103.

⁷¹ See HIMES, "Returning to Our Ancestral Lands", p. 21. The author contends that there is only one vow with two further explications. See GALOT, "Challenges and Obligations", for a presentation of the counsels as a therapy for the idolatry of created things, by making the living God visible in a special way, p. 104. See also W. BARCLAY, *The Beatitudes and the Lord's Prayer for Everyman,* New York, Harper & Row, 1975, pp. 20-28, for an interpretation of the meaning of poverty in the Gospel.

⁷² See ibid., pp. 20-21. The author invokes the saying attributed to St. Augustine, "Our hearts are restless until they rest in you." This he evidences as the fundamental state of the human — the perpetual experience of being *empty.* This is what unites as creatures, making poverty the key value in the vows.

⁷³ See H. URS VON BALTHASAR, *Love Alone,* translated by A. DRU,

New York, Herder and Herder, 1969, pp. 110-111.

74 See TROELTSCH, *The Social Teaching of the Christian Churches*, pp. 106-107. See also P.R. BROWN, *The Body and Society: Men, Women and Sexual Renunciation in Early Christianity*, New York, Columbia University Press, 1988, pp. 34-56. See also McNAMARA, *Sisters in Arms*, pp. 26-33.

75 J.M.R. TILLARD, "Les religieuses et les religieux sont-ils et seront-ils encore parmi les forces prophétiques de l'Église?", in *La vie des communautés religieuses,* 58 (2000), p. 16.

76 See S.M. PASINI, "Vita consacrata e consigli evangelici (II): La distinzione tra 'consacrazione' e 'professione'", in *Commentarium pro religiosis,* 77 (1996), pp. 349-353, where the author states that consecration is distinct from profession (of the three vows). The consecration is realised by virtue of profession (for persons in institutes of consecrated life) p. 358.

77 The opportunity of a temporary commitment for some members will probably not replace the reality that the core of any community will consist of members who are committed for life. See C.J. YUHAUS, "Religious Life: A Prophetic Dynamic Movement", in C.J. YUHAUS (ed.), *The Challenge for Tomorrow: Religious Life,* New York, Paulist Press, 1994, pp. 186-188.

78 See E.H. ERIKSON, *The Life Cycle Completed,* London, W. W. Norton & Company, 1997, p. 70. The author defines "authoritism" as a form of ritualism, which is the ungenerous and ungenerative use of sheer power for regimentation of economic and familial life.

79 For a profile of community types and of persons needed for such communities see C. LEAVEY, and R. O'NEILL, *Gathered in God's Name,* pp. 29-34 and, also, D. MURPHY, *The Death and Rebirth of Religious Life,* pp. 106-110.

80 Many articles are being written on the relationships involved in obedience and in the role of leadership. See, for example, S. SCHNEIDERS, "Congregational Leadership and Spirituality in the Postmodern Era", pp. 6-33; D.J. MARKHAM, "Leadership for the Common Good", in *Review for Religious,* 57 (1998), pp. 34-47 (including a bibliography); and A. MUNLEY, "Hearts Afire: Leadership in the New Millennium", in *Review for Religious,* 57 (1998), pp. 48-59.

[81] See MOLONEY, *Disciples and Prophets*, p. 127.

[82] See D. COUTURIER, "A Spirituality of Refounding", in G.A. ARBUCKLE and D.L. FLEMING (eds), *Religious Life: Rebirth through Conversion*, New York, Alba House, 1990, p. 88.

[83] See MOLONEY, *Disciples and Prophets*, p. 167. See also ARBUCKLE and FLEMING (eds), *Religious Life*, p. 25.

[84] See the first hypothesis of DE PAOLIS, *La vita consacrata nella Chiesa*, pp. 82. See G. ROCCA, "La 'consacrazione' dei coniugi", in ISTITUTO CLARETIANUM (ed.) *L'identità dei consacrati nella missione della Chiesa e il loro rapporto con il mondo,* Città del Vaticano, Libreria editrice Vaticana, 1994, pp. 376-378, where the author outlines the history of commitment of married people in a radical way. He also outlines their involvement in the more recent ecclesial communities such as the *Communità mariana — Oasi della Pace, il Piccolo Gruppo di Christo, Padre Nostro* and *Communità della Guedrara* as well as the pontifically approved, *Opera della Chiesa*. He foresees possibilities for the future when the theological, canonical and structural parameters have been more closely studied.

[85] Historically, there were married people in military orders which received approbation from the Church. See A. MARCHETTI, "Avremo religiosi sposati?" in *Rivista di vita spirituale,* 25 (1971), pp. 643-646. See also E. SASTRE SANTOS, "Votum castitatis coniugalis, votum religiosum", in *Commentarium pro religiosis,* 58 (1977), pp. 246-260; 59 (1978), pp. 50-65; 60 (1979), pp. 46-87. The author discusses the question at length and confirms that there were married religious in the order of St. James, which was approved by Gregory VIII. It was confirmed by ALEXANDER III, Bull, *Benedictus Deus,* 5 July 1175, in *Bullarum diplomatum et privilegiorum sanctorum Romanorum pontificum, Taurinensis editio (cura Tomassetti), locupletior facta collectione novissima plurium brevium, epistolorum, decretorum actorumque S. Sedis a S. Leone Magno usque ad praesens [i.e. 1740],* (= *Bull. Rom. Taur.*), A. Taurinorum, S. Franco et Filiis editoribus, 1857-1872, vol. 2, pp. 781-785. Several other military orders sprung up at this time but most were disbanded in later centuries when wealth, power and questionable dealings brought them into disrepute (*New Catholic Encyclopaedia*). It is a good example of congregations arising to meet particular needs in Church and society. The Order of Malta, a lay religious order (Constitutions, § 1), persists to this day and claims married members among its ranks. After their profession the Pope generally dispenses members from some of the canonical effects of the

vow of poverty to enable living in the world. Sastre Santos points out that these married religious were true religious and were regarded as juridically equal and having equal rights as their celibate brothers (p. 259).

86 See JOHN PAUL II, "This is the Day that the Lord has Made!", in *L'Osservatore romano,* (English edition), 3 June 1998, p. 1.

87 See G. SHEEHY, et al. (eds), *The Canon Law, Letter and Spirit: A Practical Guide to the Code of Canon Law*prepared by THE CANON LAW SOCIETY OF GREAT BRITAIN AND IRELAND, in association with THE CANADIAN CANON LAW SOCIETY, Dublin, Veritas, 1995, p. 116.

88 The Taizé Community has existed as an ecumenical one since 1950. Other such communities are to be found in Australia, and North and South America. In Australia, two such communities are profiled in LEAVEY and O'NEILL, *Gathered in God's Name,* pp. 41-44. Both are based on Franciscan spirituality. In North America, one example is the ecumenical community, Benedictine Women of Madison, WI, Inc. as described in L.W. SMITH, "Ecumenical Monasticism for a New Millennium", <http://www.osb.org/aba/aba2000/lwsmith.html> (10 March 2000). None of the three communities listed has received formal approval from the Catholic Church. The first two are under non-Catholic auspices, the third is a Benedictine community. Numerous others are listed on the web pages, some following a traditional monastic spirituality and others immersed in an apostolic life.

89 See *VC,* 100, 101.

90 See P.J. BURKE, "The Spirituality of Taizé", in *Spirituality Today,* 42 (1990), pp. 233-245, < http://www.op.org/domcentral/library/spir2day/90423burke.htm> (10 March 2000).

91 "The Taizé Community", < http://www.almac.co.uk/taize/1gb-taiz.html> (10 March 2000).

92 B.W. THURSTON, *The Widows: A Women's Ministry in the Early Church,* Minneapolis, Fortress Press, 1989, p. 41. The author refers to 1 Tim. 5:3-16. The first group are discussed in 1 Tim. 5:3, 5-7, 9-10. See MCNAMARA, *Sisters in Arms,* pp. 2,18. The author suggests that these widows, with their apostolate to the sick and needy, were the fountainhead from which many springs flowed: communities of virgins, recluses, cloistered nuns, and caregivers down through the centuries.

[93] THURSTON, *The Widows,* pp. 45-46. See J. IHNATOWICZ, *Consecrated Life among the Laity: A Theological Study of a Vocation in the Church,* Rome, Pontificia studiorum Universitas a S. Thomas Aquinas in Urbe, 1984, pp. 393-394. This author adds another dimension to the state of widowhood. He states that the widow's commitment to perfect and lifelong celibacy is a specially poignant way of keeping faith with her husband... a powerful sign of the dignity and exclusivity of Christian married love (p. 398). These sentiments are echoed in the group of consecrated French widows from World War II.

[94] Ibid., pp. 114-116.

[95] J. BEYER, *Le droit de la vie consacrée,* Paris, Tardy, 1988, vol. 1, pp. 153-164. This ritual was for a particular group; the author claims that it cannot be used for other groups without specific approval.

[96] Codex canonum Ecclesiarum orientalium auctoritate Ioannis Pauli PP. II promulgatus, Roma, Typis polyglottis Vaticanis, 1990, 381 p. English translation: Code of Canons of the Eastern Churches, Latin-English edition, translation prepared under the auspices of THE CANON LAW SOCIETY OF AMERICA, Washington, DC, Canon Law Society of America, 1992, p. 289.

[97] See BEYER, *Le droit de la vie consacrée,* p. 160. The men have formed *Fraternité de la Résurrection.* Widowers could be involved in religious institutes, secular institutes, or in the diaconate or priesthood.

[98] A. NERI, *Nuove forme di vita consacrata, (can. 605 C.I.C.),* Roma, Editrice Pontificia Università Lateranense, pp. 105-107. The author suggests thirteen such combinations of elements.

[99] V. DE PAOLIS, *La vita consacrata nella Chiesa,* Bologna, Dehoniane, 1991, pp. 82-83.

[100] ROCCA, "Le nuova comunità", p. 170.

[101] See *Société du Christ Seigneur* and *Opera della Chiesa.* The Order of Malta has had such a structure for more than 900 years.

[102] Neither the Benedictines nor the Dominicans, for example, pronounce three vows. Both profess a vow of obedience which they see as incorporating the other two. The Benedictines take an additional vow of stability. In other words, there is a history of pluriformity in the Church

on this matter.

[103] S. RECCHI, "Assunzione dei consigli evangelici e consacrazione di vita nelle associazioni" in*Quaderni di diritto ecclesiale,* 12 (1999), p. 345. See also B. ZADRA, "L'assunzione dei consigli evangelici negli statuti delle associazioni che prevedono la consacrazione di vita", in *Quaderni di diritto ecclesiale,* 12 (1999), pp. 353-362. At page 354, the author explains the nature of the sacred bonds for consecration in new communities that include priests, virgins, married couples and celibates. Some use vows, others use pledges or promises or *engagement,* all defined in the statutes.

[104] The apostolic exhortation, *Vita consecrata,* does not give a definition of "consecration" but uses many analogies and metaphors to plumb its depths. For a further discussion on "consecration", see E. GAMBARI, *The Canonical Establishment of a Religious Institute,* pp. 128-129, where the author stresses that consecration bespeaks a reference to God in a particularly binding offering of oneself. He adds that the terminology is used in different contexts with different meanings.

[105] See A. VON SPEYR, *The Christian State of Life,* (ed. H. URS VON BALTHASAR), translated by M.F. McCARTHY, San Francisco, Ignatius Press, 1986, pp. 179-183. The author discusses the understanding of vocation in the Gospel, explaining that there is an original meeting with the Lord who calls an individual, and the answer is always contained in the call. See also C. POZO, "The Theology of the Consecrated Life at the Recent Synod of Bishops", in *Consecrated Life,* 20-21 (1999), (combined edition), p. 125 where the author stresses the action of God in consecration.

[106] See F. MORLOT, "Qu'est-ce que la vie consacrée? Une description à partir de 'Vita consecrata'", in *Vie consacrée,* 69 (1997), pp. 29-42.

[107] See J.P. McINTYRE, "*Lineamenta* for a Christian Anthropology: Canons 208-223", in *Periodica,* 85 (1996), p. 270.

[108] See M. BRENNAN, "A White Light Still and Moving: Religious Life at the Crossroads of the Future", in C. J. YUHAUS (ed.), *The Challenge for Tomorrow: Religious Life,* New York, Paulist Press, 1994, p.104.

GENERAL CONCLUSION

In this study we explored the development of new forms of consecrated life. We examined the place of consecrated life in the experience of the Second Vatican Council and in some of the Conciliar and post-Conciliar documents and analysed how that teaching was expressed in the 1983 Code of Canon Law. We gave particular attention to the evolution of c. 605 and its implications for new forms, against current ecclesial and world backgrounds, proposed some criteria for discerning new charisms as well as new forms, and highlighted the possibilities for the application of the canon in the new millennium. In the course of the study we noted the following points:

Consecrated life is a gift to the Church. Since the earliest centuries the Holy Spirit has graced the Church with many charisms that were expressed in lives lived totally for God, in the desert hermitages, in monastic and, later, in apostolic forms. The consistent elements included the following of Christ through a commitment to the evangelical counsels of chastity, poverty and obedience, expressed through one or more vows, or other sacred bonds; a stable form of living and a withdrawal from the world. This withdrawal was signified by cloister, especially for women religious.

There is a sustained continuity in the evolution of new forms. New forms do not herald the death of existing forms but develop side by side with them, building on the experiences of the past. While consecrated life enjoys a definite continuity, even while evolving and changing, individual institutes do not have such a guarantee. The evolution of consecrated life is an organic process, with birthing, maturing, and dying phases. Sometimes, a dying institute can renew and then continue in a revitalised fashion. New institutes and new forms arise in response to needs of particular moments in history and are situated in particular ecclesial, social and cultural environments. Until the twentieth century, the dominant form was religious life, with variants such as monastic, mendicant, apostolic, and contemplative. In 1947 a new form, distinct from religious life was recognised, the secular institute whose members continued to live in the world and live lives of consecrated secularity.

The right to interpret, regulate and protect the living of consecrated life belongs to Church authorities. In the beginning, the religious life was essentially a lay movement lived somewhat independently of Church authorities. The proliferation of monasteries and ensuing problems prompted legislation at some of the early Councils. Thus the Church assumed responsibility for this form of Christian living and continued this responsibility over the centuries. The systematisation and control gave recognition to new institutes and often enhanced the flowering and development of the charisms but, at times, constricted them, resulting not only in a near stifling of the gifts of the Spirit, but also in eliciting creative ways of circumventing the laws.

The Second Vatican Council was an axial moment in the history of consecrated life. The Council Fathers recognised that consecrated life was a gift to the Church, and undeniably belonged to its life and holiness. While it was a structure **in** the Church, it was not a structure of the Church. It had a share in the mission **of** the Church to the world with which it reviewed relationships. The renewed place of consecrated life was verbalised in Chapter VI of Lumen gentium, the Dogmatic Constitution on the Church.

The Second Vatican Council called for a renewal of consecrated life. Having recognised the place of consecrated life in its mission, the Church, in Perfectae caritatis, called for a renewal so that consecrated life would be more effective to give witness by the lives and holiness of the members. The renewal was to take away lifeless accretions of centuries and make institutes more attuned to the Church and world in which they gave witness. The renewal was not to be mere rearranging of structures and externals but a deep conversion for each member and institute.

Renewal was to be based on the teachings of the Council. As constitutions were revised to express the new visions and structures, institutes and their members were to take cognisance of the ecclesiology of communio, of the "signs of the times", and of major issues such as inculturation and ecumenism. The institutes were to become missionaries anew and take the Gospel message to all with sensitivity to the cultural heritage, customs and languages of the people.

The teachings of the Council were translated into legislative norms in the 1983 Code of Canon Law. These norms replaced those in the 1917 Code where the legislation on consecrated life was first codified. The Code defined consecrated life in terms of consecration by the profession of the evangelical counsels by vow, or other sacred bond. It established some general norms for all institutes of consecrated life, with more specific canons for religious institutes and secular institutes. It also included canons for societies of apostolic life, which were not recognised as institutes of consecrated life, but were considered as related. For the first time, hermits (distinct from those attached to religious institutes) and the restored order of virgins were included as individual forms of consecrated life. Of great significance was the inclusion of the new canon 605, which gave legal and canonical grounding to the reality of new forms of consecrated life in the Church.

The Holy Spirit continues to grace the Church with new forms of consecrated life. The "form" of consecrated life is the embodiment of the charism in an entire way of life, with its own comprehensive culture and rituals. It is not merely a collection of norms and practices, but a living organic experience that evolves over time. It is the mode of life through which and from which the members partake in a special way in the mystery of Christ and his mission. The Code recognises religious life and secular institutes as forms of consecrated life, as well as hermits and virgins. However, within religious institutes there are a variety of forms, which could be regarded as sub-species. New forms must include the constitutive theological and biblical bases — since these are immutable. They may have different juridical structures since these are dependent on history and, therefore, subject to change, though they may not in any way contradict the theological prescriptions. The new form enshrines the charism and legally integrates it into the Church so that it may function in the name of the Church.

New forms arise in particular ecclesial, social and cultural conditions. As in each of the previous historical eras, new needs bring forth new gifts of the Spirit. The world of today is characterised by a new poor, by great inequities in social and monetary arenas, by a sense of alienation despite an unprecedented development in communication, by a world torn apart by wars and starvation, by a growing desire for spirituality separate from the established Church, and by a desire for the nations to have their culture respected both in the Church and in society. It is against this background that new forms of consecrated life are emerging.

The 1994 Synod of Bishops on Consecrated Life treated new forms as well as the traditional ones. New forms of consecrated life were alluded to in both preparatory documents for the synod. They were the subject of interventions at the synod and were treated in the Apostolic Exhortation, Vita consecrata. A commission was established and, later, disbanded, to set criteria for discerning new forms. It was judged to be too early in their history to systematise and codify new forms. Their treatment prior to, during and after the synod established beyond doubt that new forms have been emerging in the Church, especially since the Second Vatican Council.

Canon 605 confirmed indisputably that new forms are to be approved by the Apostolic See. This practice reflects a historical reality that the Apostolic See approved new forms, often by special bull or decree from the reigning Pontiff. Pastor bonus has assigned this task of approval to the Congregation for Consecrated Life and Societies of Apostolic Life.

****

Our study of c. 605 has shown that it not only acknowledges that new forms of consecrated life are a reality in the Church but it strives to pose the questions being shaped by the historical and social exigencies of this moment in the life of the Church. The search for answers gives rise to the following considerations:

1. Discernment of new charisms is the prerogative of the diocesan bishop. While Mutuae relationes gives guidelines for discernment of a charism for new institutes of consecrated life, these are somewhat outmoded and do not necessarily fully apply to charisms for new forms. The variety of new forms emerging and currently existing in temporary situations without pontifical approval precludes definitive systematisation and characterisation at this time. However, there are some unofficial guidelines from other sources as noted. A list of principles has been proposed as part of this study. They are not exhaustive and need to be used in partnership with the norms of the Code of Canon Law. They highlight the diocesan bishop's responsibility to assist the founder/s to discern the charism and to express it in suitable statutes that enshrine it and preserve it.

2. The possibilities for new forms in c. 605 are varied. Canon 605, having stated the respective roles of the Apostolic See and the diocesan bishop in relation to new forms of consecrated life, gives the liberating directive that the diocesan bishop is to undertake his responsibility "using especially the general norms contained in this part." The use of the word "especially", praesertim in the Latin, both delineates the parameters for new forms and, concomitantly, offers wide scope for their development and acceptance. While not limiting a diocesan bishop to these general norms, the canon offers the protection and stability for the forms of consecrated life. At the same time, it permits a generous flexibility to accept and work with the creative gifts with which the Spirit endowed the founders and, hence, the Church. Therefore, the norms on associations of the faithful may be used as guides, as well as other norms throughout the Code that have application to institutes of consecrated life. However, there is not a constraint to use these norms, because they may not suit an emerging charism. The flexibility permitted by the canon, within the scope of the general principles, is a gift for consecrated life in the new millennium. It opens the following possibilities for new forms:

An institute where all members are committed to living the evangelical counsels, either through vow, or other sacred bond, in a single sex institute. The newness could be in the structures that enshrine this form of living.

An institute where all the members are as in (i) but with mixed male and female, clerical and lay. These could be in separate branches, or all in one group with a superior chosen without distinction of state or sex.

An institute where all the members are committed to living the evangelical counsels, but not all are professed with chastity lived in perfect continence. This allows for a mixture of states of life — married, single, fully consecrated according to the norms of cc. 573- 606. The unity of consecration rests in conforming the person to Christ, the Way to all holiness.

An institute where some members are committed to living the evangelical counsels according to their state in life, while others are associated and live the spirit of the charism in the manner of third orders, associates or oblates.

An institute where some members have a permanent commitment and others may commit themselves to the life for a temporary period. Their consecration to God would be on-going but the manner of expressing it would change with time and circumstances.

Our study has indicated that the elements just described could be incorporated into structures that are either already canonically recognised in the Code of Canon Law or are recognised by virtue of the fact that they exist. Such structures include:

Associations of the faithful. Many of these associations already include members who have professed the living of the evangelical counsels by vow or other sacred bond according to their constitutions. Some of these associations are permanent and have official pontifical recognition through the Pontifical Council of the Laity. Some are temporary, in that they are an intermediate step on the way to the group's becoming an institute of consecrated life. They have their recognition through the Congregation for Institutes of Consecrated Life and Societies of Apostolic Life. These latter may become an institute as currently canonically recognised or a new form.

Ecclesial families. Two such families have received pontifical approval and include single, married and clergy with consecration according to the constitutions. They also include associates and affiliates. There are different levels of belonging according to state of life and other circumstances, all spelled out in the constitutions. One such family has integrated leadership, (there are not separate branches), while the other has an overall president as well as a superior for each branch. This model appears to be the most common among the new movements or new communities.

Ecumenical communities. These groups exist but are not pontifically approved, c. 597 §1 precluding persons who are not Catholics from institutes of consecrated life.

Communities with a mixture of types of consecrated life. Such communities could include some or all of the "traditional" types of consecrated life, that is, contemplative members, apostolic members, hermits and consecrated virgins, or a mixture of the different types, their relationships specified in their constitutions.

****

It has been ascertained that some areas need further treatment. We suggest that the following be studied at greater depth:

1. General Terminology. In the 1983 Code of Canon Law the use of the term "consecrated life" refers to institutes of consecrated life canonically recognised. The term is also used to refer to those who have taken vows or other sacred bonds to profess the evangelical counsels in associations of the faithful. Vita consecrata used the term "evangelical life". The result is some confusion between what is accepted as theological consecration and what is canonical consecration, between what is consecrated life and what is life consecrated. Some of the confusion arises from the understanding of the term "consecration".

2. Consecration. In the Code of Canon Law, the term "consecration" is used in several contexts that are not dealt with in this study, which is confined to consecrated life. We have established that there is a difference between consecration as applied to the canonical entity of consecrated life and that which is lived in associations or movements by persons living the evangelical counsels according to their constitutions. Various authors, as well as the Pope in Vita consecrata, say that married couples seeking to live the counsels according to their state in life cannot be considered a part of consecrated life. However, the Pope also spoke, in Vita consecrata, of married couples having their own "consecration". Therefore, what is needed is a broader definition of what types of persons, and with what commitment, can be included in the definition of consecrated life. The present Code confines these to profession of the evangelical counsels, in a public manner by vow or other sacred bond, lived in a stable form of life.

Consecration involves the call of God to deepen the baptismal consecration, a response on the part of the one called and a confirmation of that response in some manner by a competent ecclesiastical authority. Its purpose is to conform the person more to Christ so that he, Christ, is more present to the world. We suggest that the evangelical counsels remain the basis of consecrated life and that the living of the counsels be according to the state of life of the individuals undertaking the commitment. This re-definition may already be understood, since two of the pontifically recognised new forms of consecrated life include consecrated married couples.

3. Changes in canonical legislation. The general norms governing institutes of consecrated life would need to be changed to incorporate the broader meaning of consecration. The legislation on associations of the faithful would need to incorporate some norms for the regulation of the profession of the evangelical counsels in these associations. Both these changes would bring the lived experience of the faithful more into congruence with the law and acknowledge the gifts which the Spirit has caused to blossom in the recent decades in the Church.

Appendix One

The development of c. 605 is shown in the table on the following pages.

APPENDIX 1

DEVELOPMENT OF CANON 605

1977 Schema, Canon 14.	1978 Schema; C. 40 discussed on 30/5/1979	1979 Schema; C. 30 approved on 30/5/1979
Competentis Ecclesiae Auctoritatis est, duce Spiritu Sancto, consilia evangelica interpretari, eorumdem praxim legibus moderari atque stabiles inde vivendi formas canonicas approbatione constituere necnon curare ut secundum spiritum fundatorum crescant et floreant.	Vigilanti cura Episcopi (Auctoritates Ecclesiae ad quas spectat) nova vitae consecratae dona (charismata) a Spiritu Sancto Ecclesiae concredita discernere satagant et promotores adiuvare ut inspirationem receptam quam melius exprimant et aptis statutis protegant (adhibitis praesertim generalibus normis in hac parte contentis.	Novas formas vitae consecratae approbare uni Sedi Apostolicae reservatur. Episcopi diocesani autem nova vitae consecratae dona a Spiritu Sancto Ecclesiae concredita discernere satagant et promotores adiuvent ut proposita quam melius exprimant et aptis statutis protegant, adhibitis praesertim generalibus normis in hac parte contentis.

1980 Schema; C. 532 (same as in 1979 schema)	1982 Schema; C. 606.	1983 Code; C. 605.
Novas formas vitae consecratae approbare uni Sedi Apostolicae reservatur. Episcopi diocesani autem nova vitae consecratae dona a Spiritu Sancto Ecclesiae concredita discernere satagant et promotores adiuvent ut proposita quam melius exprimant et aptis statutis protegant, adhibitis praesertim generalibus normis in hac parte contentis.	Novas formas vitae consecratae approbare uni Sedi Apostolicae reservatur. Episcopi diocesani autem nova vitae consecratae dona a Spiritu Sancto Ecclesiae concredita discernere satagant iidemque promotores adiuvent ut proposita meliore quo fieri potest modo exprimant et aptisque statutis protegant, adhibitis praesertim generalibus normis in hac parte contentis.	Novas formas vitae consecratae approbare uni Sedi Apostolicae reservatur. Episcopi diocesani autem nova vitae consecratae dona a Spiritu Sancto Ecclesiae concredita discernere satagant iidemque adiuvent promotores ut proposita meliore quo fieri potest modo exprimant et aptisque statutis protegant, adhibitis praesertim generalibus normis in hac parte contentis.

APPENDIX 2

CRITERIA FOR APPROVAL OF NEW FORMS OF CONSECRATED LIFE ACCORDING TO CANON 605*

When dealing with a *new form of consecrated life* it is understood that it includes the following essential elements described in cc. 573-605, that is to say:

The profession of the evangelical counsels by sacred bonds assumed according to common and proper law.

Stability of life.

Dedication, with a new and special title, to the honour of God, to the edification of the Church and to the salvation of the world.

Fraternal life, proper to each institute.

Internal superiors, given power according to common and proper law.

A just autonomy of life, especially of governance.

A fundamental code, approved by the competent ecclesiastical authority.

Erection by a competent ecclesiastical authority.

A *new form of consecrated life* is accepted as such when the new institute cannot, without forcing, be included in any of the other forms already established, that is to say: religious institutes;

secular institutes; societies of apostolic life, that assume the evangelical counsels; eremitical life, (solitary or associated); consecrated virginity, (individual or associated).

The institutes could include diverse types of persons: clerics, laity (men and women) bound in a common desire to attain the goals of the institute. When these institutes contain all the elements described in n. 1, but their complex organisation impedes them from entering a category described in n. 2, then these institutes can be recognised as institutes with *a new form of consecrated life.*

If a *new form of consecrated life* includes a *clerical branch,* it is not necessary that the institute be recognised as "clerical"; it is enough that the clergy incardinated in the institute be dependent on a priest-member, with the necessary powers, whether or not he is, at that same time, president of the institute.

As regards the number of members (in any branch), follow the criteria given for other institutes of consecrated life and societies of apostolic life.

Given the originality of *new forms of consecrated life*, it would be more opportune to foresee the examination and approval by the Dicastery, and to authorise the diocesan bishop to erect the institute of diocesan right as a new form of consecrated life, and to approve its constitutions *ad experimentum et ad nutum Sanctae Sedis,* without a time-limit. It will present itself for the approval of the Holy See when the institute has demonstrated the validity and ecclesial viability of the experiment. Both the bishop, who erects the institute, and the supreme moderator must report every year (or every two years) to the Holy See on the state of the institute, so that it can follow the progress of these "new forms", the approval of which is reserved solely to the Apostolic See.

*This is a translation of the notes by G. ROCCA, "Le nuova comunità", in *Quaderni di diritto ecclesiale*, 5 (1992), pp. 171-172, footnote 25. Original in Italian.

APPENDIX 3

STAGES IN THE DEVELOPMENT OF A NEW INSTITUTE OR A NEW FORM OF CONSECRATED LIFE*

Canon 579 states: Provided the Apostolic See has been consulted, diocesan bishops can, by formal decree, establish institutes of consecrated life in their own territories.

Canon 605 states: The approval of new forms of consecrated life is reserved to the Apostolic See. Diocesan bishops, however, are to endeavour to discern new gifts of consecrated life which the Holy Spirit entrusts to the Church. They are also to assist promotors to express their purposes in the best possible way, and to protect these purposes with suitable statutes, especially by the application of the general norms contained in this part of the code.

The beginning of a new institute is the work of the Spirit. A new charism is given **to** the Church **for** the Church. There are four possible stages in the development.

Inspiration

The inspiration, received by the founder/foundress, is a gift of the Spirit and needs to be discerned as such by the Bishop together with the People of God. See Chapter four for principles in discerning this gift.

Association (cc. 298-329)

This stage is a well recognised step in the way to

recognition of a new institute, which usually begins without formality. This is a stage of growth, of clarification of identity, of proof of stability and authenticity. It is a time for developing statutes or constitutions. While this stage occurs after the discernment of the charism, the discernment is on-going. This stage signifies the beginning of the formal recognition by the Church. There is as yet no spiritual patrimony; the founder/foundress is at the point of determining its elements: the nature, the end, the spirit and the character of the institute.

What is to be the juridic nature of the institute? Is it to be religious? Monastic? Apostolic? Secular? Clerical? Lay? Or a new form of consecrated life?

The end: What is the particular purpose of the founder? Why make a new foundation? To what particular needs does it respond?

The spirit: What is the spirituality of the institute? What particular Gospel values does it enshrine? What are the characteristics of the spirituality and how are they brought to life?

The character: How would a synthesis of the nature, end and spirit of the institute be presented in order to express its particular identity? Is it conventual or apostolic?

The statutes or constitutions will be written to express the reality of this identity, including the most appropriate form of consecration in a life of the evangelical counsels, the apostolate, the norms for formation and other pertinent information.

An Institute of Diocesan Right

This third step in the juridic development of a new institute comes with diocesan erection, which is the prerogative of the diocesan bishop after consultation with the Apostolic See. There are documents that need to accompany such a request.

- The name of founder/foundress, and also of the first Supreme Moderator, together with a *curriculum vitae*.

- An historical-juridical account of the institute from the beginning. A copy of the document, which gave approval as an association by a competent ecclesiastical authority, must be attached.

- The Constitutions and Directory. These, from the Association, could be the basis for the constitutions as an institute.

- Current statistics of membership (including personal data such as date of birth and profession), of houses (location in dioceses, number), and of the apostolic works of the institute. **Note:** to erect a new institute there is a requirement of 40 members, most of whom must have taken final or perpetual profession in the association.

- An account of the financial patrimony of the institute, including a declaration of debts. Detail must be sufficient to show that there is financial stability, capacity to support members and the works of the apostolate.

- A statement regarding:

+ Any facts of an extraordinary nature with reference to the institute such as visions etc.

+ Particular devotions or exercises of piety, specific to the institute.

+ Whether, in the diocese of origin, there exists another institute of the same name or with the same purpose.

+ Testimonial letters from the bishops of those dioceses where members of the institute live and work.

When all the documentation is ready and received by the Congregation for Institutes of Consecrated Life and Societies of Apostolic Life, it will be presented for a decision prior to granting the diocesan bishop the *nihil obstat* to erect a new institute. The diocesan bishop issues a decree of erection.

An Institute of Pontifical Right

The fourth step, pontifical recognition, is a possibility but not an obligation. It is encouraged where an institute is spread across several dioceses. The documentation is essentially the same as above. The number of members required is 100. The diocesan bishop forwards the request and the Apostolic See issues the Decree.

Note: The process for approval of a new form of consecrated life is similar. However, the approval of a new form rests with the Apostolic See.

*This appendix is based on notes from a workshop given by Sr. Sharon Holland, from the Congregation for Institutes of Consecrated Life and Societies of Apostolic Life, at Minneapolis in October 1999.

BIBLIOGRAPHY

1. Sources

Acta Leonis XIII Pontificis Maximi, Romae, ex Typographica Vaticana, 1881-1905, 23 vols.

Acta Apostolicae Sedis: commentarium officiale, Romae, 1909-1928; in Civitate Vaticana, Typis polyglottis Vaticanis, 1929-.

Acta et documenta concilio oecumenico Vaticano II apparando, Series I, (*Antepraeparatoria*), 4 vols with 2 appendices to vol. 2: Series II, (*Praeparatoria*), 3 vols, Roma, Typis Vaticanis, 1960-1988.

Acta Sanctae Sedis, Romae, Typis polyglottis Vaticanis, 1865-1909, 41 vols.

Acta synodalia sacrosancti concilii oecumenici Vaticani II, Roma, Typis polyglottis Vaticanis, 1970-, 5 vols, 2 vols of appendices, index.

Annuario Pontificio, Città del Vaticano, Tipografia poliglotta Vaticana, 1716- .

Benedicti XIV Pont. opt. max olim. Prosperi cardinalis de Lambertinis Bullarium, Prati, in typographia Aldina, 1845-1847, 4 vols.

Bullarium Ordinis Fratrum Praedicatorum, T. RIPOLL (ed.), Romae, 1729-1740, 8 vols.

Bullarum diplomatum et privilegiorum sanctorum Romanorum pontificum, Taurinensis editio (cura Tomassetti), locupletior facta collectione novissima plurium brevium, epistolorum, decretorum actorumque S. Sedis a S. Leone Magno usque ad praesens [i.e. 1740], A. Taurinorum, S. Franco et H. Dalmazzo editoribus, 1857-1872, 24 vols.

Canon Law Digest, T. BOUSCAREN (ed.), vols. 1-3; T. BOUSCAREN and J. O'Connor (eds), Milwaukee, Bruce Publishing Co., vols. 4-6; J. O'CONNOR (ed.), Mundelein, Ill., vols. 7-10; E. PFNAUSCH (ed.), Washington, DC, Canon Law Society of America, vol. 11.

Catechism of the Catholic Church, Strathfield, NSW, St Pauls, (Pocket Edition), 1998, xii, 803 p.

CHERUBINI, L. (ed.), *Magnum bullarium Romanum a beato Leone magno usque ad S.D.N. Benedict XIV,* editio novissima, Luxemburgi, Gosse, 1742, 6 vols; English translation in Archives of the Institute of the Blessed Virgin Mary, Toronto.

Codex canonum Ecclesiarum orientalium auctoritate Ioannis Pauli PP. II promulgatus, *Roma, Typis polyglottis Vaticanis, 1990, xxxiv, 381 p.;*

English language transation: *Code of Canons of the Eastern Churches,* Latin-English edition, translation prepared under the auspices of THE CANON LAW SOCIETY OF AMERICA, Washington, DC, Canon Law Society of America, 1992, xlvii, 785 p.

Codex iuris canonici auctoritate Ioannis Pauli PP. II promulgatus, Roma, Libreria editrice Vaticana, 1983, xxx, 317 p.;

American version of English-language translation: *Code of Canon Law,* Latin-English edition, translation prepared under the auspices of THE CANON LAW SOCIETY OF AMERICA, Washington, DC, Canon Law Society of America, 1999, xliii, 751 p.;

British commonwealth version of English-language translation: *The Code of Canon Law in English Translation,* new revised edition prepared by THE CANON LAW SOCIETY OF GREAT BRITAIN AND IRELAND, in association with THE CANON LAW SOCIETY OF AUSTRALIA AND NEW ZEALAND and THE CANADIAN CANON LAW SOCIETY, London, Collins: Ottawa, Canadian Conference of Catholic Bishops, 1997, xvi, 509 p.

Codex iuris canonici Pii X Pontificis Maximi iussu digestus, Benedicti Papae XV auctoritate promulgatus, Romae, Typis polyglottis Vaticanis, 1917, xliv, 852 p.

Communicationes: Romae, vols 1-15, Pontificia Commissio Codici iuris canonici recognoscendo; vols 16-20, Pontificia Commissio Codici iuris canonici authentice interpretando; vols 21-, Pontificium Consilium de legum textibus interpretandis, 1969- .

Congregation for Institutes of Consecrated Life and Societies of Apostolic Life, *Congregavit nos in unum Christi amor: Fraternal Life in Common,* Rome, 1994; English translation, Médiaspaul, Sherbrooke, QC, 1994, 68 p.

Council of the General Secretariat of the Synod of Bishops, *De vita consecrata deque eius munere in Ecclesia et in mundo: lineamenta,* Roma, Libreria editrice Vaticana; English translation, *The Consecrated Life and its Role in the Church and in the World, Lineamenta,* Ottawa, Canadian Conference of Catholic Bishops, 1992, 71 p.

————, *De vita consecrata deque eius munere in Ecclesia et in mundo: Instrumentum laboris,* Roma, Libreria editrice Vaticana; English translation, The *Consecrated Life and Its Role in the Church and in the World, Instrumentum laboris,* Ottawa, Canadian Conference of Catholic Bishops, 1994, 153 p.

Dictionnaire de spiritualité ascétique et mystique: doctrine et histoire, Paris, Beauchesne, 1937- 1995, 17 v. en 21.

Flannery, A. (ed.), vol.1: *Vatican Council II: The Conciliar and Post Conciliar Documents,* new revised edition, Dublin, Dominican Publications, 1992, xxi, 1036 p.: vol. 2: *Vatican Council II: More Post Conciliar Documents,* Northport, NY, Costello Publishing Co., (1982), xxi, 920 p.

Friedberg, A., *Corpus iuris canonici,* Lipsiae, ex Officina B. Tauchnitz, 1879-1881, 2 vols.

Hite, J., S. Holland and D. Ward (eds), *Religious Institutes, Secular*

Institutes, Societies of Apostolic Life: A Handbook on Canons 573-746, revised edition, Collegeville, MN, Liturgical Press, 1990, 493 p.

JOHN PAUL II, Allocution: "Iis qui coetui Conferentiae Mundialis Institutorum Secularium Romae habito affuere in Arce Gandulfi coram admissis", 28 August 1980, in *AAS,* 72 (1980), pp. 1018-1024, (original text in French): English translation, in *Secular Institutes: The Official Documents,* Rome, Conférence mondiale des Instituts séculiers, 1981, pp. 103-113.

————, "The Task of the Latin American Bishop", in *Origins,* 12 (1982-1983), pp. 569-662.

————, "Your Dignity Depends on What You Are: Witnesses of New and Eternal Life", in *Consecrated Life,* 12 (1987), pp. 201-207.

————, *Angelus* address, "Associazioni e movimenti come fattori di arricchimento della communione e della missione della Chiesa", 23 August 1987, in *Insegnamenti di Giovanni Paoli II, X/3, 1987,* Roma, Libreria editrice Vaticana, 1988, pp. 239- 242.

————, "Address to the Catholic Health Care Ministry", September 14, 1987, Phoenix, Arizona, reprinted in *Catholic Health Ministry in Transition: A Handbook for Responsible Leadership,* Silver Spring, MD, National Coalition on Catholic Health Care Ministry, 1995, Section three, Resource 1, pp. 1-3.

————, "Apostolic Constitution on the Roman Curia", *Pastor bonus,* 28 June 1988, in *AAS,* 80 (1988), pp. 841-924; English translation in *Code of Canon Law,* Latin-English edition, prepared under the auspices of THE CANON LAW SOCIETY OF AMERICA, Washington, DC, Canon Law Society of America, 1999, pp. 681-751.

————, "Apostolic Exhortation", *Christifideles laici,* 30 December 1988, in *AAS,* 81 (1989), pp. 393-521; English translation in *Origins,* 18 (1988-1989), pp. 561, 563-595.

————, "Letter of the Holy Father John Paul II to All Consecrated Persons Belonging to Religious Communities on the Occasion of the Marian Year", in *Consecrated Life,* 14 (1989), pp. 199-210.

JOHN PAUL II, "The Value and Efficacy of Religious Life Always Depend on Ecclesial Communion", in *Consecrated Life,* 15 (1990), pp. 17-19.

————, "Toward the Fifth Centenary of New World Evangelization", in *Origins,* 20 (1990-1991), pp. 208-216.

————, Encyclical letter, *Redemptoris missio,* 7 December 1990, in *AAS,* 83 (1991), pp. 249-340; English translation in *Origins,* 20 (1990-1991), pp. 541, 543-568.

————, "The Gospel and the World: Essential Points of Reference of Your Vocation", in *Consecrated Life,* 17 (1992), pp. 22-25.

————, "The Church Has a Great Need Today of Your Spirit of Sacrifice", in *Consecrated Life,* 17 (1992), pp. 35-40.

————, "The New Evangelization Demands Love in Strict Fidelity to the Gospel", in *Consecrated Life,* 17 (1992), pp. 64-66.

————, "Make the Three Evangelical Counsels Be the Foundation of Your Religious Life", in *Consecrated Life,* 17 (1992), pp. 71-76.

————, "Christ Invites Us: 'Come, follow me'," in *L'Osservatore romano,* (English edition), 5 October 1994, pp. 1-2.

————, "Religious Live Baptismal Vows Intensely", in *L'Osservatore romano* (English edition), 5 October 1994, p. 11.

————, "Spirit Continues Giving New Charisms" in *L'Osservatore romano,* (English edition), 12 October 1994, p. 15.

————, "Apostolic Letter for the Jubilee of the Year 2000", *Tertio millennio adveniente,* 24 April 1994, in *AAS,* 87 (1995), pp. 5-44; English translation in *Origins,* 24 (1994-1995), pp. 401, 403-416.

————, "Your Fidelity to the Observance of the Evangelical Counsels Sustains the Character of the Christian Community", in

Consecrated Life, 19 (1995), p. 12.

JOHN PAUL II, "Be Present with Love and Prophetic Dedication Wherever Life is Endangered", in *Consecrated Life,* 19 (1995), pp. 20-23.

————, "To Choose God Means to Contemplate His Word", in *Consecrated Life,* 19 (1996), pp. 9-11.

————, Post-synodal Apostolic Exhortation *Vita consecrata,* 25 March 1996, in *AAS,* 88 (1996), pp. 377-486; English translation, *Consecrated Life,* Sherbrooke, QC, Médiaspaul, 1996, 208 p.

————, "Witnessing Christ in Secular Life", 1 February 1997; English translation in *The Pope Speaks,* 42 (1997), pp. 230-233.

————, "This is the Day that the Lord has Made!", in *L'Osservatore romano,* (English edition), 3 June 1998, p. 1.

————, "You Express the Church's Fruitful Vitality: Message for the World Congress of Ecclesial Movements and New Communities", in *L'Osservatore romano,* (English edition), 10 June 1998, p. 2.

L'Attività della Santa Sede; Pubblicazione non ufficiale, Città del Vaticano, Libreria editrice Vaticana, 1941- .

Magnum bullarium Romanum: bullarum, privilegiorum ac diplomatum Romanorum Pontificum amplissima collectio continuatio, Graz, Akademische, Druck-u, Verlagsanstalt, 1963-1964, 19 vols.

MANSI, J.D. (ed.), *Sacrorum conciliorum nova et amplissima collectio,* Parisiis, H.Welter, 1901- 1927, 53 vols.

MIGNE, J. (ed.), *Patrologiae cursus completus,* Series latina, Parisiis, Montrouge, 1844-[1960], 221 vols.

Normae secundum quas S. Cong. Episcoporum et regularium procedere solet in approbandis novis institutis votorum simplicium, Romae, Typis S. C. propagande fide, 1901, 59 p.

Normae secundum quas S. Congregatio de Religiosis in novis religiosis congregationibus approbandis procedere solet, Romae, Typis polyglottis Vaticanis, 1922, 16 p.

PAUL VI, Encyclical Letter on Paths of the Church, *Ecclesiam suam,* in *AAS,* 56 (1964), pp. 650- 653. English translation, "Paths of the Church", in *Conciliar and Post-conciliar Documents,* Catholic Desktop Library, Pauline Books and Media, 1994-1995 on diskette.

_____, Apostolic Exhortation on the Renewal of Religious Life, *Evangelica testificatio,* 29 June 1971, in *AAS,* 63 (1971), pp. 497-526; English translation in FLANNERY 1, pp. 680-706.

_____, "The Unique Witness of Secular Institutes", 2 February 1972, in *L'Osservatore romano,* 3 February 1972; English translation in *The Pope Speaks,* 17 (1972), pp. 26-32.

_____, "Apostolic Exhortation", *Evangelii nuntiandi,* 8 December 1975 in *AAS,* 68 (1976), pp. 5-76; English translation in FLANNERY 2, pp. 711-761.

_____, "Ad repraesentantes institutorum saecularium", 25 August, 1976; English translation in *Secular Institutes: The Official Documents,* Rome, Conférence mondiale des Instituts séculiers, 1981, pp. 95-99.

_____, "Allocutione Die festo Praesentationis Domini, in Basilica Vaticana, tricesimo anno ex quo Pius XII P. M. Constitutionem Apostolicam *Provida Mater* de institutis saecularibus promulgavit", 2 February 1977, in *AAS,* 69 (1977), pp. 140-142; English translation in in *Secular Institutes: The Official Documents,* Rome, Conférence mondiale des Instituts séculiers, 1981, pp. 101-102.

PELLICIA, G. and G. ROCCA, (eds), *Dizionario degli istituti di perfezione,* Romae, Edizione Paoline, (G. PELLICIA 1962-1968 and G. ROCCA 1969-), 9 vols.

PIUS XII, Apostolic Constitution *Provida Mater Ecclesia,* 2 February

1947, in *AAS,* 39 (1947), pp. 114-124; English translation in *Canon Law Digest,* Milwaukee, Bruce Publishing Co., vol. 3, pp. 135-146.

Pius XII, Motu proprio *Primo feliciter,* 12 March 1948, in *AAS,* 40 (1948), pp. 283-286; English translation in *Canon Law Digest,* vol. 3, pp. 147-151.

Pontificia Commissio Codici Iuris Canonici Interpretando, *Codex iuris canonici auctoritate Ioannis Pauli PP.II promulgatus, fontium annotatione et indice analytico- alphabetico auctus,* Romae, Libreria editrice Vaticana, 1989, xxxii, 669 p.

_____, *Schema canonum de institutis vitae consecratae per professionem consiliorum evangelicorum,* English translation, *Schema of Canons on Institutes of Life Consecrated by Profession of the Evangelical Counsels; Draft,* Washington, DC, Publications Office, United States Catholic Conference, 1977, xxv, 73 p.

Pontificia Commissio Codici Iuris Canonici recognoscendo, *Schema codicis iuris canonici. schema Patribus Commissionis reservatum,* Romae, Libreria editrice Vaticana, 1980, xxiii, 382 p.

Sacra Congregatio Episcoporum et Regularium, *Collectanea in usum Secretariae Sacrae Congregationis Episcoporum et Regularium,* A. Bizzarri (ed.), Romae, Ex typographia polyglotta, S.C. Propaganda fide, 1885, 881 p.

Sacred Congregation for Bishops and Sacred Congregation for Religious and Secular Institutes, Directives for Mutual Relations Between Bishops and Religious in the Church, *Mutuae relationes,* 14 May 1978, in *AAS,* 70 (1978), pp. 473-506; English translation in Flannery 2, pp. 209-243.

Sacred Congregation for Religious, Instruction *Cum Sanctissimus Dominus,* 19 March 1948, in *AAS,* 40 (1948), pp. 293-297; English translation in *Canon Law Digest,* vol. 3, pp. 151-157.

SACRED CONGREGATION FOR RELIGIOUS AND SECULAR INSTITUTES, Instruction on the Renewal of Religious Life, *Renovationis causam,* 6 January 1969, in *AAS,* 61 (1969), pp. 103-120; English translation in Flannery 1, pp. 634-655.

————, "Riflessioni sugli istituti secolari desunte dall'esperienza di vita", in *Informationes SCRIS,* 3 (1977), pp. 33-53; 179-195.

SCHROEDER, H.J. (ed.), *Canons and Decrees of the Council of Trent,* St. Louis, Herder, 1941, xxxiii, 608 p.

SCHROEDER, H.J.(ed. and translator), *Disciplinary Decrees of the General Councils: Text, Translation and Commentary,* St. Louis, Herder, 1937, viii, 669 p.

SECOND VATICAN COUNCIL, Decree on the Apostolate of Lay People, *Apostolicam actuositatem,* 18 November 1965, in *AAS,* 58 (1966), pp. 837-864; English translation in Flannery 1, pp. 766-798.

————, "Dogmatic Constitution on the Church", *Lumen gentium,* 21 November 1964, in *AAS* 57 (1965), pp. 5-75; English translation in Flannery 1, pp. 350-426.

————, "Decree on the Up-To-Date Renewal of Religious Life", *Perfectae caritatis,* 28 October 1965, in *AAS,* 58 (1966), pp. 702-712; English translation in Flannery 1, pp. 611-623.

————, "Pastoral Constitution on the Church in the Modern World", *Gaudium et spes,* 7 December 1965, in *AAS,* 58 (1966), pp. 1025-1115; English translation in Flannery 1, pp. 903-1001.

————, "Decree on the Church's Missionary Activity", *Ad gentes,* 7 December 1965, in *AAS,* 58 (1966), pp. 947-990; English translation in Flannery 1, pp. 813-856.

————, "Council's Message to Women, 8 December 1965", in *AAS,* 58 (1966), pp. 13-14; English translation in *Conciliar and Post-conciliar Documents,* Catholic Desktop Library, Pauline Books and Media, 1994-1995 on diskette.

TANNER, N.P. (ed.), *Decrees of Ecumenical Councils,* original text established by G. Alberigo et al. in consultation with H. Jedin, London, Sheed and Ward; Washington, Georgetown University Press, 1990, 2 vols.

2. Rules and Constitutions

CHRISTIAN COMMUNITY FOR THE SOCIAL APOSTOLATE, *Constitutions and Statutes,* Perth, Privately published, 1981, 8 p.

Constitutional Charter and Code of the Sovereign Military Hospitaller Order of St. John of Jerusalem, of Rhodes and of Malta, promulgated 27 June 1961, revised by the Extraordinary Chapter General, 28-30 April 1997, Roma, Tipografia Arte della Stampa, 1998, 149 p.

Constitutions of the Institute of Saint Joseph, La Crosse, Privately published, 1998.

SOCIÉTÉ DU CHRIST SEIGNEUR, *Constitutions,* Montréal, Centre Leunis, 1997, 40 p.

3. Books

AA.VV., *Les 'mouvements' dans l'Église,* Paris, Éditions Lethielleux, 1984, 236 p.

———, *Il nuovo diritto dei religiosi,* Roma, Editrice Rogate, 1984, 254 p.

———, *Questions juridiques et canoniques: Hommage au R.P. P.-E Bouchet,* Toulouse, Institut Catholique de Tulouse, Faculté de Droit canonique, 1987, 66p.

———, *La teologia della vita consacrata,* Roma, Centro Studi USMI-Roma, 1990, 220 p.

ABBASS, J., *Two Codes in Comparison,* Roma, Pontificio Istituto Orientale, 1997, 303 p.

ABBOTT, E., *A History of Celibacy,* Toronto, Harper Collins, 1999, 559 p.

ALBERIONE, J. et al., *Religious Life in the Light of Vatican II,* Boston, Daughters of St Paul, 1967, 479 p.

ALEXANDER, C., *The Missionary Dimension: Vatican II and the World Apostolate,* Milwaukee, The Bruce Publishing Co., 1967, viii, 117 p.

AMOS, J.R., *Associations of the Christian Faithful in the 1983 Code of Canon Law: A Canonical Analysis and Evaluation,* Ann Arbor, MI, University Microfilms International, 1988, xi, 424 p.

ANDRÉS, D.J., *Il diritto dei religiosi: commento esegetico al codice,* 2a ed. italiana, Roma, Ediurcla, 1996, 757 p.

ANSON, P.F., *The Call of the Desert: The Solitary Life in the Early Christian Church,* S.P.C.K., London, 1964, xiii, 278 p.

ARBUCKLE G.A., and D.L. FLEMING (eds), *Religious Life: Rebirth through Conversion,* New York, Alba House, 1990, xi, 142 p.

ARRIBAS, A.S (ed.), *The Laity and the Religious: Toward the Church of the Future,* Quezon City, Philipines, Claretian Publications, 1988, v, 163 p.

ARRUPE, P., *Challenge to Religious Life To-day,* vol. 1 of *Selected Letters and Addresses,* edited by J. Aixala, Anand, India, Gujarat Sahitya Prakash, and St. Louis, The Institute of Jesuit Sources, 1979, xi, 297 p.

————, *L'insertion dans le monde,* Ottawa, Conférence religieuse canadienne, 1981, 16 p.

ASPEGREN, K., *The Male Woman: A Feminine Ideal in the Early Church,* Stockholm, Almqvist & Wiksell International, 1990, 189 p.

AUBRY, J. et al., *Vita consacrata: un dono del Signore alle sua Chiesa,* Torino, Editrice Di Ci, 1994, 407 p.

AZEVEDO, M., *The Consecrated Life: Crossroads and Directions:* translated by Guillermo Cook, Maryknoll, NY, 1995, xv, 141 p.

BANGERT, W.V., *A History of the Society of Jesus,* St. Louis, The Institute of Jesuit Sources, 1972, xii, 558 p.

BARAÚNA, G. (ed.), *L'Église de Vatican II: Études autour de la Constitution conciliaire sur l'Église,* Paris, Éditions du Cerf, 1966, 3 vols.

BARCLAY, W., *The Beatitudes and the Lord's Prayer for Everyman,* New York, Harper & Row, 1975, 256 p.

BARRY, G.F., *Violation of the Cloister: An Historical Synopsis and Commentary,* Washington, DC, Catholic University of America, 1942, xii, 260 p.

BARTOLAC, V.L., *The Practice of the Evangelical Counsels in Secular Institutes,* Ann Arbor, Michigan, UMI, 1991, viii, 363 p.

BATTELLI, G., *Religious Life in the Light of the New Canon Law,* Nairobi, Kenya, St Paul Publications – Africa, 1990, x 110 p.

BERLIÉRE, U., *L'ordre monastique des origines au XIIᵉ siècle,* Lille, Desclée, 1924, xii, 310 p.

———, *L'ascèse bénédictine des origines à la fin du XII siècle: essai historique,* Bruges, Desclée de Brouwer, 1927, xi, 282 p.

———, *La* familia *dans les monastères bénédictins du Moyen âge,* Bruxelles, M. Lamertine, 1931, 123 p.

BERLIOZ, J., (ed.), *Moines et religieux au Moyen Age,* Paris, Seuil, 1994, 341 p.

BEYER, J., *Les instituts séculiers,* Bruges, Belgium, Desclée de Brouwer, 1954, 402 p.

———, *La consécration à Dieu dans les instituts séculiers,* Roma, Presses de l'Université Grégorienne, 1964, viii, 224 p.

———, *Religious Life or Secular Institute,* Rome, Gregorian University Press, 1970, 207 p.

BEYER, J., *Vers un nouveau droit des Instituts de vie consacrée: commentaire du projet et premières observations,* Paris, Éditions St Paul, 1978, 352 p.

————, *Du concile au Code de droit canonique: la mise en application de Vatican II,* Paris, Éditions Tardy, 1985, 126 p.

————, *Le droit de la vie consacrée,* Paris, Tardy, 1988, 2 vols.

————, *Communione ecclesiale e strutture di corresponsabilità: dal Vaticano II al nuovo Codice di diritto canonico,* Roma, Pontificia Università Gregoriana, 1990, 80 p.

BLAIS, A., *Consecrated Secularity, the Pope Speaks: A Commentary on the Speech of Paul VI to Secular Institutes on February 2nd, 1972 and the Original Inspiration of the Institute of Christ the Priest,* Hammerskraal, Republic of S. Africa, Servants of Christ the Priest, 1972, 94 p.

BLAIS, Y-M., *Document de recherches sur les nouvelles oeuvres mixtes dans l'Église,* Brossard, Québec, Y-M. Blais, 1984, 179 p.

BOISVERT, L., *La consécration religieuse: consécration baptismale et formes de vie consacrée,* Paris, Éditions du Cerf, 1988, 119 p.

BONFILS, J., *Les sociétés de la vie apostolique: identité et législation,* Paris, Les Éditions du Cerf, 1990, 209 p.

BOUSCAREN, T.L. and A.C. ELLIS, *Canon Law: A Text and Commentary,* 4th rev. ed., Milwaukee, Bruce Publishing Co., 1966, xvi, 1011 p.

BRADY, M.L., *The Quinquennial Report of Religious Institutes to the Holy See: A Historical Synopsis and a Commentary,* Washington, DC, Catholic University of America, 1963, xiii, 114 p.

BRESSAN, G. et al., *Lumen gentium: guida alla lettura della costituzione* Roma, Salles, 1996, 369 p.

BROCKHAUS, T.A., *Religious Who Are Known as Conversi: An Historical Synopsis and Commentary,* Washington, DC, Catholic

University of America, 1946, ix, 127 p.

BROWN, P.R., *The Body and Society: Men, Women and Sexual Renunciation in Early Christianity,* New York, Columbia University Press, 1988, xx, 504 p.

BROWN, P.R., *The Rise of Western Christendom: Triumph and Diversity AD 200-1000,* Malden, MA, Blackwell, 1997, xi, 368 p.

BUTLER, B., *The Theology of Vatican II,* London, Darton, Longman & Todd, 1981, x, 230 p.

CADA, L. et al., *Shaping the Coming Age of Religious Life,* New York, Seabury Press, 1979, 197 p.

CAIN, J.R., *The Influences of the Cloister on the Apostolate of Congregations of Religious Women,* Rome, Pontificia Universitas Lateranensis, 1965, xxiv, 107 p.

CALLAHAN, F.J., *The Centralisation of Government in Pontifical Institutes of Women with Simple Vows,* Rome, Gregorian University, 1948, 112 p.

CAMISASCA, M. et M. VITALI, *Les mouvements dans l'Église,* Paris, Lethielleux, 1984, 239 p.

CANALS NAVARRETE, S., *Secular Institutes and the State of Perfection: The Priesthood and the State of Perfection,* Dublin, Scepter, 1959, 173 p.

CAPARROS, E, M. THÉRIAULT and J. THORN (eds), *Code of Canon Law Annotated,* Latin-English edition of the *Code of Canon Law* and English language translation of the 5th Spanish language edition of the commentary prepared under the responsibility of the Instituto Martín de Azpilcueta, Montréal, Wilson & Lafleur, 1993, 1631 p.

CHALENDARD, M., *La promotion de la femme à l'apostolat, 1540-1650,* Paris, Éditions Alsatia, 1950, 207 p.

CHITTISTER, J., *The Fire in These Ashes: A Spirituality of Contemporary Religious Life,* Kansas City, Sheed and Ward, 1996, xi, 178 p.

————, *Le feu sous les cendres,* traduit de l'anglais par M. GAGNON, Montréal, Bellarmin, 1998, 371 p.

CHITTY, D., *The Desert a City: An Introduction to the Study of Egyptian and Palestinian Monasticism under the Christian Empire,* Oxford, Basil Blackwell, 1966, xvi, 222 p.

CLANCY, P.M., *Secular Institutes,* Washington DC, Catholic University of America, 1951, 16 p.

CLARKE, T.J., *Parish Societies,* Washington, DC, The Catholic University of America Press, 1943, xii, 147 p.

CLEAR, C., *Nuns in Nineteenth Century Ireland,* Dublin, Gill and MacMillan; Washington, DC, Catholic University of America Press, 1988, xix, 214 p.

CODINA, V., *Vita religiosa: storia e teologia,* Assissi, Cittadella editrice, 1990, 213 p.

CODINA, V. and N. ZEVALLOS, *La vie religieuse: Histoire et théologie,* traduit de l'espagnol par E. URIBE-CARRENO, Paris, Les Éditions du Cerf, 1992, 238 p.

COLRAT, M., *Vie consacrée,* Strasbourg, Université des sciences humaines, 1984, x, 139 p.

COMITÉ CANONIQUE DES RELIGIEUX, *Vie religieuse, érémitisme, consécration des vierges, communautés nouvelles: études canoniques,* Paris, Éditions du Cerf, 1993, 253 p.

CONFERENCE OF MAJOR RELIGIOUS SUPERIORS OF WOMEN'S INSTITUTES IN THE UNITED STATES OF AMERICA, *Proposed Norms for Consideration in the Revision of the Canons Concerning Religious as Submitted to the Pontifical Commission on the Revision of the Code of Canon Law,* Washington, DC, CMSW National Secretariat, 1968, vii, 99 p.

CONFERENCE OF RELIGIOUS, INDIA, *Consecrated Life - A Call to Communion in the Light of "Vita consecrata" for the Third Millennium,* New Delhi, CRI House, 1997, 90 p.

CONFERENCE OF RELIGIOUS OF IRELAND, (CORI), Annual Report, *Discovering God in the Now,* Dublin, CORI, 1997, 67 p.

CONGAR, Y., *Report from Rome,* London, Geoffrey Chapman, 1963, 132 p.

————, et B.D. DUPUY (eds), *L'Episcopat et l'Église universelle,* (Unam Sanctam, 39), Paris, Cerf, 1962, pp. 229-260.

CONGREGATIO PRO RELIGIOSIS ET INSTITUTIS SAECULARIBUS, *The Secular Institutes: Their Identity and Mission,* Rome, Conférence mondiale des Instituts séculiers, 1985, 99 p.

CONGREGATIONS FOR CATHOLIC EDUCATION, FOR THE ORIENTAL CHURCHES, FOR INSTITUTES OF CONSECRATED LIFE AND FOR SOCIETIES OF APOSTOLIC LIFE, *New Vocations for a New Europe, Final Document of the Congress on Vocations to the Priesthood and to Consecrated Life in Europe,* Vatican City, Libreria editrice Vaticana, 1997, 112 p.

CONGRESSUS INTERNATIONALIS INSTITUTORUM SAECULARIUM (2ND: ROME, 1980), *Evangelisation and the Secular Institutes in the Light of "Evangelii nuntiandi": Acts of the Second Congress of Secular Institutes,* Rome, CMIS, 1984, 222 p.

CORIDEN, J.A., T.J. GREEN and D.E. HEINTSCHEL (eds), *The Code of Canon Law: A Text and Commentary;* commissioned by the Canon Law Society of America, New York, Paulist Press, 1985, xxvi, 1152 p.

COURTOIS, G., *The States of Perfection According to the Teaching of the Church: Papal Documents from Leo XIII to Pius XII,* translated from the French by J.A. O'Flynn, Dublin, M.H. Gill, 1961, xv, 400 p.

CREUSEN, J., *Religious Men and Women in the Code,* translated by E.F.

Garesché, Milwaukee, Bruce, 1940, xiii, 314 p.

CREUSEN, J., *De iuridica status religiosi evolutione, synopsis historica,* Romae, Pontificiae Universitatis Gregorianae, 1948, 46 p.

DARRICAU, R. and B. PEYROUS, *Father Noailles and the Association of the Holy Family: the Story of a Charism,* translated from the French by the Holy Family Sisters, Chambray-les-Tours, C.L.D.Editions, 1995, 329 p.

DE PAOLIS, V., *La vita consacrata nella Chiesa,* Bologna, Dehoniane, 1991, 460 p.

DEL PORTILLO, A., *Faithful and Laity in the Church,* trans. by L. Hickey, Shannon, Ireland, Ecclesia Press, 1972, 200 p.

DONOVAN, M.A., *Sisterhood as Power: The Past and Passion of Ecclesial Women,* New York, Crossroad, 1989, 136 p.

DRIOT, M., *Les Pères du désert: vie et spiritualité,* Paris, Médiaspaul, 1991, 160 p.

DUCHET-SUCHAUX G., et M. DUCHET-SUCHAUX, *Les ordres religieux: Guide historique,* Paris, Flammarion, 1993, 317 p.

DUSTER, C.J., *The Canonical Status of Members of Missionary Societies of Apostolic Life of Pontifical Right,* Rome, Pontificia studiorum Universitas a S. Thomas Aquinas in Urbe, 1994, xii, 280 p.

ECKENSTEIN, L., *Woman under Monasticism: Chapters on Saint Lore and Convent Life,* Cambridge, University Press, 1986, xv, 496 p.

ERIKSON, E.H., *The Life Cycle Completed,* London, W. W. Norton & Company, 1997, 134 p.

FARRELL, B.F., *The Rights and Duties of the Local Ordinary Regarding Congregations of Women Religious of Pontifical Approval,* Washington, DC, Catholic University of America Press, 1941, iv, 195 p.

FIAND, B., *Living the Vision: Religious Vows in an Age of Change,* New York, The Crossroad Publishing Co., 1990, 169 p.

————, *Where Two or Three are Gathered: Community Life for the Contemporary Religious,* New York, The Crossroad Publishing Co., 1992, 108 p.

————, *Wrestling with God: Religious Life in Search of Its Soul,* New York, The Crossroad Publishing Co., 1997, xiii, 208 p.

FLANAGAN, B.J., *The Canonical Erection of Religious Houses: an Historical Synopsis and Commentary,* Washington, DC, Catholic University of America, 1943, x, 147 p.

FLANNERY, A. (ed.), *Missions and Religions: A Commentary on the Second Vatican Council's Decree on the Church's Missionary Activity and Declaration on the Relation of the Church to Non-Christian Religions,* Dublin, Scepter Books, 1968, 163 p.

————, *Towards the 1994 Synod of Bishops,* Dublin, Dominican Publications, 1993, 173 p.

FLEMING, D.L. and E. McDONOUGH (eds), *The Church and Consecrated Life,* St. Louis, MO, Review for Religious, 1996, viii, 440 p.

FRIEDLANDER, C. (ed.), *La clôture des moniales: Trente ans d'expectative,* Namur, Vie consacrée, 1997, 217 p.

FRY, E.J.B., et al., *Secular Institutes: A Symposium,* London, Blackfriars Publications, 1952, 131 p.

FRY, T. (ed.), *The Rule of St. Benedict in Latin and English with Notes,* abridged edition Collegeville, Minnesota, 1981, 627 p.

GALLAGHER, M., *The Common Life: An Element of Apostolic Institutes of Women,* Doctoral dissertation, Ottawa, Faculty of Canon Law, Saint Paul University, 1995, xv, 256 p.

GAMBARI, E., *Ma vie, c'est l'Église: ecclésiologie de la vie religieuse,* traduit J. DÉSORMEAUX, Paris, Fleurus, 1970, 364 p.

GAMBARI, E., *Unfolding the Mystery of Religious Life,* trans. by M. M. Bellasis, Boston, St Paul Editions, 1974, 200 p.

————, *Consecration and Service,* translated by M.M. Bellasis, Boston, St. Paul Éditions, 1973-1974, 2 vols.

————, *I religiosi nel Codice: commento ai singoli canoni,* Milano, Ancora, 1986, 445 p.

————, *Religious Life: According to Vatican II and the New Code of Canon Law:* English translation by Daughters of St. Paul, Boston, St. Paul Editions, 1986, 668 p.

————, *The Canonical Establishment of a Religious Institute: Process and Procedures,* translated from Italian by M.M. ARMATO and T. BLESSIN, Florence, Artigraf, 1999, 220 p.

GAUSSIN, P-R., *L'Europe des ordres et des congrégations: des Bénédictins aux Mendiants (VIe-XVIe),* Paris, C.E.R.C.O.M., 1984, 210 p.

————, *Le monde des religieux des origines au temps présent: glorification de Dieu et service des hommes,* Paris, Éditions Cujas, 1988, 391 p.

GERMAIN, E., *La vie consacrée dans l'Église: approche historique,* Paris, Médiaspaul; Montréal: Éditions Paulines, 1994, 197 p.

GEROSA, L., *Carisma e diritto nella Chiesa: riflessioni canonistiche sul 'carisma originario' dei nuovi movimenti ecclesiali,* Milano, Jaca Book, 1989, xv, 273 p.

GHIRLANDA, G., V. DE PAOLIS and A. MONTAN, *La vita consacrata,* Bologna, Dehoniane, 1983, 201 p.

GHIRLANDA, G. (ed.), *Punti fondamentali sulla vita consacrata,* Roma, Editrice Pontificia Università Gregoriana, 1994, x, 91 p.

GIBSON, S.G., *"Called by the Lord": The Theme of Vocation in Lumen gentium,* Romae, Pontificia studiorum Universitas a S. Thomas

Aquinas in Urbe, 1990, xi, 218 p.

GROESCHEL, B.J., *The Reform of Renewal,* San Francisco, Ignatius Press, 1990, 227 p.

GUTIÉRREZ, D.J., *Il diritto dei religiosi: commento esegetico al codice,* Roma, Ediurcla, 1996, 757 p.

HALEY, J.E. (ed.), *Dedicated Life in the World: Secular Institutes,* St. Meinrad, Indiana, Grail Publications, 1955, 48 p.

HALLMAN, D.G., *Ecotheology: Voices from South and North,* Geneva, WCC Publications, 1994, ix, 316 p.

HARMER, C., *Religious Life in the 21st Century; A Contemporary Journey into Canaan,* Mystic, Twenty-Third Publications, 1995, 136 p.

HASTINGS, A., *A Concise Guide to the Documents of the Second Vatican Council,* London, Darton Longman & Todd, 1968, 2 vols.

HAUGHT, J.F., *The Promise of Nature: Ecology and Cosmic Purpose,* New York, Paulist Press, 1993, iii, 156 p.

HAYES, E.J., *Rightful Autonomy of Life and Charism in the Proper Law of the Norbertine Order,* Ann Arbor, MI, UMI, 1991, xii, 588 p.

HÉBRARD, M., *Les nouveaux disciples dix ans après: voyage à travers les communautés charismatiques, réflexions sur le renouveau spirituel,* Paris, Centurion, 1987, 378 p.

HOSTIE, R., *Vie et mort des ordres religieux: approches psychosociologiques,* Paris, Desclée de Brouwer, 1972, 381 p.

HOURLIER, J., *L'âge classique, 1140-1378: les religieux,* Paris, Éditions Cujas, 1971, 567 p.

HYNOUS, D.M., *The Relationship Between Religious and the Hierarchy since the Second Vatican Council,* Romae, Pontificia studiorum Universitas a S. Thomas Aquinas in Urbe, 1969, 75 p.

IHNATOWICZ, J.A., *Consecrated Life Among the Laity: A Theological Study of a Vocation in the Church,* Rome, Pontificia studiorum Universitas a S. Thomas Aquinas in Urbe, 1984, xvi, 442 p.

ISTITUTO CLARETIANUM (ed.) *L'identità dei consacrati nella missione della Chiesa e il loro rapporto con il mondo,* Città del Vaticano, Libreria editrice Vaticana, 1994, 455 p.

JARRELL, L., *The Development of Legal Structures for Women Religious Between 1500 and 1900: A Study of Selected Institutes of Religious Life for Women,* Washington, DC, Catholic University of America, 1984, xi, 336 p.

JEDIN, H. and J. DOLAN (eds), *History of the Church,* (translation of *Handbuch der Kirchengeschichte,* 1962-1979), London, Burns & Oates, 1981, 10 vols.

JOHNSON, P.D., *Equal in Monastic Profession: Religious Women in Medieval France,* Chicago, 1991, xv, 294 p.

KALLUMKAL, J., *The Patrimony of an Institute According to the Code of Canon Law,* Roma, Pontificia Università Lateranense, 1989, ix, 208 p.

KHOURY, J., *Vie consacrée (essai de commentaire des canons 573-709),* Rome, S.N., 1984, 332 p.

KNIGHTS OF MALTA, *The Rule, Statutes and Customs of the Hospitallers, 1099-1310,* with Introductory Chapters and Notes by E. J. KING, London, Methuen & Co. Ltd., 1981, xv, 224 p.

KNOWLES, D., *From Pachomius to Ignatius: A Study in the Constitutional History of the Religious Orders,* Oxford, Clarendon Press, 1966, 98 p.

────── and D. OBOLENSKY, *The Christian Centuries: A New History of the Catholic Church,* London, Darton, Longman and Todd, 1969, 5 vols.

KOMONCHAK, J.A., M. COLLINS and D.A. LANE (eds), *The New Dictionary of Theology,* Wilmington, DE, Michael Glazier Inc., 1987, viii, 1112 p.

KOWAL, J., *Uscita definitiva dall'istituto religioso dei professi di voti perpetui: evoluzione storica e disciplina attuale,* Roma, Pontificia Universitas Gregoriana, 1997, xii, 316 p.

LANSLOTS, D.I., *Handbook of Canon Law for Congregations of Women Under Simple Vows,* 9th edition revised and enlarged to conform with the new Code of Canon Law, New York, F. Pustet Co., Inc., 1920, 303 p.

LATOURELLE, R., e R. FISICHELLA (eds), *Dizionario di Teologia fondamentale,* Assisi, Cittadella editrice, 1990, 1502 p.

LAURET, B. (ed.), *Nouveau dictionnaire de théologie,* Paris, Les Éditions du Cerf, 1996, 1136 p.

LAWLESS, G., *Augustine of Hippo and His Monastic Rule,* Oxford, Clarendon Press, 1987, xix, 185 p.

LAWRENCE, C.H., *Medieval Monasticism: Forms of Religious Life in Western Europe in the Middle Ages,* London, Longman, 1984, ix, 260 p.

LEAVEY, C. and R. O'NEILL, *Gathered in God's Name: New Horizons in Australian Religious Life,* Sydney, Crossing Press, 1996, xiv, 172 p.

LECLERQ, J., F. VANDENBROUCKE and L. BOUYER, *The Spirituality of the Middle Ages,* translated from the French by the Benedictines of Holme Eden Abbey, Carlisle, London, Burns and Oates, 1968, x, 602 p.

LEFEBVRE, S., *Sécularité et instituts séculiers: Bilan et perspectives,* Montréal, Éditions Paulines & Médiaspaul, 1989, 114 p.

LENOIR, F., *Les communautés nouvelles: interviews des fondateurs,* Paris, Fayard, 1988, 362 p.

LERNER, G., *Women and History,* New York, Oxford University Press, 1986-1993, 2 vols.

LESAGE, G., *L'accession des congrégations à l'état religieux juridique,* Ottawa, University of Ottawa, 1948, 300 p.

LEYSER, H., *Hermits and the New Monasticism: A Study of Religious Communities in Western Europe, 1000-1150,* London, Macmillan Press, 1984, ix, 135 p.

LOPEZ-AMAT, A., *La vita consacrata. Le varie forme dalle origini ad oggi,* Roma, Città Nuova, 1991, 259 p.

LOZANO, J.M., *La sequela di Cristo: teologia storica-sistematica della vita religiosa,* Milano, Ancora, 1981, 366 p.

————, *Discipleship: Towards an Understanding of Religious Life,* translated by B. Wilczynski, Chicago, Claret Center for Resources in Spirituality, 1983, xv, 375 p.

LUNA BARRERA, L.A., *Las implicaciones jurídicas en las sociedades de vida apostólica que asumen los consejos evangélicos,* Ottawa, Saint Paul University, 1999, 325 p.

LYNCH, T., *Contracts Between Bishops and Religious Congregations: A Historical Synopsis and a Commentary,* Washington, DC, Catholic University of America, 1946, xiii, 232 p.

McCANN, J. (ed. and translator), *The Rule of St Benedict,* London, Burns Oates, 1952, xxiv, 214 p.

McCARTHY, M.C., *The Rule for Nuns of St. Caesarius of Arles: A Translation with a Critical Introduction,* Washington, D.C., The Catholic University of America Press, 1960, viii, 230 p.

MACDONALD, H.L., *Hermits: The Juridical Implications of Canon 603,* Ottawa, Saint Paul University, 1990, xii, 255 p.

McDONALD, W.J. (ed. in chief), *New Catholic Encyclopedia,* New York, McGraw Hill, 1967-, 17 vols.

McDonnell, E.W., *The Beguines and Beghards in Medieval Culture,* New Brunswick, 1969, xvii, 643 p.

McDonough, E., *Ready Reference for the 1980 Schema of Canons on Institutes of Consecrated Life,* Springs Press, Saint Mary of the Springs, 1981, ii, 60 p.

———, *Religious in the 1983 Code: New Approaches to the New Law,* Chicago, Franciscan Herald Press, 1985, xiii, 165 p.

———, *Canon Law in Pastoral Perspective: Principles for the Application of Law According to Antoninus of Florence,* Ann Arbor, Michigan, UMI, 1988, viii, 264 p.

McFarland, N.F., *Religious Vocation: Its Juridic Concept: A Historical Synopsis and a Commentary,* Washington, DC, Catholic University of America, 1953, ix, 132 p.

McNamara, J.A., *Sisters in Arms: Catholic Nuns through Two Millennia,* Cambridge, MA, Harvard University Press, 1996, xi, 751 p.

McNamara, K., *The Church: A Theological and Pastoral Commentary on the Constitution of the Church,* Dublin, Veritas Publications, 1983, 437 p.

MacPherson, I., *The Exercise of Authority in Apostolic Religious Institutes of Women According to the 1983 Revised Code of Canon Law,* Ottawa, Saint Paul University, 1984, xi, 276 p.

Macha, A., *The Juridical Identity of the Societies of Apostolic Life Compared to Institutes of Consecrated Life in the Light of the Present Code of Canon Law, Canon 731: A Comparative Study,* Rome, Pontificia Universitas Urbaniana, 1994, xvi, 241 p.

Makowski, E., *Canon Law and Cloistered Women: Periculoso and Its Commentators 1298-1545,* Washington, DC, The Catholic University of America Press, 1997, vii, 149 p.

Malvaux, B., *Les relations entre évêques diocésains et instituts religieux cléricaux de droit pontifical du Concile Vatican II à l'exhortation apostolique post-synodale Vita consecrata,* Ottawa, Université Saint-Paul, 1996, xiii, 252 p.

MARTÍN DE AGAR, J.T., *A Handbook on Canon Law,* Montréal, Wilson & Lafleur, 1999, xviii, 268 p.

MARZOA, A., J. MIRAS Y R. RODRIGUEZ-OCAÑA, *Comentario exegético de derecho canónico,* Pamplona, Ediciones Universidad de Navarra, 1997, 5 vols in 8.

MASCARENHAS, F., *The Identities of Societies of Apostolic Life: An Analysis of c. 731,* Rome, Pontificia Universitas Urbaniana, 1990, 98 p.

MASTERMAN, R.E. (ed.), *Religious Life: A Mystery in Christ and the Church: A Collated Study According to Vatican Council II and Subsequent Papal and Ecclesial Documents,* New York, Alba House, 1975, xv, 289 p.

MERKLE, J., *Committed by Choice, Religious Life Today,* Collegeville, MN, Liturgical Press, 1992, 158 p.

MOLINARI, P. and P. GUMPEL, *Il capitolo VI "De religiosis" della costituzione dogmatica sulla Chiesa,* Milan, Editrice Ancora, 1985, 221 p.

MOLONEY, F., *Disciples and Prophets: A Biblical Model for the Religious Life,* London, Darton, Longman and Todd, 1980, xiii, 225 p.

MOLONEY, F., *A Life of Promise: Poverty, Chastity, Obedience,* Wilmington, DE, Michael Glazier, Inc., 1984, 175 p.

MURPHY, D., *The Death and Rebirth of Religious Life,* Alexandria, N.S.W., E.J. Dwyer, 1995, xi, 243 p.

———, *A Return to Spirit; After the Mythic Church,* Alexandria, N.S.W., E.J. Dwyer, 1997, xi, 259 p.

MURRAY, B., *Les ordres monastiques et religieux,* Paris, MA Editions, 1986, 183 p.

NERI, A., *Nuove forme di vita consacrata (can. 605 C.I.C.),* Roma,

Editrice Pontificia Università Lateranense, vii, 203 p.

NICHOLLS J.A. and L.T. SHANK (eds), *Medieval Religious Women I: Distant Echoes,* Kalamazoo, MI., Cistercian Publications Inc., 1984, xi, 299 p.

NJINO, J.K., *Institutes of Consecrated Life: Religious and Secular,* Eldoret, Kenya, AMECEA Gaba Publications, 1988, 79 p.

NGUYEN, J.T., *Totally Consecrated to God and to the Service of his Church,* Roma, Pontificia studiorum Universitas a S. Thomas Aquinas in Urbe, 1992, 219 p.

NGUYEN DAN, P., *The Spiritual Patrimony of an Institute of Consecrated Life,* Rome, Pontificia Universitas Urbaniana, 1989, xvii, 207 p.

OCCHIALINI, U., *Vita religiosa, novità di vita,* Assisi, Cittadella editrice, 1983, 231 p.

O'CONNOR, D.F., *Witness and Service: Questions about Religious Life Today,* New York, Paulist Press, 1990, vi, 195 p.

O'MURCHU, D., *Religious Life: A Prophetic Vision: Hope and Promise for Tomorrow,* Notre Dame, Indiana, Ave Maria Press, 1991, 259 p.

————, *Reclaiming Spirituality,* Dublin, Gill and Macmillan, 1997, ix, 197 p.

————, *Quantum Theology,* New York, Crossroad, 1997, x, 227 p.

ORTH, C.R., *The Approbation of Religious Institutes,* Washington, DC, Catholic University of America, 1931, 166 p.

OTTINGER, B.M. and A.S. FISCHER (eds), *Secular Institutes in the 1983 Code: A New Vocation in the Church,* Westminster, MD, Christian Classics, 1988, x, 88 p.

PACAU, M., *Les ordres monastiques et religieux au Moyen Âge,* Paris, F. Nathan, 1970, 175 p.

PARENTY, F.J., *Life of St Angela Merici of Brescia: Foundress of the Order of St. Ursula,* New York, P. J. Kenedy, 1857, 251 p.

PASTOR, L., *The History of the Popes from the Close of the Middle Ages: Drawn from the Secret Archives of the Vatican and Other Original Sources,* from the German, London, Routledge and Kegan Paul, Trench, Trübner, 1929-1953, 40 vols.

PEACOCKE, A., *Theology for a Scientific Age,* Oxford, Basil Blackwell, 1990, x, 221 p.

PENNINGTON, M.B. (ed.), *The Cistercian Spirit: A Symposium in Memory of Thomas Merton,* Spencer, MA, Cistercian Publications, 1970, xv, 284 p.

PERRIN, J.M., *Secular Institutes: Consecration to God and Life in the World,* translated by R. Capel, London, G. Chapman, 1961, xvii, 122 p.

PINGAULT, P., *Renouveau de l'Église: les communautés nouvelles,* Tournai, Le Sarment, 1989, 224 p.

PINGAULT, P., *Livre de vie de la communauté du Pain de Vie,* Paris, Centurion, 1993, 363 p.

Pontificale Romanum; Ordo consecrationis virginum, Civitate Vaticana, Typis polyglottis Vaticanis, 1970, 64 p.

POLKINGHORNE, J., *Serious Talk: Science and Religion in Dialogue,* Valley Forge, PA, Trinity Press International, 1995, ix, 117 p.

PROU, J., *La clôture des moniales,* Paris, Les éditions du Cerf, 1996, 270 p.

QUIGLEY, C. (ed.), *Turning Points in Religious Life,* Wilmington, DE, M. Glazier, 1987, 257 p.

QUINN, S., *Relation of the Local Ordinary to Religious of Diocesan Approval: A Historical Synopsis and a Commentary,* Washington, DC, Catholic University of America, 1949, xii, 153 p.

RADCLIFFE, T., *Sing a New Song: the Christian Vocation,* Springfield, IL, Templegate Publishers, 1999, p. 252.

RAHNER, K., *The Dynamic Element in the Church,* translated by W. J. O'HARA, Montreal, Palm Publishers, 1964, 170 p.

RAHNER, K, *The Church after the Council,* Montreal, Palm Publishers, 1966, 106 p.

RANFT, P., *Women and the Religious Life in Premodern Europe,* New York, St. Martin's Press, 1996, xvi, 159 p.

RAPLEY, E., *The Dévotes: Women and Church in Seventeenth Century France,* Kingston, ON, McGill-Queen's University Press, 1990, 283 p.

RAUSCH, T.P., *The Roots of the Catholic Tradition,* Wilmington, DE, M. Glazier, 1986, 247 p.

——, *Authority and Leadership in the Church: Past Directions and Future Possibilities,* Wilmington, DE, M. Glazier, 1989, 158 p.

——, *Radical Christian Communities,* Collegeville, MN, Liturgical Press, 1990, 216 p.

——, *Catholicism at the Dawn of the Third Millennium,* Collegeville, MN, Liturgical Press, 1996, xvii, 253 p.

RAVIER, A., *Ignatius of Loyola and the Founding of the Sociey of Jesus,* translated by M. DALY et al., San Francisco, Ignatius Press, 1987, 504 p.

RECCHI, S., *Consacrazione mediante i consigli evangelici: dal Concilio al Codice,* Milano, Ancora, 1988, 247 p.

RENARD, A.C., *Le concile et les religieuses,* Mulhouse, Salvator, 1966, 87 p.

RISTUCCIA, B.J., *Quasi-Religious Societies: A Historical Synopsis and a Commentary,* Washington, DC, The Catholic University of

America Press, 1949, xvi, 318 p.

Roof, W.C., *A Generation of Seekers: The Spiritual Journeys of the Baby Boom Generation,* San Francisco, Harper Collins, 1993, x, 294 p.

Rouleau, J-P et J. Zylberberg (eds), *Les mouvements religieux aujourdhui: théories et pratiques,* Montréal, Bellarmin, 1984, 282 p.

Ryan, J., *Irish Monasticism: Origins and Early Development,* Dublin, Four Courts Press, Reprinted 1992, xv, 492 p.

Rovira, J., *Commitment To-day: Crises, Challenges and Hopes,* Quezon City, Philippines, Claretian Publications, 1988, xiii, 117 p.

Sastre Santos, E., *Las condiciones y posibilidades de nuevas formas de vida consagrada,* Roma, Urbaniana University Press, 1999, 312 p.

Schaaf, V.T., *The Cloister,* Cincinnati, OH, St Anthony Messenger Press, 1921, x, 185 p.

Schillebeeckx, E., *God Among Us: The Gospel Proclaimed,* translated by J. Bowden, New York, Crossroad, 1983, 258 p.

Schoenmaeckers, M.J., *Genèse du chapitre VI 'De religiosis' de la constitution dogmatique sur l'Église 'Lumen gentium',* Rome, Gregorian University Press, 1983, 328 p.

Schneiders, S., *New Wineskins,* Mahwah, NJ, Paulist Press, 1986, 309 p.

Scott, W., *A History of the Early Christian Church,* Nashville, Cokesbury Press, 1936, 375 p.

Sebott, R., *Ordensrecht: Kommentar zu Den Kanones 573-746 des Codex Iuris Canonici,* Frankfurt am Main, Verlag Josef Knecht, 1995, 348 p.

SECONDIN, B., *Sequela e profezia: eredità e avvenire della vita consacrata: intervista sulla vita religiosa ieri e oggi,* Roma, Edizioni Paoline, 1983, 148 p.

Secular Institutes: The Official Documents, Rome, Conférence mondiale des Instituts séculiers, 1981, 304 p.

SHAHAR, S., *The Fourth Estate: A History of Women in the Middle Ages,* translated by C. GALAI, London, Methuen, 1983, xii, 351 p.

SHEEHY, G. et al. (eds), *The Canon Law, Letter and Spirit: A Practical Guide to the Code of Canon Law* prepared by THE CANON LAW SOCIETY OF GREAT BRITAIN AND IRELAND, in association with THE CANADIAN CANON LAW SOCIETY, Dublin, Veritas, 1995, xxv, 1060 p.

SHELTON, J.R., *The Nature of the Secular Institute: Provida Mater to CIC 83,* Romae, Pontificia studiorum Universitas a S. Thomas Aquinas in Urbe, 1995, vii, 167 p.

SILLS, D.L., (ed.), *International Encyclopedia of the Social Sciences,* New York, Macmillan Co. and the Free Press, 1968, 18 vols.

SILVESTRI DI, G.M., *Life in Common: An Integral Part of Religious Life as Exemplified in the Congregation of the Sisters of St. John the Baptist,* Roma, Pontificia studiorum Universitas a S. Thomas Aquinas in Urbe, 1986, 254 p.

SIRE, H.J.A., *The Knights of Malta,* New Haven, Yale University Press, 1994, xiii, 305 p.

SMITH, I.G., *Christian Monasticism: From the Fourth to the Ninth Centuries of the Christian Era,* London, A. D. Innes, 1892, viii, 351 p.

SWEENEY, B.J., *The Patrimony of an Institute in the Code of Canon Law: A Study of Canon 578,* Roma, Pontificia studiorum Universitas a S. Thomas Aquinas in Urbe, 1995, 197 p.

THÉRIAULT, M., and J. THORN (eds), *Le nouveau code de droit canonique: Actes du Ve Congrès de droit canonique,* Ottawa, Université Saint Paul, 1986, 2 vols.

THÉRIAULT, M., and J. THORN (eds), *Unico Ecclesiae servitio: études de droit canonique offertes à Germain Lésage, o.m.i., en l'honneur de son 75e anniversaire de naissance et du 50e anniveraire de son ordination presbytérale,* Ottawa, Faculty of Canon Law, Saint Paul University, 1991, 355 p.

THURSTON, B.W., *The Widows: A Women's Ministry in the Early Church,* Minneapolis, Fortress Press, 1989, 141 p.

TILLARD, J.M.R, *Dilemmas of Modern Religious Life,* Wilmington, DE, Glazier, 1984, 87 p.

TORJESEN, K.J., *When Women Were Priests: Women's Leadership in the Early Church and the Scandal of their Subordination in the Rise of Christianity,* San Francisco, Harper San Francisco, 1995, x, 278 p.

TRAPET, M.A., *Pour l'avenir des nouvelles communautés dans lÉglise,* Paris, Desclée de Brouwer, 1987, 222 p.

TROELTSCH, E., THE SOCIAL TEACHING OF THE CHRISTIAN CHURCHES, TRANSLATED BY O. Wyon, KENTUCKY, WESTMINSTER/JOHN KNOX PRESS, REPRINTED 1992, 2 VOLS.

UNION DES SUPÉRIEURS GÉNÉRAUX, *Charismes dans l'église pour le monde,* Paris, Médiaspaul, 1994, 298 p.

UNION OF SUPERIORS GENERAL, *Religious Life 20 Years after Vatican II: Evaluation and Prospective,* Roma, Unione superiori generali, 1986, iv, 90 p.

————, *Consecrated Life Today: Charisms in the Church for the World,* Middlegreen, Slough, St Pauls, 1994, 288 p.

VALDRINI, P. et al, *Droit canonique,* Paris, Dalloz, 1990, xxvi, 749 p.

VAN LIER, R., *Les nouvelles communautés religieuses dans lÉglise catholique du Quebec,* Quebec, Université Laval, 1996, 316 p.

VANDERWILT, J., *A Church without Borders,* Collegeville, MN, The

Liturgical Press, 1998, x, 189 p.

VENDRAME, C., *Essere religiosi oggi: Riflessioni di un superiore generale,* Roma, Edizioni Dehoniane, 1989, 317 p.

VERNAY, J., *Le droit dans l'Église catholique,* Paris, Desclée de Brouwer, 1995, 225 p.

VON BALTHASAR, H. URS, *Church and World,* translated by A.V. LITTLEDALE and A. DRU, MONTREAL, Palm Publishers, 1967, 176 p.

———, *Love Alone,* translated by A. DRU, New York, Herder and Herder, 1969, 124 p.

———, *New Elucidations,* translated by M.T. SKERRY, San Francisco, Ignatius Press, 1986, 305 p.

VON GALLI, M. (ed.), *The Council and the Future,* New York, McGraw Hill Book Company, 1966, 299 p.

VON SPEYR, A., *The Christian State of Life,* (ed. H. URS VON BALTHASAR), translated by M. F. MCCARTHY, San Francisco, Ignatius Press, 1986, 213 p.

VORGRIMLER, H., *Commentary on the Documents of Vatican II,* Freiburg, Herder and Herder, 1967-1969, 5 vols.

WALSH, D.A., *The New Law on Secular Institutes: A Historical Synopsis and a Commentary,* Washington, DC, Catholic University of America, 1953, xiii, 145 p.

WILBER, K., *A Sociable God,* New York, McGraw Hill, 1982, xiii, 160 p.

WILTGEN, R.M. (ed.), *The Religous Life Defined: An Official Commentary on the Deliberations of the Second Vatican Council,* Techny, IL, Divine Word Publications, 1970, 135 p.

WILTGEN, R.M., *The Rhine Flows into the Tiber: A History of Vatican II,* Devon, Augustine Publishing Co., 1979, 340 p.

WITTBERG, P., *Creating a Future for Religious Life: A Sociological Perspective*, New York, Paulist Press, 1991, vi, 185 p.

————, *The Rise and Fall of Catholic Religious Orders: A Social Movement Perspective*, Albany, State University of New York Press, 1994, xii, 423 p.

————, *Pathways to Re-creating Religious Communities*, New York, Paulist Press, 1996, iii, 266 p.

WOODWARD, E., *Poets, Prophets and Pragmatists: A New Challenge to Religious Life*, Notre Dame, Indiana, Ave Maria Press, 1987, 248 p.

WRIGHT, M., *The Canonical Development of the Institute of the Blessed Virgin Mary*, Sydney, Crossing Press, 1997, xvi, 248 p.

YUHAUS C.J., (ed.), *The Challenge for Tomorrow: Religious Life*, New York, Paulist Press, 1994, iv, 213 p.

4. Articles

ABBASS, J., "Forms of Consecrated Life Recognized in the Eastern and Latin Codes", in *Commentarium pro religiosis*, 76 (1995), pp. 5-38.

AMBROGI, T., "Goal for 2000: Unchaining Slaves of National Debt", in *National Catholic Reporter*, 26 March 1999, 35 (1999), pp. 3-5.

ANAND, S., "Consecrated Secularity: Theological Basis and Practical Implications", in *Vidyajyoti*, 59 (1995), pp. 145-160.

ANDRÉS, D.X., "Le innovazioni nel libro II parte III del nuovo Codice di diritto canonico sugli IVC e sulle SVA (cc. 573-746)", in *Vita consacrata*, 19 (1983), pp. 545-603.

ANDRÉS, D.X., "Innovazioni del Codice all'esterno degli Istituti di vita consacrata", in *Vita consacrata*, 20 (1984), pp. 37-60, 129-148.

ANSON, J., "The Female Transvestite in Early Monasticism: The Origin and Development of a Motif", in *Viator,* 5 (1974), pp. 1-32.

ARCHIBALD, R., et al, "Associate Relationship: An Emerging Sense of Identity", in *Review for Religious,* 56 (1997), pp. 295-301.

ARDITO, S., "Vita consacrata e vita religiosa nel nuovo Codice di diritto canonico: fondamento ecclesiologico e norme communi", in *Salesianum,* 47 (1985), pp. 529-554.

ARRAGAIN, J., "Est-il canoniquement possible que des Sociétés de vie apostolique soient des Instituts de vie consacrées?" in *Commentarium pro religiosis,* 69 (1988), pp. 31-53.

_____, "La Vie consacrée par la profession des conseils évangéliques", in *Claretianum,* 36 (1996), pp 259-283.

BALDUCCI, A.M., "The Co-responsibility of Sisters in Evangelization", in *Consecrated Life,* 17 (1992), pp. 168-171.

BANDERA, A., "*Vita consecrata*: Il numero iniziale", in *Vita consacrata,* 33 (1997), pp. 244-264.

——, "L'identità ecclesiale della vita religiosa", in *Vita consacrata,* 33 (1997), pp. 372-389.

BARBIERO, F., "La donna consacrata", in *Claretianum,* 35 (1995), pp. 176-180.

BARILE, R., "Battesimo e vita religiosa", in *Rivista di pastorale liturgica,* 34 (1996), pp. 47-57.

BETTI, U., "Si sono consacrati a te", in *L'Osservatore romano,* 3 July 1996, n.150, pp. 1, 4.

BEYER, J., "Religious Life or Secular Institute", in *Supplement to the Way,* 7 (1969), pp.112-132.

—— , "The New Law of the Church for Institutes of Consecrated Life II", in *The Way Supplement,* 23 (1974), pp. 75-96.

BEYER, J., "Le deuxième projet de droit pour la vie consacrée", in *Studia canonica,* 15 (1981), pp. 87-134.

_____, "Religious in the New Code and Their Place in the LocalChurch", in *Studia canonica,*17 (1983), pp. 171-183.

_____, "De novo iure circa vitae consecratae instituta et eorum sodales quaesita et dubia solvenda", in *Periodica,* 73 (1984), pp. 411-450, 525-554.

_____, "*Redemptionis donum:* un documento di attissimo valore che spiega la legislazione del Codice nuovo", in *Vita consacrata,* 21 (1985), pp. 158-176.

_____, "Religiosi e chiesa locale da *"Mutuae relationes"* al nuovo Codice", in *Vita consacrata,* 21 (1985), pp. 840-859.

_____, "I movimenti ecclesiali", in *Vita consacrata,* 23 (1987), pp. 238-252.

_____, "Il nuovo diritto dei religiosi e la vita associativa della Chiesa", in *Vita consacrata,* 24 (1988), pp. 344-358, 826-839.

_____, "La pratica dei consigli evangelici", in *Vita consacrata,* 26 (1990), pp. 677-684.

_____, "Charisms, Religious Institutes and Particular Churches", in *Consecrated Life,* 15 (1990), pp. 315-329.

_____, "Vita associativa e corresponsibilità ecclesiale", in *Vita consacrata,* 26 (1990), pp. 923-941.

_____, "I movimenti nuovi nella Chiesa", in *Vita consacrata,* 27 (1991), pp. 61-77.

_____, "La vita consacrata in Occidente", in *Vita consacrata,* 28 (1992), pp. 358-369.

_____, "La Chiesa si interroga sulla vita consacrata", in *Quaderni di diritto ecclesiale,* 6 (1993), pp. 363-387.

BEYER, J. "La vita consacrata: prospettive di avvenire", in *Vita consacrata,* 30 (1994), pp. 696-715.

———, "Il Sinodo dei Vescovi sulla vita consacrata 2-29 ottobre 1994", in *Quaderni di diritto ecclesiale,* 8 (1995), pp. 143-153.

———, "La clausura", in *Quaderni di diritto ecclesiale,* 10 (1997), pp. 230-236.

BISIGNANO, S., "A New Way of Talking about Formation", in *Consecrated Life,* 16 (1991), pp.1-12.

BOAGA, E., "La clausura. Origine e sviluppo storico-giuridico-spirituale", in *Vita consacrata,* 29 (1993), pp. 492-512.

BÖHLER, H., "Vita consacrata e Chiesa particolare", in *Quaderni di diritto ecclesiale,* 10 (1997), pp. 355-364.

BOISVERT, L., "La consécration religieuse", in *La vie des communautés religieuses,* 52 (1994), pp. 3-14.

———, "La consécration d'après l'Exhortation apostolique", in *La vie des communautés religieuses,* 54 (1996), pp. 229-240.

———, "Conseils et voeux", in *La vie des communautés religieuses,* 57 (1999), pp. 67-77.

BONADIO, J. DE LA CROIX "Notes Toward a Definition of the Secular Institute", in *The Way Supplement,* 12 (1971), pp. 16-23.

BONFILS, J., "*'Mutuae relationes'* - Ten Years Later", in *Consecrated Life,* 17 (1992), pp. 122-134.

BONI, A., "Codice e costitutizioni religiose nel nuovo ordinamento giuridico della Chiesa", in *Apollinaris,* 58 (1985), pp. 451-508.

BORRAS, A., "Le droit canonique et la vitalité des communautés nouvelles", in *Nouvelle revue théologique,* 118 (1996), pp. 200-218.

Braux, J., "Pour les communautés nouvelles, quel statut?", in *Les cahiers du droit ecclésial,* 4 (1987) pp. 121-137.

Brink, L., "Another Woman Religious Breaks Camp", in *National Catholic Reporter,* 18 February 2000, pp. 22-23.

Burke, P.J., "The Spirituality of Taizé", in *Spirituality Today,* 42 (1990), pp. 233-245, <http://www.op.org/domcentral/library/spir2day/90423burke.htm> (10 March 2000).

Cabra, P.G., "A Reflection for the Synod on the Consecrated Life", in *Consecrated Life,* 19 (1995), pp. 45-59.

————, "La nuova evangelizzazione", in *Informationes SCRIS,* 20-21 (1994-1995), (combined edition), pp. 164 – 173.

Cain, J.R., "Cloister and the Apostolate of Religious Women", in *Review for Religious,* 27 (1968), pp. 243-280, 427-448, 652-671, 916-937; 28(1969) pp. 101-121.

Callahan, S., "A Witness of Unique Witnessing", in *Review for Religious,* 57 (1998), pp. 138-145.

Cantalamessa, R., "The Ideal of Separation from the World in Religious Life Today", in *Consecrated Life,* 17 (1992), pp. 99-115.

Castaño, J., "Consécration et sécularité dans les instituts séculiers", in *Dialogue,* 5 (1977), pp. 9-15.

————, "Lo 'status consecratorum' nell'attuale legislazione della Chiesa", in *Angelicum,* 60 (1983), pp. 190-223.

————, "'Condicio laicalis' e 'status consecratorum' nel nuovo Codice", in *Angelicum,* 65 (1988), pp. 325-339.

Castillo-Lara, R., "De ecclesialitate vitae religiosae in Codice iuris canonici", in *Periodica,* 74 (1985), pp. 419-437.

Champagne, C., "La nouvelle évangélisation: la pensée de Jean-Paul II", in *Kerygma,* 26 (1992), pp. 247-270.

CHOLVY, G., "Crise révolutionnaire et initiatives religieuses féminines dans la France du XIXe siècle", in *Vie consacrée,* 69 (1997), pp. 43-56.

COATES, K., "Speaking out for the World's Poorest People", in *The Month,* 259 (1998), pp. 219-221.

CODY, A., "The New Canons on Consecrated Life and the Mind of the Council", in *Concilium,* 147 (1981), pp. 64-88.

COMUNITÀ MARIANA "OASI DELLA PACE", "Nuove Forme di vita consacrata: Communità mariana 'Oasi della pace'", in *Vita consacrata,* 34 (1998), pp. 181-196.

CONGRESS OF MOVEMENTS, "The Ecclesial Movements: Communion and Mission on the Threshold of the Third Millennium, Rome 27-29 May 1998", <http://www.newevng.org/mov/english/congreso.htm> (8 March 2000).

CONNER, P.M., *Vita consecrata*: An Ultimate Theology of the Consecrated Life", in *Angelicum,* 76 (1999), pp. 245-273.

CONNOR, E., "The Royal Abbey of Las Huelgas and the Jurisdiction of its Abbesses", in *Cistercian Studies,* 23 (1988), pp.128-155.

CONTI, M., "La vita consacrata e la sua missione nella chiesa e nel mondo", in *Antonianum,* 68 (1993), pp. 45-90.

CORDES, P.J., "Nouveaux mouvements spirituels dans l'Église", in *Nouvelle revue théologique,* 109 (1987), pp. 49-65.

COTIGNOLI, C., "Nuove forme di vita consacrata; Il movimento dei focolari", in *Vita consacrata,* 34 (1998), pp. 521-530.

COUNCIL OF THE "16", "An Overall View of the Document *Mutual Relations*", in *Consecrated Life,* 18 (1993), pp. 115-132.

DAGENS, C., "Les mouvements spirituels contemporains: Jalons pour un discernment", in *Nouvelle revue théologique,* 106 (1984), pp. 885-899.

DALBESIO, A., "La vita religiosa come attuazione della sequela radicale di cristo secondo il nuovo testamenti", in *Antonianum,* 68 (1993), pp. 301-326.

DAMMERTZ, V., "Gli istituti di vita consacrata nel nuovo Codice di Diritto canonico", in *Vita consacrata,* 19 (1983), pp. 110-136.

———, "What Do Religious Expect of Bishops?" in *Consecrated Life,* 14 (1989), pp. 11-16.

DARRICAU, R et B. PEYROUS, "Les communautés nouvelles en France", in *Nouvelle revue théologique,* 109 (1987), pp. 712-729.

DE PAOLIS, V., "The New Forms of Consecrated Life", in *Consecrated Life,* 19 (1996), pp. 62-85.

———, "Associations Founded with the Intent of Becoming Religious Institutes", in *Consecrated Life,* 20-21 (1999) (combined edition), pp. 158-183.

DELANEY, A., "Bishops and Religious — the Document *Mutuae relationes*", in *The Furrow,* 34 (1983), pp. 233- 241.

DIIANNI, A., "Religious Vocations: New Signs of the Times", in *Review for Religious,* 52 (1993), pp. 745-763.

———, "Religious Life: Directions for a Future", in *Review for Religious,* 55 (1996), pp. 342-364.

DION, M-P., "Les effets du rite de la consécration des vierges", in *Église et Théologie,* 16 (1985), pp. 275-318.

———, "La virginité", in *Église et Théologie,* 17 (1986), pp. 5-39.

DORRONSORO, J., "Cinquantesimo della 'Provida Mater'", in *Informationes SCRIS,* 23 (1997), pp. 53-68.

DORTEL-CLAUDOT, M., "Le strutture di governo e di partecipazione delle Congregazioni religiose", in *Vita consacrata,* 21 (1985), pp. 773-792.

DORTEL-CLAUDOT, M., "The Evolution of the Canonical Status of Religious Institutes with Simple Vows from the 16th Century Until the New Code", in *Periodica,* 74 (1985), pp. 439-458.

DOWNEY, M., "In the Ache of Absence: Spirituality at the Juncture of Modernity and Postmodernity", in *Liturgical Ministry,* 3 (1994), pp. 92-99.

DOYLE, T.P., "The Canonical Status of Religious Institutes: Additional Considerations", in *Monitor ecclesiasticus,* 110 (1985), pp. 227-245.

DUBAY, T., "Consecrated Life in the New Canon Law", in *Homiletics and Pastoral Review,* 83 (1983), pp. 9-15.

DUBAY, T., "Religious Life in the New Code of Canon Law", in *Homiletics and Pastoral Review,* 84 (1984), pp. 55-59.

DULLES, A., "John Paul II and the New Evangelization", in *America,* 166 (1992), pp. 52-59, 69-72.

EDITORIAL COMMENT, "East of Eden", in *The Month,* 247 (1986), pp. 316-317.

ERRÁZURIZ, F., "An Event of Grace", in *Consecrated Life,* 19 (1996), pp. 29-44.

ETZI, P., "Il concetto di 'consacrazione religiosa' nel supremo magistero dal concilio vaticano II all'esortazione apostolica post-sinodale 'Vita consecrata'", in *Antonianum,* 72 (1997), pp. 571-602.

EUART, S.A., "A Canonical Analysis of *Essential Elements* in Light of the 1983 Code of Canon Law", in *The Jurist,* 15 (1985), pp. 438-501.

————, "Religious Institutes and the Juridical Relationship of the Members to the Institute", in *The Jurist,* 51 (1991), pp.103-118.

FAGIOLO, V., "Appartenenza *iure divino* della vita consacrata alla costituzione della Chiesa", in *Vita consacrata,* 21 (1985), pp. 424-430.

FAGIOLO, V., "The Conferences of Major Superiors in the Discussions of the Council", in *Consecrated Life,* 14 (1989), pp. 25-36.

FEDELE, G., "L'Opera della Chiesa: una famiglia ecclesiale nuovo e profetico dono di vita consacrata", in *L'Osservatore romano,* 16 November 1990, p. 5.

FERNANDES DE ARAÚJO, S., "Le 'Nuove comunità' o 'Famiglie ecclesiali'", in archival ms, p. 1-3; Summary and translation in *L'Osservatore romano,* (English edition), 2 November 1994, p. 20.

FERRARI, S. e F. TRAPLETTI, "Le forme della proposta dei movimenti religiosi alternative: utenza, consonanza, adesione", in *Quaderni di diritto ecclesiale,* 3 (1999), pp. 310-330.

FINKE, R., "The Rewards of a Costly Religious Community", in *Review for Religious,* 56 (1997), pp. 412-427.

FINN, T.J., "An Old Entity: A New Name: Societies of Apostolic Life", in *Studia canonica,* 20 (1986), pp. 439-456.

FOLEY, N., "The Nature and Future of Religious Life", in *Religious Life Review,* 29 (1990), pp. 70-79.

FREUND, J., "From Parchment to Cyberspace: New Technologies Can Serve Charisms", in *Review for Religious,* 56 (1997), pp. 491-502.

FUERTES, I.B., "Status matrimonialis, status religiosus?" in *Commentarium pro religiosis,* 57 (1976), pp. 3-38.

FUERTES, I.B., "Religio-Religiosus", in *Commentarium pro religiosis,* 68 (1987), pp. 125-150.

GALANTE, J.A., "Consecrated Life: New Forms and New Institutes", in *CLSA Proceedings,* 48 (1986), pp. 118-125.

GALLAGHER, C., "The Church and Institutes of Consecrated Life", in *The Way Supplement,* 50 (1984), pp. 3-15.

GALLEN, J.F., "Canon Law for Religious after Vatican II: *Mutuae relationes"*, in *Review for Religious,* 39 (1980), pp. 105-111.

GALOT, J., "Valore e necessità della vita consacrata", in *Vita consacrata,* 32 (1996), pp. 108-119.

———, "Challenges and Obligations", in *Consecrated Life,* 22 (1999), pp. 103-117.

GAMBARI, E., "La Costituzione *'Lumen gentium'* e la vita religiosa", in *Vita religiosa,* 2 (1966), pp. 34-44.

———, "The Canonical Establishment of a Religious Institute: Process and Procedures", Florence, Artigraf, 1999, xiv, 220 p. English translation by M. M. ARMATO and T. BLESSIN.

GHIRLANDA, G., "La tipologia degli Istituti di vita consacrata dal Concilio al nuovo Codice", in *Vita consacrata,* 21 (1985), pp. 210-227.

———, "Iusta autonomia et exemptio Institutorum religiosarum: fundamenta et extensio", in *Periodica,* 78 (1989), pp. 113-142.

———, "Relations Between Religious Institutes and Diocesan Bishops", in *Consecrated Life,* 14 (1989), pp. 37-71.

———, "Les formes de consécration à la lumière du nouveau Code", in *Documents épiscopat: Bulletin du sécretariat de la Conférence des Évêques de France,* 3 (1990), pp. 69-79.

———, "La vita consacrata nel Codice di diritto canonico", in *Credere oggi,* 66 (1991), pp. 93-105.

———, "Charisma di un istituto e sua tutela", in *Vita consacrata,* 28 (1992), pp. 465-477, 554-562.

———, "*L'instrumentum laboris* per il Sinodo sulla vita consacrata", in *Periodica,* 83 (1995), pp. 437-446.

———, "Dimensione ecclesiologica della vita consacrata nel Sinodo dei Vescovi del 1994", in *Periodica,* 84 (1995), pp. 655-685.

GHIRLANDA, G., "'Istituti misti' e nuove aggregazioni", in *Quaderni di diritto ecclesiale,* 9 (1996), pp. 483-494.

_____, "L'Esortazione apostolica *'Vita consecrata':* aspetti teologici ed ecclesiologici", in *Periodica,* 85 (1996), pp. 555-596.

_____, "L'Esortazione apostolica *'Vita consecrata':* aspetti canonici", in *Periodica,* 85 (1996), pp. 555-596.

_____, "La vie consacrée dans l'église", in *Vie consacrée,* 68 (1996), pp. 88-101.

_____, "The Consecrated Life in the Church", in *Consecrated Life,* 20-21 (1999), (combined edition), pp. 86-122.

GIRARDI, O.G., "Vita consacrata e Chiesa locale", in *Quaderni di diritto ecclesiale,* 6 (1993), pp. 388-402.

GIROTTI, G., "Apostolato degli Istituti di vita consacrata", in *Monitor ecclesiasticus,* 110 (1985), pp. 119-138.

GONZALEZ SILVA, S.M., "In the Church and for the Church", in *Consecrated Life,* 22 (1999), pp. 41-67.

GOTTEMOELLER, D., "Looking at Associate Membership To-day", in *Review for Religious,* 50 (1991), pp. 390-397.

_____, "Apostolic Women Religious: Identity and Mission", in *Origins,* 24 (1994-1995), pp. 325-326.

_____, "*Vita consecrata:* The Post-synodal Exhortation on Consecrated Life", in *CLSA Proceedings,* 58 (1996), pp. 176-186.

_____, "Religious Life: Where Does It fit in Today's Church?" in *Review for Religious,* 57 (1998), pp. 146-160.

GRANFIELD, P., "Changes in Religious Life: Freedom, Responsibility, Community", in *America,* 161 (1984), pp 120-123.

GREGERSEN, N.H., "The Idea of Creation and the Theory of Autopoietic

Processes", in *Zygon: Journal of Religion and Science,* 33 (1998), pp. 333-367.

GUERRO, J.M., "L'engagement socio-politique et la vie religieuse", in *Vie consacrée,* 56 (1984), pp. 345-357.

GUTIERREZ, A., "Professio religiosa ad tempus", in *Commentarium pro religiosis,* 64 (1983), pp. 107-123.

————, "Lo stato della vita consacrata: valori permanenti e innovazioni", in *Monitor ecclesiasticus,* 110 (1985), pp. 37-63.

HALSTEAD, J., "Attachment, Belonging, and Membership: Commitment Styles in Male Religious Communities", in *Review for Religious,* 54 (1995), pp. 881-903.

HAMER, J., "De munere Episcopi erga vitam religiosam", in *Commentarium pro religiosis,* 67 (1986), pp. 136-139.

————, "Religious Life and Evangelization", in *Consecrated Life,* 17 (1992), pp. 77-81.

HAUSMAN, N., "La vie religieuse apostolique comme vie ecclésiale", in *Vie consacrée,* 56 (1984), pp. 331-344.

————, "Sur le rapport de la vie consacrée avec les conseils évangéliques", in *Vie consacrée,* 68 (1996), pp. 252-264.

HENNAUX, J-M., "Consécration des vierges et hiérarchie", in *Vie consacrée,* 61 (1989), pp. 239-242.

HERR, É., "La mondialisation: pour une évaluation éthique?", in *Nouvelle revue théologique,* 122 (2000), pp. 51-67.

HIMES, M., "Returning to Our Ancestral Lands", in *Review for Religious,* 59 (2000), pp. 6-25.

HINNEBUSCH, P., "Is an Outmoded Rule a Holy Rule?", in *Sisters Today,* 37 (1966), pp. 295-303.

HINNEBUSCH, W., "Origins and Development of Religious Orders", in *Review for Religious,* 28 (1969), pp. 910-930, 29 (1970), pp. 59-78.

HOGAN, W.F., "Canonical Room for Charisms", in D.L. FLEMING and E. McDONOUGH (eds), *The Church and Consecrated Life,* St. Louis, MO, Review for Religious, 1996, viii, 440 p.

HOLLAND, S., "Religious Life", in *Chicago Studies,* 23 (1984), pp. 77-96.

———, "Instituta saecularia et Codex 1983", in *Periodica,* 74 (1985), pp. 511-534.

———, "Secular Institutes: Can They Be Both Clerical and Lay?", in *CLSA Proceedings,* 49 (1988), pp. 135-144.

———, "Consecrated Virgins for Today's Church", in *Informationes SCRIS,* 24 (1998), pp. 72-91.

HOURCADE, J., "L'ordre des vierges consacrées", in *Vie consacrée,* 65 (1993), pp. 297-301.

HUFTIER, M., "Le Code de droit canonique: les Instituts de vie consacrée selon le Code", in *Esprit et vie,* 84 (1984), pp. 254-255.

HUME, G.B., *Relatio post disceptationem,* Rome, e. Civitate Vaticana, 1994, 32 p.

———, "Note on Church Teaching Concerning Homosexual People", in *Origins,* 24 (1994-1995), pp. 765, 767-769.

———, "Relatio ante disceptationem", in *Consecrated Life,* 20-21 (1999) (combined edition), pp. 61-85.

IGLESIAS, F., "Fraternal Life in Common", in *Consecrated Life,* 16 (1991), pp. 113-131.

INSTITUTE OF ST. JOSEPH, *To Make God Present to the World, and the World Present to God,* Chippewa Falls, Institute of St. Joseph, 1987, pp. 1-11.

INTERNATIONAL LABOUR ORGANIZATION: WORKING PARTY ON THE SOCIAL DIMENSIONS OF THE LIBERALIZATION OF INTERNATIONAL TRADE, "Final Report: Globalization: Perceptions, Definition and Measurement", November 1999, <http://www.ilo.org/public/english/standards/relm/gb/docs/gb276/sdl-1.htm> (3 May 2000).

JARRELL, L., "The Legal and Historical Context of Religious Life for Women", in *The Jurist*, 45 (1985), pp. 419-437.

JASINSKI, R.M., "The Associate Movement in Religious Life", in *Review for Religious*, 49 (1990), pp. 353-357.

——, "Envisioning Associate Identity", in *Review for Religious*, 51 (1992), pp. 575-580.

JOHANNING, M., "Mission, A Constitutive Element of Apostolic Life", in *UISG Bulletin (Special Supplement)*, 62 (1964), pp. 50-55.

JOHNSON, E., "Between the Times: Religious Life and the Postmodern Experience of God", in *Review for Religious*, 53 (1994), pp. 6-28.

KALLUMKAL, J., "The Patrimony of an Institute", in *Commentarium pro religiosis*, 70 (1989), pp. 263-303.

KASPER, W., "Church as *Communio*," in *Communio: International Catholic Review*, 13 (1986), pp. 100-117.

——, "The Church as Sacrament of Unity", in *Communio: International Catholic Review*, 14 (1987), pp. 4-11.

KING, M.H., "The Desert Mothers: A Survey of the Feminine Anchoretic Tradition in Western Europe", <http://www.peregrina.com/matrologia/ desertmothers.html> (5 June 2000).

KOBLER, J.F., "Toward a History of Vatican II", in *Chicago Studies*, 38 (1999), pp. 17-191.

KOLVENBACH, P.H., "La vita consacrata è un dono dello Spirito!" in *Vita consacrata*, 31 (1995), pp. 419-429.

LAUDAZI, C., "La vita consacrata nella dimensione ecclesiale", in *Vita consacrata,* 33 (1997), pp. 170-191.

LAZZATI, K., "Pluralism Amongst Secular Institutes", in *The Way Supplement,* 12 (1971), pp. 73-80.

———, "Consacrazione e secolarità", in *Vita consacrata,* 7 (1971), pp. 294-306.

LECLERCQ, H., "The Second Council of Nicaea", <http://www. newadvent.org/ cathen/11045a.htm> (15 March 2000).

LECLERQ, J., "Nouvelle formes de vie religieuse. Histoire et actualité", in *Vie consacrée,* 58 (1986), pp. 107-112.

LEROY, H., "Chronique du droit de la vie consacrée", in *L'Année canonique,* 40 (1998), pp. 269-291.

LESAGE, G., "The Principle of Subsidiarity: A New Way of Governing: A Psycho-Canonical Study", in *Consultations,* 1 (1968), Ottawa, Canadian Conference of Religious, pp. 3-20.

LINSCOTT, M., "The Personal Identity of the Apostolic Woman Religious", in *Consecrated Life,* pp. 13-25.

———, "Leadership, Authority and Religious Government", in *Review for Religious,* 52 (1993), pp. 166-193.

LOBO, G., "Vie religieuse en Inde", in *Vie consacrée,* 57 (1985), pp. 28-36.

LORENZONI, L.N., "The *Annuario Pontificio:* The Vatican's 'Pontifical Yearbook' and a Recent Editorial Decision", in *Review for Religious,* 58 (1999), pp. 261-265.

MCDERMOTT, R., "Women in the New Code", in *The Way Supplement,* 50 (1984), pp. 27-37.

———, "Recent Developments in Consecrated Life", in *Bulletin on Issues of Religious Law,* 9 (1993), pp. 1-9.

McDermott, R., "Two Approaches to Consecrated Life: The *Code of Canons of the Eastern Churches* and the *Code of Canon Law*", in *Studia canonica,* 29 (1995), pp. 193-239.

————, "The Ninth Ordinary Session of the Synod of Bishops: Four Moments and Six Canonical Issues", in *Commentarium pro religiosis,* 77 (1996), pp. 261 - 294.

————, "*Vita consacrata:* A Vocation for the Third Millennium", in *Review for Religious,* 55 (1996), pp. 454-461.

————, "Recent Developments in Consecrated Life", in *Selected Issues in Religious Law,* P. Cogan (ed.), Washington, DC, Canon Law Society of America, 1997, 168 p.

MacDonald, H.L., "Hermits: The Juridical Implications of Canon 603", in *Studia canonica,* 26 (1992), pp. 163-189.

McDonough, E., "The Past is Prologue: Quid agis?", in *Review for Religious,* 51 (1992), pp. 78-97.

————, "Hermits and Virgins", in *Review for Religious,* 51 (1992), pp. 303-308.

————, "*Lumen gentium's* Chapter 6: Religious", in *Review for Religious,* 52 (1993), pp. 927- 932.

————, "The Conciliar Decree *Perfectae caritatis*", in *Review for Religious,* 53 (1994), pp. 143-148.

————, "Life Consecrated by Profession of the Evangelical Counsels", in *Review for Religious,* 57 (1998), pp. 94-99.

McIntyre, J.P., "*Lineamenta* for a Christian Anthropology: Canons 208-223", in *Periodica,* 85 (1996), pp. 249-276.

McSweeney, A., "Consecrated for Mission", in *Consecrated Life,* 17 (1992), pp. 125-133.

————, "Charisms in the Church for the World: Consecrated Life Today", in *Consecrated Life,* 19 (1996), pp. 44-61.

MALVAUX, B., "La vie consacrée, signe de communion dans l'Église", in *Vie consacrée,* 69 (1997), pp. 161-174.

———, "Les relations mutuelles entre évêques et instituts religieux: quelques propositions canoniques à la suite du Synode sur la vie consacrée et de l'Exhortation apostolique postsynodale *Vita consecrata*", in *Studia canonica,* 32 (1998), pp. 293-320.

MANCUSO, T., "The Urban Hermit: Monastic Life in the City", in *Review for Religious,* 55 (1996), pp. 133-142.

MARCHETTI, A., "Avremo religiosi sposati?", in *Rivista di vita spirituale,* 25 (1971), pp. 643-646.

MARKHAM, D., "Religious Life To-morrow", in *Human Development,* 18 (1997), pp. 5-9.

———, "Leadership for the Common Good", in *Review for Religious,* 57 (1998), pp. 34-47.

MARTINEZ SAEZ, J., "Fraternità 'Verbum Dei'", in *Vita consacrata,* 34 (1998), pp. 87-97.

MARTINEZ SOMALO, E., "Animated by the Spirit in Service of the Missions", in *Consecrated Life,* 19 (1995), pp. 35-44.

———, "Conformity to Christ", in *Consecrated Life,* 19 (1996), pp. 25-28.

———, "Presentation of the Apostolic Exhortation, *Vita consecrata*", in *Consecrated Life,* 22 (1999), pp. 1-9.

MARTINI, C.M., "Verso nuove forme di vita consacrata? *I.L.* 37 e 38", in archival ms, pp. 1-2; Summary and translation in *L'Osservatore romano,* (English edition), 16 November 1994, p. 7.

MEYERS, B., "Fire, Flood, Earthquake – *Sursum Corda,* Sisters", in *Sisters Today,* 10 (1967), pp. 333-344.

MIDALI, M., "La theologia della vita consacrata dal Vaticano II a oggi", in *Vita consacrata,* 28 (1992), pp. 312-327.

MIDALI, M., "Verso una comprensione teologica corale delle varie forme di vita consacrata", in *Vita consacrata,* 32 (1996), pp. 363-383.

MILLIGAN, M., "The Future of Apostolic Religious Life", in *The Way Supplement,* 23 (1974), pp. 68-74.

MOLINARI, P., *"Perfectae caritatis* — Introduction and Commentary", in *Supplement to the Way,* 2 (1966), pp. 3-64.

MOLONEY, F., "Religious Life Beyond 2000", private ms, lecture given in Perth, Australia, September 1998, 25 p.

MONROE, T.M., "Reclaiming Competence", in *Review for Religious,* 51 (1992), pp. 432-452.

MORLOT, F., "Un statut original: les laics consacrés dans un institut séculier", in *L'année canonique,* 29 (1986), pp. 141-151.

———, "Qu'est-ce que la vie consacrée? Une description à partir de 'Vita consecrata'" in *Vie consacrée,* 69 (1997), pp. 29-42.

MORRISEY, F., "Canon 303 and the Establishment of Third Orders and Related Associations", in *Informationes SCRIS,* 25 (1999), pp. 74-92.

MUELLER, J.J., "Second-Stage Inculturation: Six Principles of the American Mind", in *Review for Religious,* 53 (1994), pp. 658-674.

MUNLEY, A., "Community and Prophetic Witness", in *Review for Religious,* 56 (1997), pp. 143-155.

———, "Hearts Afire: Leadership in the New Millennium", in *Review for Religious,* 57 (1998), pp. 48-59.

NERI, A., "Il can. 605 CIC e le nuove forme di vita consacrata", in *Claretianum,* 36 (1996), pp. 445-496.

NINTH ORDINARY SESSION OF THE SYNOD OF BISHOPS, "Message of the Synod on Consecrated Life", in *L'Osservatore romano,* (English edition), 2 November 1994, pp. 6-7.

NONA ASSEMBLEA GENERALE ORDINARIA DEL SINODO DEI VESCOVI, "*Propositiones* del sinodo al papa: Identità, comunione, missione", in *Il regno-documenti,* 21 (1994), pp. 662-673.

OBERTI, A., "Gli Istituti secolari nel nuovo Codice di diritto canonico", in *Monitor ecclesiasticus,* 110 (1985), pp. 171-180.

————, "A cinquant'anni dalla *'Provida Mater'"*, in *Vita consacrata,* 33 (1997), pp. 35-50.

O'CONNOR, D.F., "Two Forms of Consecrated Life: Religious and Secular Institutes", in *Review for Religious,* 45 (1986), pp. 205-219.

O'DONOHUE, J., "To Awaken the Divinity Within: Towards a New Theory of Evangelization", in *The Way,* 34 (1994), pp. 265-272

O'LEARY, B., "Prophecy, Refounding, Conversion", in *Review for Religious,* 49 (1990), pp. 707-713.

————, "Discernment and Decision Making", in *Review for Religious,* 51 (1992), pp. 56-63.

O'MALLEY, J.W., "To Travel to any Part of the World: Jeronimo Nadal and the Jesuit Vocation", in *Studies in the Spirituality of the Jesuits,* 16/2(1984), pp. 1-20.

————, "Priesthood, Ministry, and Religious Life: Some Historical and Historiographical Considerations", in *Theological Studies,* 49 (1988), pp. 223-257.

O'MURCHÚ, D., "Whither Religious Life: Missing Dimensions of the *FORUS* Study", in *Sisters To-Day,* 66 (1994), pp. 354-360.

O'NEILL, U., "Community for Mission", in *The Way Supplement,* 61 (1988), pp. 62-75.

O'REGAN, J., "Religious Community: Group or Association - or What?" in *Études Oblates,* 28 (1969), pp.231-239.

PAGÉ, R., "Note sur les 'critères d'ecclésialité pour les associations de laïcs'", in *Studia canonica,* 24 (1990), pp. 455-463.

PARDILLA, A., "Theological Identity of Religious Life", in *Consecrated Life,* 12 (1987), pp. 243-262.

PARIJIS, J-M., "Communautés religieuses et fidélités apostoliques", in *Vie consacrée,* 63 (1991), pp. 386-400.

PASINI, S.M., "Vita consacrata e consigli evangelici (I): Il concetto teologico-giuridico di 'Vita consacrata'", in in *Commentarium pro religiosis,* 77 (1996), pp. 157-177.

———, "Vita consacrata e consigli evangelici (II): La distinzione tra 'consacrazione' e 'professione'", in *Commentarium pro religiosis,* 77 (1996), pp. 345-361.

PASSICOS, J., "Catégories canoniques, nouvelles communautés et nouveaux mouvements religieux", in *L'année canonique,* 36 (1994), pp. 49-55.

PEDRETTI, A., "Una prospettiva per le nuove forme di vita consacrata presente nel canone 605", in *Commentarium pro religiosis,* 80 (1999), pp. 155-175.

PFAB, J., "Neue Formen des geweihten Lebens", in S. HAERING, (Hg.), *In unum congregati: Festgabe für Augustinus Kardinal Mayer OSB zur Vollendung des 80. Lebensjahres,* Metten, Abtei-Verlag, 1991, 604 p.

———, "The Particular Church and the Consecrated Life", in *Consecrated Life,* 19 (1995), pp. 59-68.

PIAT, M., "Commentaire de la bulle *Conditae,* de Léon XIII, sur les instituts à voeux simples", in *Nouvelle revue théologique,* 33 (1901), pp. 453-470, 565-573.

PIERCE, B., "The Vatican II Generation and Religious Life", in *Review for Religious,* 56 (1997), pp. 14-27.

PIGNA, A., "Sulla teologia della consecrazione", in *Vita consacrata,* 31 (1995), pp. 515-536.

—————, "Fondamenti teologici della vita consacrata", in *Rivista di vita spirituale,* 51 (1997), pp. 72-97.

PINHEIRO, A., "Bishop-Religious Relationship: The 'Apostolic Subjection' of Religious to the Power of the Diocesan Bishop in the Exercise of Apostolic Activities in the Diocese (c. 678 §§1&2)", in *Commentarium pro religiosis,* 68 (1987), pp. 35-76.

POGGI, A., "New Institutes", in *Consecrated Life,* 11 (1986), pp. 262-269.

POLI, G.F., "Bibliografia sul sinodo", in *Vita consacrata,* 31 (1995), pp. 9-51; pp. 196-200; p. 276.

POZO, C., "The Theology of the Consecrated Life at the Recent Synod of Bishops", in *Consecrated Life,* 20-21 (1999), (combined edition), pp. 122-131.

RACICOT, L., *La Société du Christ Seigneur: une forme de vie consacrée pour les laïcs,* Montréal, Centre Leunis, 1994, 28 p.

—————, "La Société du Christ Seigneur: Une nouvelle forme de vie consacrée", in *La vie des communautés religieuses,* 57 (1999), pp. 78-93.

RADCLIFFE, T., "Inculturation", in *Review for Religious,* 53 (1994), pp. 646-657.

RATZINGER, J., "The Theological Locus of Ecclesial Movements", in *Communio: International Catholic Review,* 25 (1998), pp. 480-504.

RECCHI, S., "La natura della consacrazione mediante i consigli evangelici nel Codice", in *Vita consacrata,* 24 (1988), pp. 740-755.

—————, "Il verbo 'accedere' nei cc. 694 e 731 del Codice di diritto canonico", in *Vita consacrata,* 26 (1990), pp. 950-965.

RECCHI, S., "L'ordine delle vergini", in *Quaderni di diritto ecclesiale,* 5 (1992), pp. 141-150.

————, "La missione della vita consacrata nella Chiesa missione", in *Quaderni di diritto ecclesiale,* 6 (1993), pp. 403-411.

————, "La consacrazione mediante i consigli evangelici nel dibattito sinodale", in *Quaderni di diritto ecclesiale,* 8 (1995), pp. 154-164.

————, "Le nuove forme di vita consacrata", in *Vita consacrata,* 32 (1996), pp. 666-674; 33 (1997), pp. 676-686.

————, "Assunzione dei consigli evangelici e consacrazione di vita nelle associazioni" in *Quaderni di diritto ecclesiale,* 12 (1999), pp. 339-352.

RÉGAMEY, P.R., "Carismi", (art.) in G. PELLICCIA e G. ROCCA, *Dizionario degli istituti di perfezione,* Roma, Edizioni Paoline, 1975, vol. 2, pp. 299-315,

REGAN, T., "New Needs... New Paradigms: the Changing Character of Religious Life", in *Review for Religious,* 49 (1990), pp. 220-226.

REISER, W., "Reformulating the Religious Vows", in *Review for Religious,* 54 (1995), pp. 594-599.

RENKEN, J., "The Ecclesiology of *Communio* as Hermeneutic for Canon Law", in Lecture presented at Saint Paul University, 14 February 2000, 30 p.

Report of the Congress of the Large Family of the Daughters of Saint Angela Merici, Rome, privately printed, 1968, 180 p.

RINERE, E., "Dialogue Between Bishops and Religious", in *Review for Religious,* 45 (1986), pp. 368-375.

ROCCA, G., "Le nuova comunità", in *Quaderni di diritto ecclesiale,* 5 (1992), pp. 163-176.

ROFE, D., "Journey into Freedom", in *The Way Supplement,* 53 (1985), pp. 4-13.

ROSANNA, E., "The Synod's Discussion of the Consecrated Life of Women", in *Consecrated Life,* 20-21 (1999), (combined edition), pp. 191-208.

SAMMON, S.D., "Last Call for Religious Life", in *Human Development,* 20 (1999), pp. 12-27.

SASTRE SANTOS, E., "Votum castitatis coniugalis, votum religiosum", in *Commentarium pro religiosis,* 58 (1977), pp. 246-260; 59 (1978), pp. 50-65; 60 (1979), pp. 46-87.

———, "Communio institutorum vitae consecratae cum Sede Apostolica", in *Commentarium pro religiosis,* 66 (1985), pp. 5-41.

———, "Some Suggestions on the Concept of the *Vita apostolica"*, in *Commentarium pro religiosis,* 67 (1986), pp. 387-394.

———, "The Diocesan and Pontifical Approval of an Institute of Consecrated Life", in *Consecrated Life,* 15 (1990), pp. 41-63.

———, "Las nuevas formas de vida consagrada. Variaciones sobre el canon 605", in *Claretianum,* 35 (1995), pp. 7-141.

———, "On Church Approbation of Religious Institutes and of their Rules and Constitutions: (*Historical excursus)*", in *Consecrated Life,* 21 (1999), pp. 127-157.

SAUVAGE, A., "Est-il canoniquement possible que des Sociétés de vie apostolique (SVA) soient des Instituts de vie consacrées (IVC)?", in *Commentarium pro religiosis,* 70 (1989), pp. 39-48.

SCHINDLER, D.L., "Reorienting the Church on the Eve of the Millennium: John Paul II's 'New Evangelization'", in *Communio,* 24 (1997), pp. 728-779.

SCHNEIDERS, M.J., "Religious Death to the World in the Post-Conciliar

Church", in *Sisters Today,* 9 (1967), pp. 299-307.

SCHNEIDERS, S., "Non-Marriage for the Sake of the Kingdom", in *Widening the Dialogue: Reflection on 'Evangelica testificatio',* Ottawa, Canadian Religious Conference, 1974, pp. 125-197.

————, "Congregational Leadership and Spirituality in the Postmodern Era", in *Review for Religious,* 57 (1998), pp. 6-33.

SCHREITER, R., "Reflecting upon Religious Life's Future", in *Origins,* 28 (1998-1999), pp. 165-169.

SCHWARZ, K., "Alternative Membership in Religious Congregations", in *Review for Religious,* 50 (1991), pp. 559-563.

SECOND EXTRAORDINARY GENERAL ASSEMBLY OF THE SYNOD OF BISHOPS, "Final *Relatio*: The Church in the Word of God Celebrates the Mysteries of Christ for the Salvation of the World", in *L'Ossevatore romano,* (English edition), 16 December 1985, pp. 6-9.

SECONDIN, B., "Horizons of the Charism of an Institute: The 'New' Participation of the Lay Faithful", in *Consecrated Life,* 17 (1992), pp. 83-97.

————, "Le nuove forme di vita religiosa", in *Claretianum,* 35 (1995), pp. 170-176.

————, "La théologie de la vie consacrée", in *Vie consacrée,* 66 (1994), pp. 225-270.

————, "Incarnare la vita consacrata nel cuore delle culture", in *Vita consacrata* 32 (1996), pp. 38-49; 196-202; 471-478.

SILVA, G., "Fundamenti teologici della vita religiosa", in *Monitor ecclesiasticus,* 110 (1985), pp.16-36.

SMITH, L.W., "Ecumenical Monasticism for a New Millennium", <http://www.osb.org/aba/aba2000/lwsmith.html > (10 March 2000).

Soullard, R., "Chronique de la vie consacrée", in *L'année canonique,* 34 (1991), pp. 291-300.

"The Taizé Community", < http://www.almac.co.uk/taize/1gb-taiz.html> (10 March 2000).

Tassone, F., "'Comunità Casa del Giovane' il progetto di don Enzo Boschetti continua", in *Vita consacrata,* 34 (1998), pp. 398-404.

Thompson, R., "Scientific and Religious Understanding: Towards a Post-modern Spirituality", in *The Way,* 34 (1992), pp. 258-267.

Tillard, J.M.R., "Les religieuses et les religieux sont-ils et seront-ils encore parmi les forces prophétiques de l'Église?" in *La vie des communautés religieuses,* 58 (2000), pp. 3-19.

Trapet, M., "Les dangers d'une réduction de la vie consacrée à la vie religieuse", in *L'année canonique,* 30 (1987), pp. 83-99.

Tryon-Montalembert, R. de, "La vierge consacrée signe de l'amour de l'église pour le Christ", in *Vie consacrée,* 61 (1989), pp. 226-238.

Turcotte, J.C., "Les communautés nouvelles: en lien avec *l'Instrumentum laboris,* par. 37, 38, 40 et 87", archival ms., pp. 1-4; English translation from the CCCB.

Veilleux, A., "The Evolution of the Religious Life in its Historical and Spiritual Context", in *Cistercian Studies,* 6 (1971), pp. 8-34.

Viganò, E., "The Animation of Consecrated Life", in *Consecrated Life,* 18 (1993), pp. 37-46.

Vilnet, J., "Secular Institutes and the Local Churches", in *Consecrated Life,* 14 (1989), pp. 333-347.

Vitali, T., "A Question of Life or Death: Is 'Temporary Vocation' a Valid Concept?", in *Review for Religious,* 30 (1971), pp. 41-46.

Walter, P.F., "Religious Life in Church Documents", in *Review for Religious,* 51 (1992), pp. 550-561.

WEAKLAND, R., "Le renouveau de la vie religieuse aujourd'hui", in *La vie des communautés religieuses,* 52 (1994), pp. 259-271.

———, "Globalisation and the Need for a Cultural Vision", in *Origins,* 27 (1997-1998), pp. 433-434.

WEISENBECK, J.D., "Ecumenism a Scripture Mandate for Religious", in *Review for Religious,* 54 (1995), pp. 675-680.

WEISENBECK, M., "Emerging Expressions of Consecrated Life in the United States: Pastoral and Canonical Implications", in *CLSA Proceedings,* 58 (1996), pp. 368-390.

———, "Emerging Forms of U.S. Religious Life", in *Review for Religious,* 55 (1996), pp. 396-413.

WILKINS, J., "My Three Dreams: An Interview with Cardinal Martini", in *The Tablet,* 253 (1999), pp. 1489-1490.

WILLIAMSON, E., "The Notion of Charism in the Religious Life", in *Studia canonica,* 19 (1985), pp. 99-114.

WITTBERG, P., "'Real' Religious Communities: A Study of Authentication in New Roman Catholic Religious Orders", in *Religion and the Social Order,* 6 (1996), pp. 149-174.

WITTBERG, P., "Deep Structure in Community Cultures: The Revival of Religious Orders in Roman Catholicism", in *Sociology of Religion,* 58 (1997), pp. 239-259.

ZADRA, B., "L'assunzione dei consigli evangelici negli statuti delle associazioni che prevedono la consacrazione di vita", in *Quaderni di diritto ecclesiale,* 12 (1999), pp. 353-362.

ZENIT REPORT ON ROME ENCOUNTER, "World Congress of Ecclesial Movements Held in Rome", < http://www.its.caltech.edu./~bwilson/movement/ zw980531-3> (6 March 2000).

BIOGRAPHICAL NOTE

Maria Casey grew up in Ireland and, having completed secondary education there, entered the Sisters of Saint Joseph of the Sacred Heart in Sydney, Australia. After profession and teacher training she taught in secondary schools, returning later to further tertiary studies. She completed degrees in Science, Arts and education. She had wide experience in the classroom and in educational administration as well as being in leadership in her own congregation. In recent years she received her PhD and JCD in Canon Law from Ottawa University and Saint Paul University in Ottawa. Currently, she is Director of the Marriage Tribunal for the diocese of Ballarat as well as working as a consultant in Canon Law for religious congregations.